The Green Dip
Covering the City with a Forest
by The Why Factory
(TU Delft)

Authors: Winy Maas,
Javier Arpa Fernández,
Adrien Ravon

nai010 publishers

Table of contents

Table of contents

Urgent Earth

The need to act

Earth is our home. Its intricate ecosystems and diverse landscapes support us, providing a haven for all life forms. However, our home faces daunting challenges.

Climate breakdown marches on relentlessly. The unstoppable warming of our planet due to human activities is disrupting weather patterns, causing extreme weather events and endangering countless species. Rising sea levels threaten coastal communities, and changing climates impact agriculture and food security.

As if that weren't enough, the United Nations estimates that the global population will reach 10.4 billion individuals by 2100. Balancing the needs of a growing population with our planet's limited resources is a complex puzzle.

Deforestation erodes biodiversity and disrupts vital carbon cycles, as forests act as crucial carbon sinks, absorbing carbon dioxide and mitigating the impacts of climate change.

Air and water pollution not only harm ecosystems but also jeopardize the well-being of human populations.

Moreover, income disparities persist, reinforcing a world where some thrive while others struggle to meet basic needs. Addressing this gap is essential for fostering stability and ensuring that every human can lead dignified lives.

These challenges are undeniably daunting, but they should do more than appall us: they should stir our collective imagination and inspire us to think about alternative futures. We must face these urgencies with urgency itself, considering them not just as problems but as levers for radical change. Although not the sole solution and unlikely to resolve all these issues, greening our cities is a promising step toward creating a better existence on our planet.

Earth, with all its beauty and complexity, is where we must make our stand.

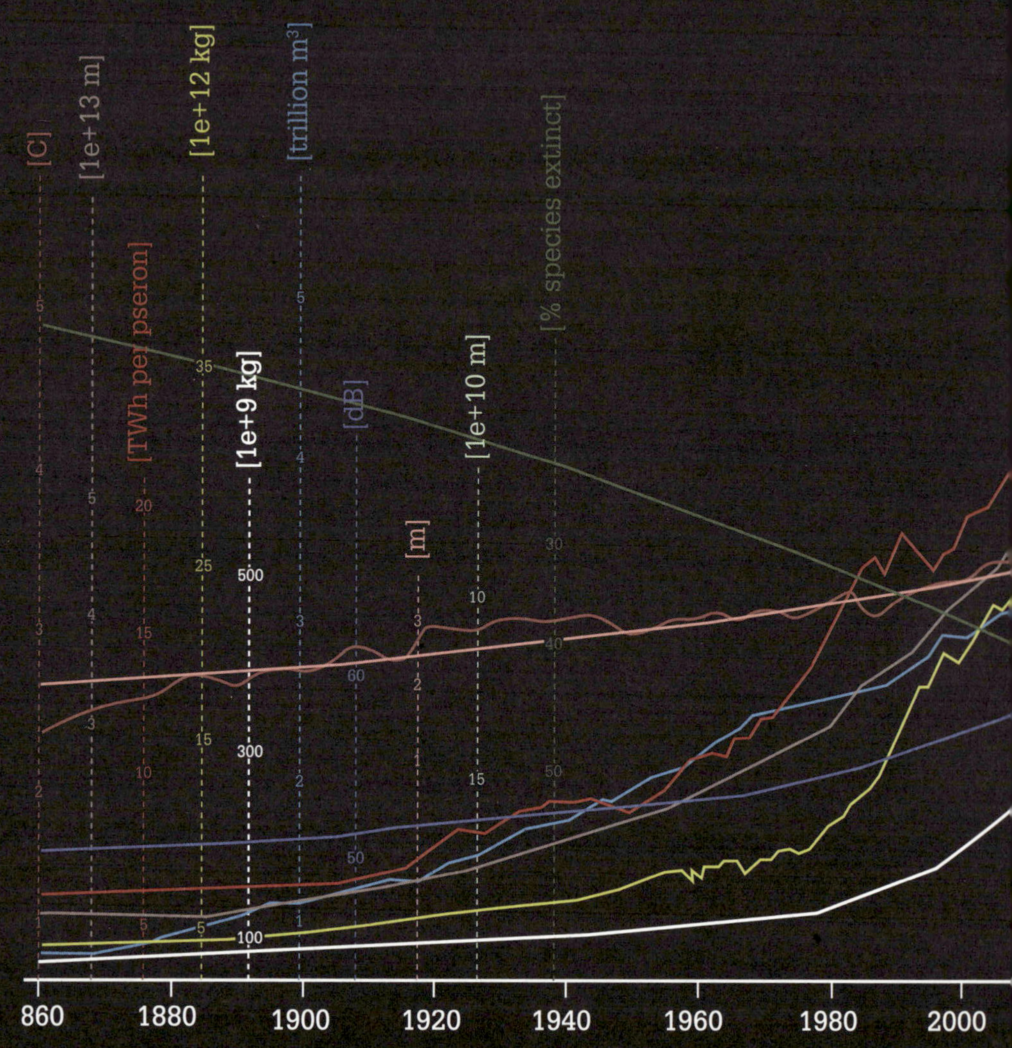

A timeline of urgencies

Starting in 1860, this timeline displays the past century's global trends. It highlights two significant tendencies: the rise in population growth and its consumption of resources, which directly and indirectly impact factors such as carbon emissions, sea level rise, energy consumption, land use for agriculture, global temperatures, and noise pollution.

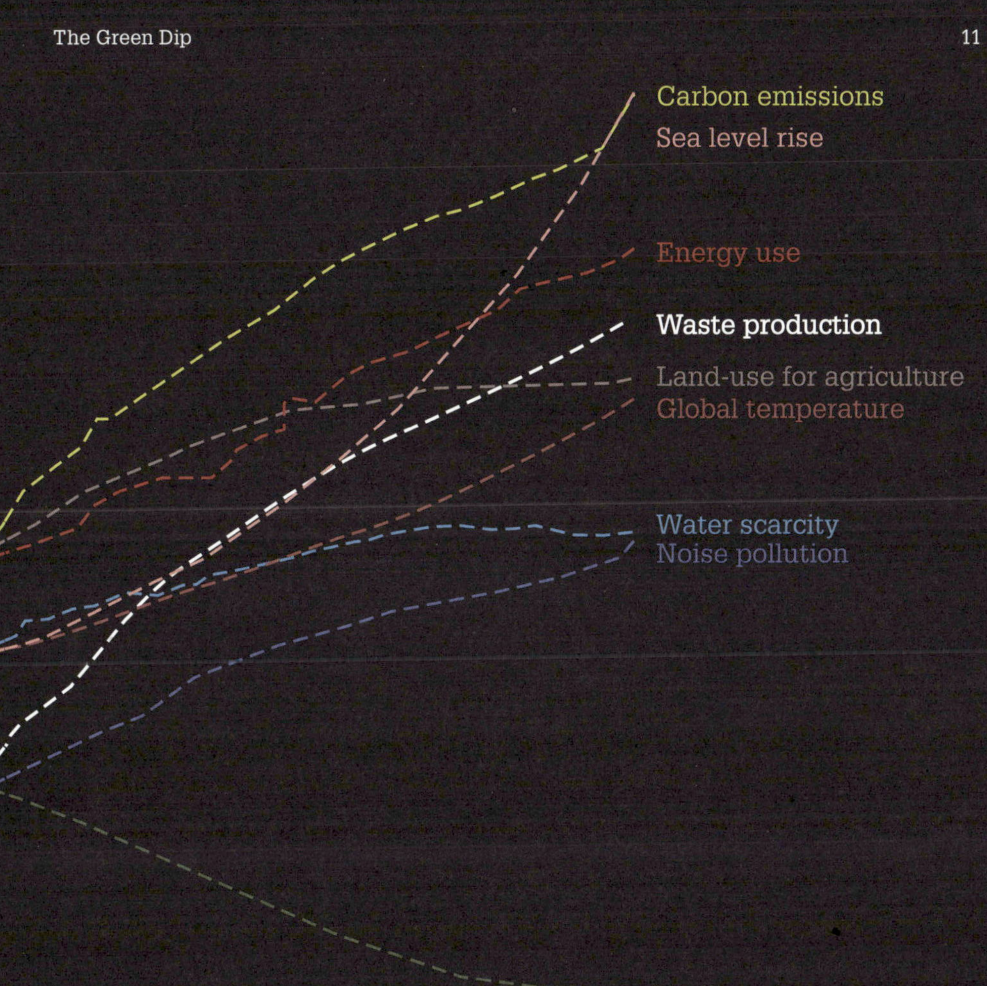

Resources deplete at an unsustainable rate, with growing concerns related to the scarcity of water, loss of biodiversity, and deforestation. This timeline projects into the future to reveal the urgency of these planetary challenges. As the population rises and inequalities persist, urgencies become increasingly interrelated.

The crust section

How can we unveil the complexity and interrelation of the impact of human activities on the planet? Raising awareness about the urgency of this question was the objective undertaken by students at The Why Factory during the spring of 2021. Their approach involved presenting a cross-sectional visual representation of the Earth's crust, illustrating the interwoven connections between various urgencies and activities.

The urban heat island effect, air pollution, the increase in extreme weather events, sinking cities, declining biodiversity, noise pollution, global carbon emissions, desertification sensitivity, rising global temperatures, deforestation, energy supply, health risks, food scarcity, sea level rise, and depleting biodiversity are all interconnected challenges requiring critical attention.

Killing animals
Humans kill 72 billion animals per year for meat.
Land-use
77% of all agriculture land is used for animal farming.
Nitrogen Dentrification
Denitrification bacteria
Assimilation
Nitrifying
Milk
544.000.000 ton per year.
For 1 kg beef
99.9 kg CO2 is produced, 15 L water and 326 m2 land are used.
Humans are only a small part of all life
Humans make up only 0.1% of all biomass.
Our livestock is 10x bigger than wildlife.

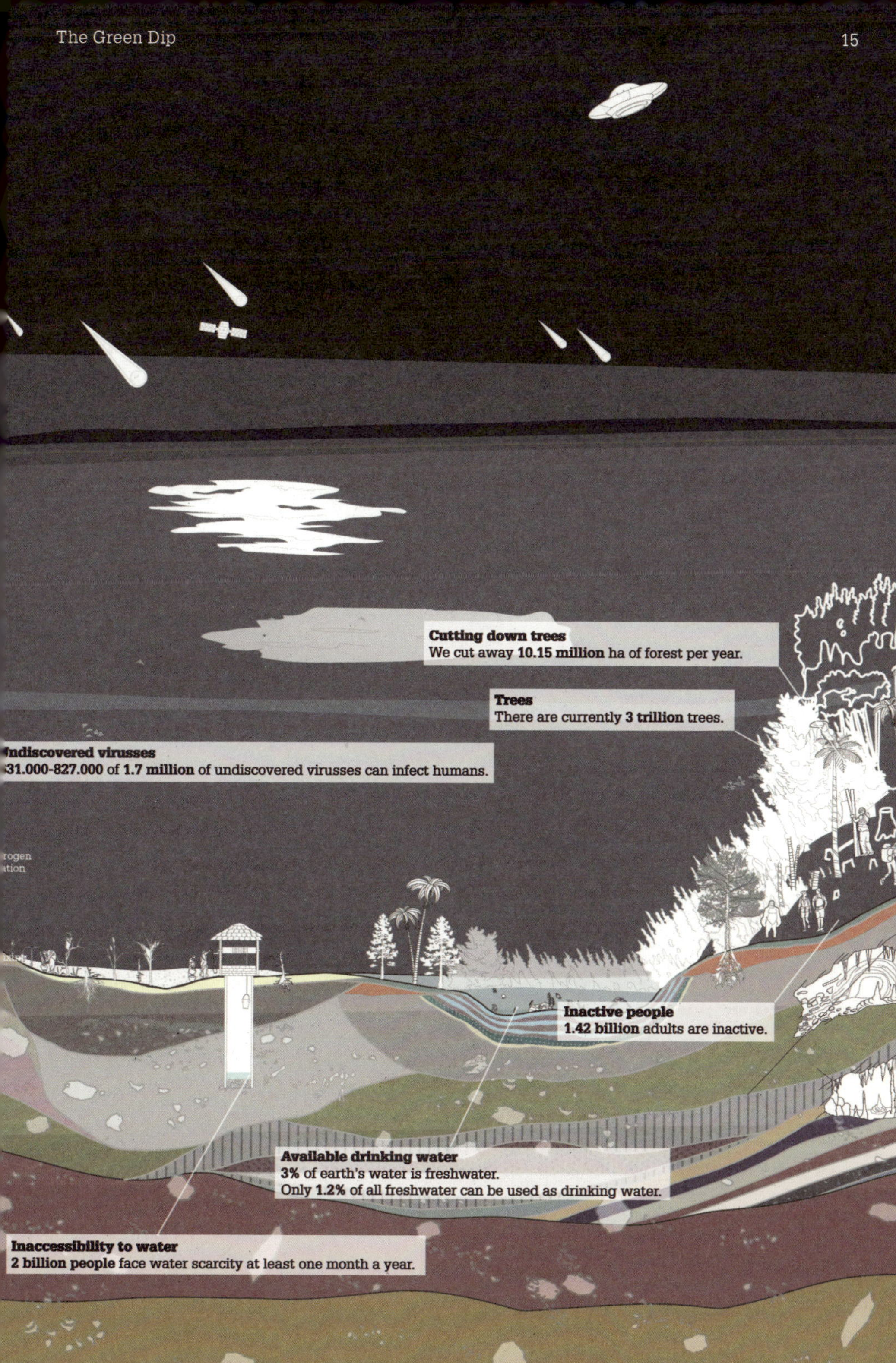
Cutting down trees
We cut away **10.15 million** ha of forest per year.
Trees
There are currently **3 trillion** trees.
ndiscovered virusses
31.000-827.000 of **1.7 million** of undiscovered virusses can infect humans.
rogen
ation
Inactive people
1.42 billion adults are inactive.
Available drinking water
3% of earth's water is freshwater.
Only **1.2%** of all freshwater can be used as drinking water.
Inaccessibility to water
2 billion people face water scarcity at least one month a year.

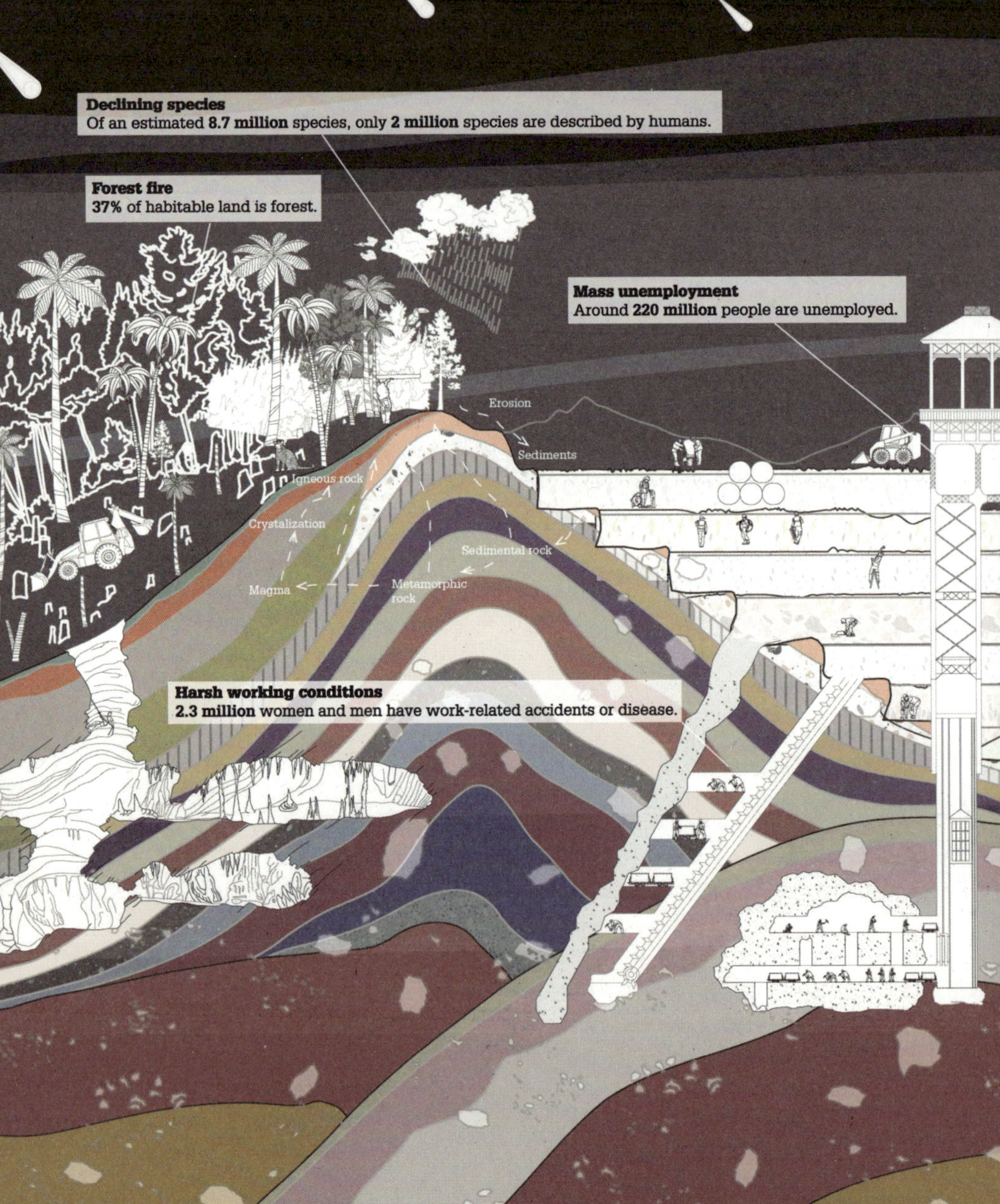

Declining species
Of an estimated **8.7 million** species, only **2 million** species are described by humans.
Forest fire
37% of habitable land is forest.
Mass unemployment
Around **220 million** people are unemployed.
Erosion
Sediments
Igneous rock
Crystalization
Sedimental rock
Magma
Metamorphic rock
Harsh working conditions
2.3 million women and men have work-related accidents or disease.

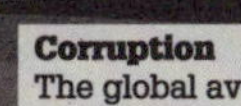

Corruption
The global average for CPI (Corruption Perception Index) is **43/100**.

Extreme poverty
689 million people live in absolute poverty.

Rapid population growth
In 2100, there is a chance population will increase to 12 billion people.

dequate economic security
billion people do not have adequate economic security.

Not able to read
Around **759 million** adults are illiterate.

Unequal power
There are **52** countries ruled by a dictator in the world.

Children not learning
72 million children do not have access to adequate education

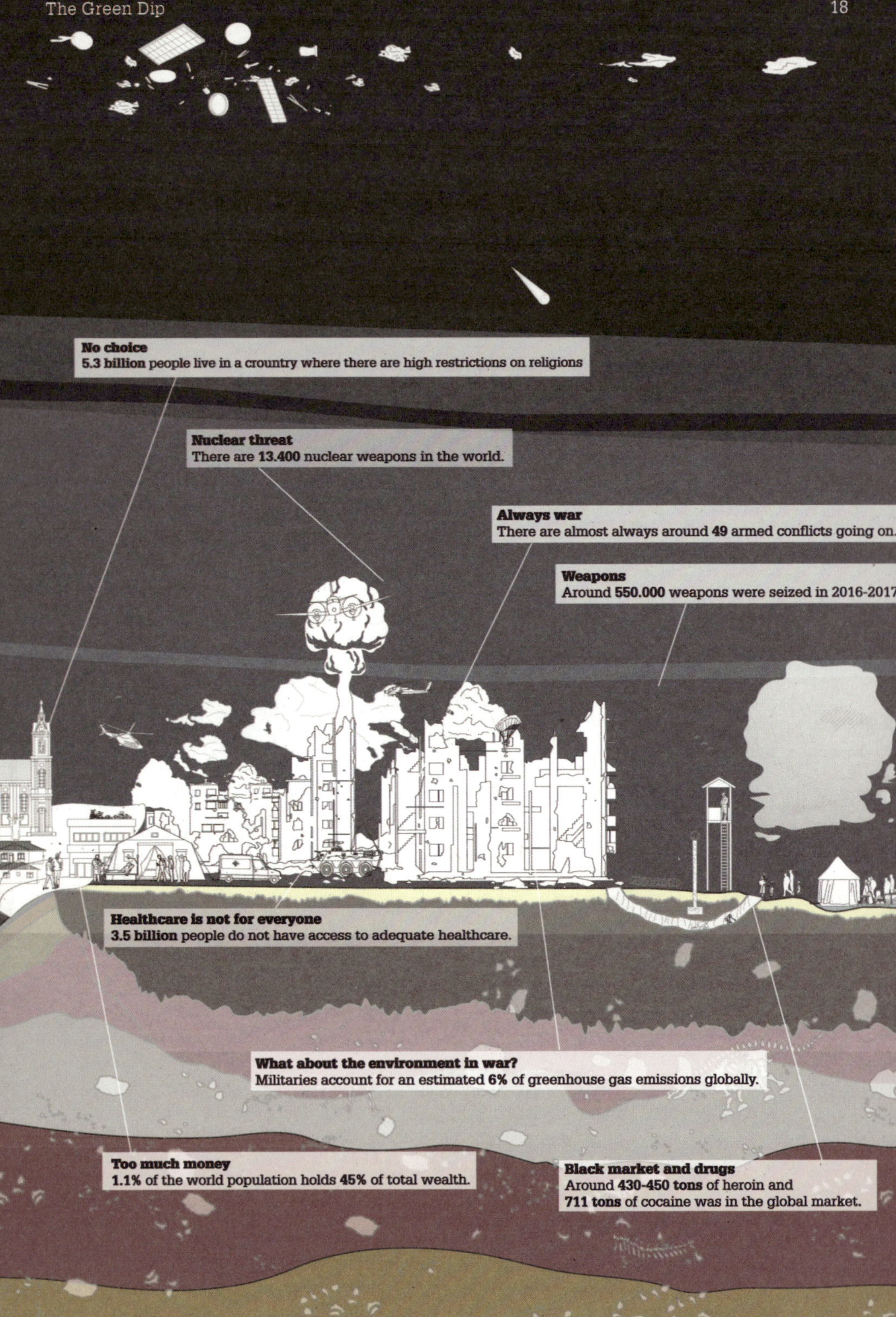
No choice
5.3 billion people live in a crountry where there are high restrictions on religions
Nuclear threat
There are **13.400** nuclear weapons in the world.
Always war
There are almost always around **49** armed conflicts going on.
Weapons
Around **550.000** weapons were seized in 2016-2017
Healthcare is not for everyone
3.5 billion people do not have access to adequate healthcare.
What about the environment in war?
Militaries account for an estimated **6%** of greenhouse gas emissions globally.
Too much money
1.1% of the world population holds **45%** of total wealth.
Black market and drugs
Around **430-450 tons** of heroin and
711 tons of cocaine was in the global market.

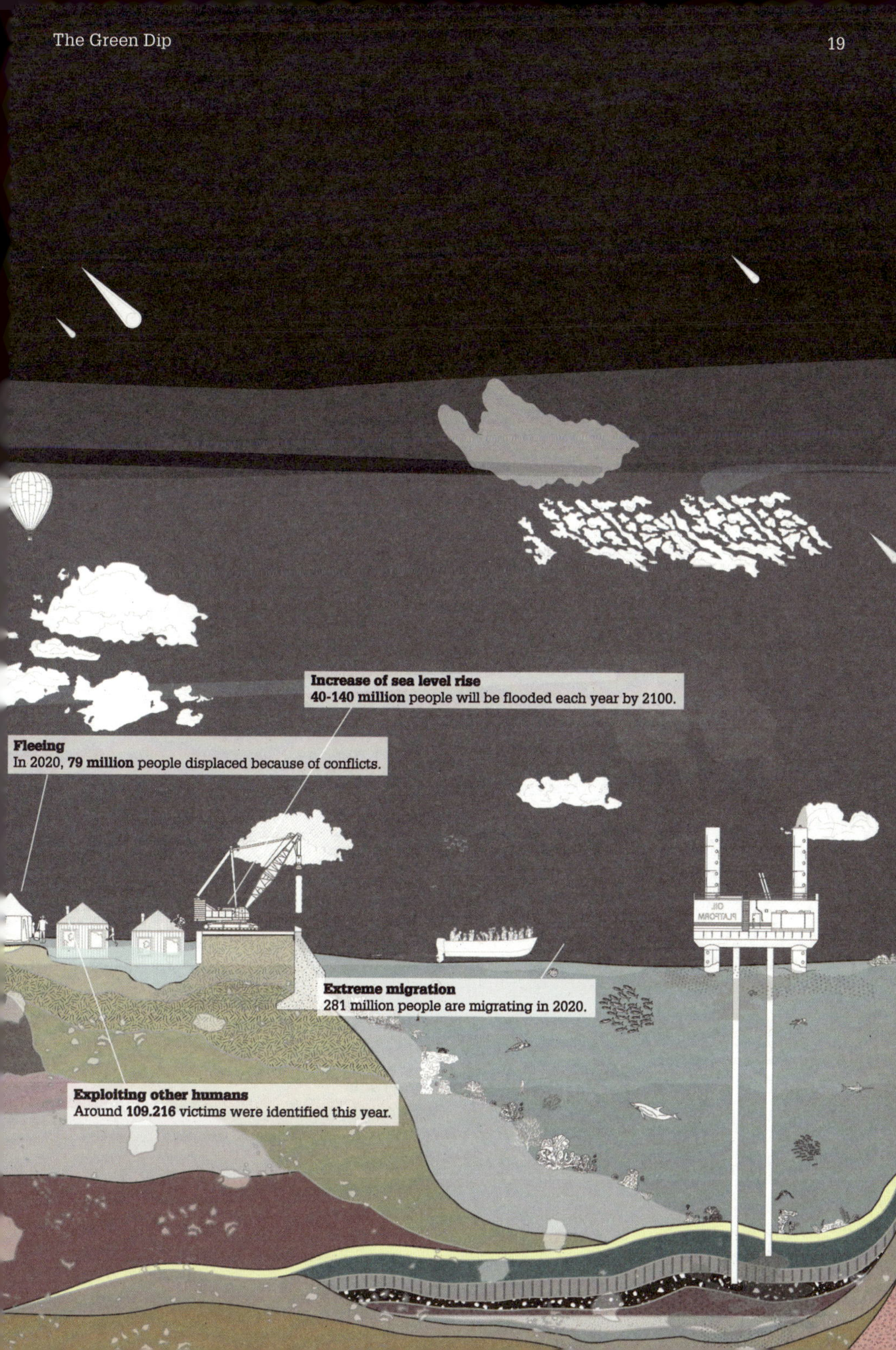
Increase of sea level rise
40-140 million people will be flooded each year by 2100.
Fleeing
In 2020, **79 million** people displaced because of conflicts.
OIL PLATFORM
Extreme migration
281 million people are migrating in 2020.
Exploiting other humans
Around **109.216** victims were identified this year.

Bycatch
Around 40% or 38 million tons of annual marine catch is bycatch.
Waste island
There is 5.25 trillion macro and micro pieces of plastic in the ocean.
Ice melting
Because of global warming, 750 billion tons of ice is melting every year.
Unsustainable
90% of all fishing is unsustainable.
Electric waste production
Humans produce 50 million metric tons of electric waste every year.
HAB
Harmful Algae Bloom can cause death to humans and fish
Warming ocean
The ocean's temperature increases 0.11 degrees Celcius ever 10 years.

Increasing global temperature
Currently, the earth temperature changed by **+1.2** degrees Celcius since the preindustrial area.

Increase of extreme wildfires
It is expected that wildfires will increase with **50%** by **2100**.

Extreme weather
An extreme weather event will occur everyday, killing **115** people on average per day.

More extreme weather casualties
From 1970 to 2019, weater, climate and water hazards accounted for **50%** of disasters.

Increase of tsunamis
A **50 cm** increase in sealevel doubles the chance for tsunamis.

Coastal erosion
Around **14.000 km2** land was lost between 1984 and 2015.

So much waste
2.01 billion tons of municipal waste is produced every year.

Unethical internet practices.
Ransomware has increased by 435% in 2020.
Adequate housing
Estimate 1.6 billion people lack adequate hous
Depression
350 million people suffer from depression worldwide.
Homeless
100 million people are homeless.
Rural slowly decreasing
Currently, 44% lives in rural areas and continues to decline.
Mental health issues
20% of the world's population has a mental health issue.

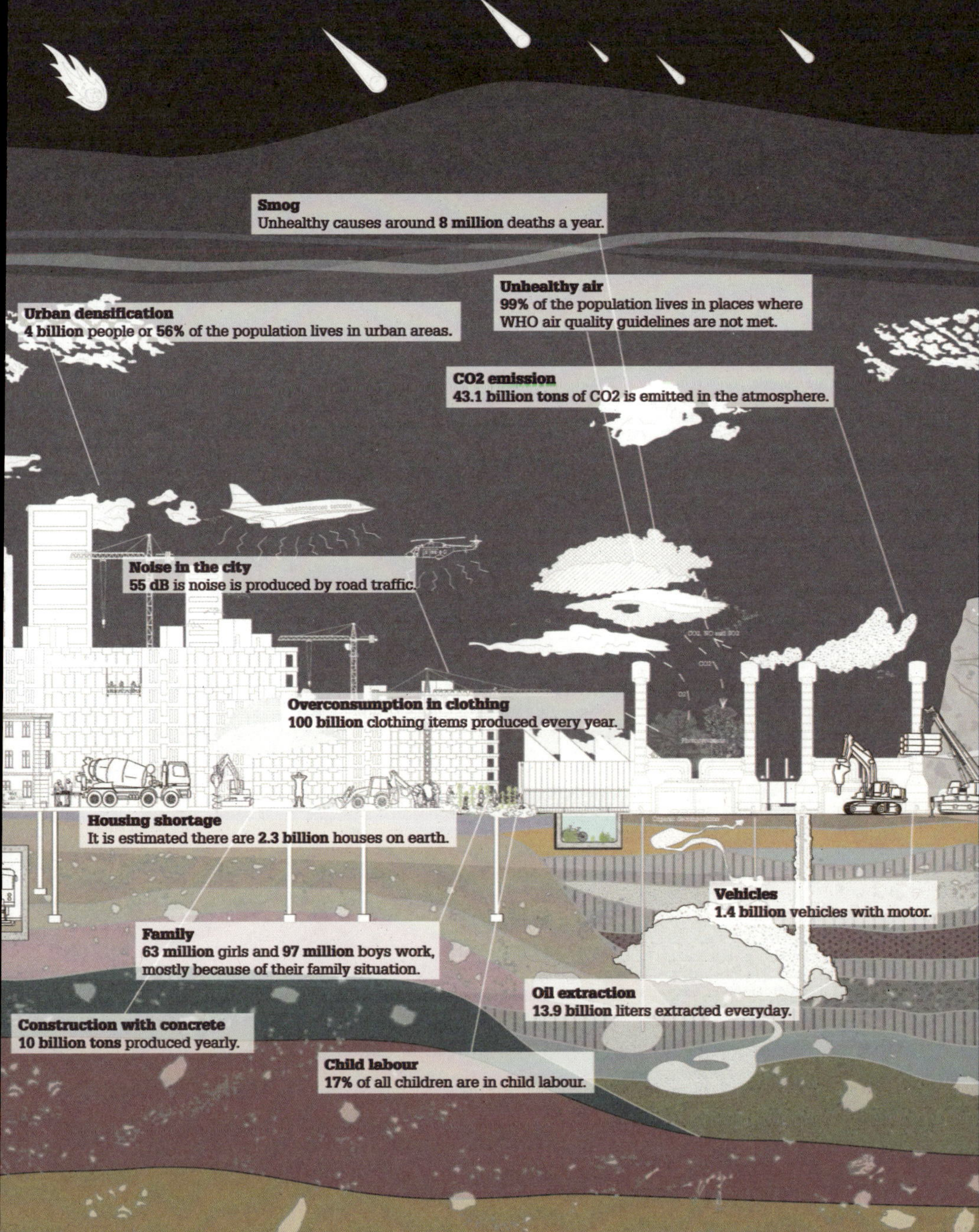

Smog
Unhealthy causes around **8 million** deaths a year.

Unhealthy air
99% of the population lives in places where WHO air quality guidelines are not met.

Urban densification
4 billion people or **56%** of the population lives in urban areas.

CO2 emission
43.1 billion tons of CO2 is emitted in the atmosphere.

Noise in the city
55 dB is noise is produced by road traffic.

Overconsumption in clothing
100 billion clothing items produced every year.

Housing shortage
It is estimated there are **2.3 billion** houses on earth.

Vehicles
1.4 billion vehicles with motor.

Family
63 million girls and **97 million** boys work, mostly because of their family situation.

Oil extraction
13.9 billion liters extracted everyday.

Construction with concrete
10 billion tons produced yearly.

Child labour
17% of all children are in child labour.

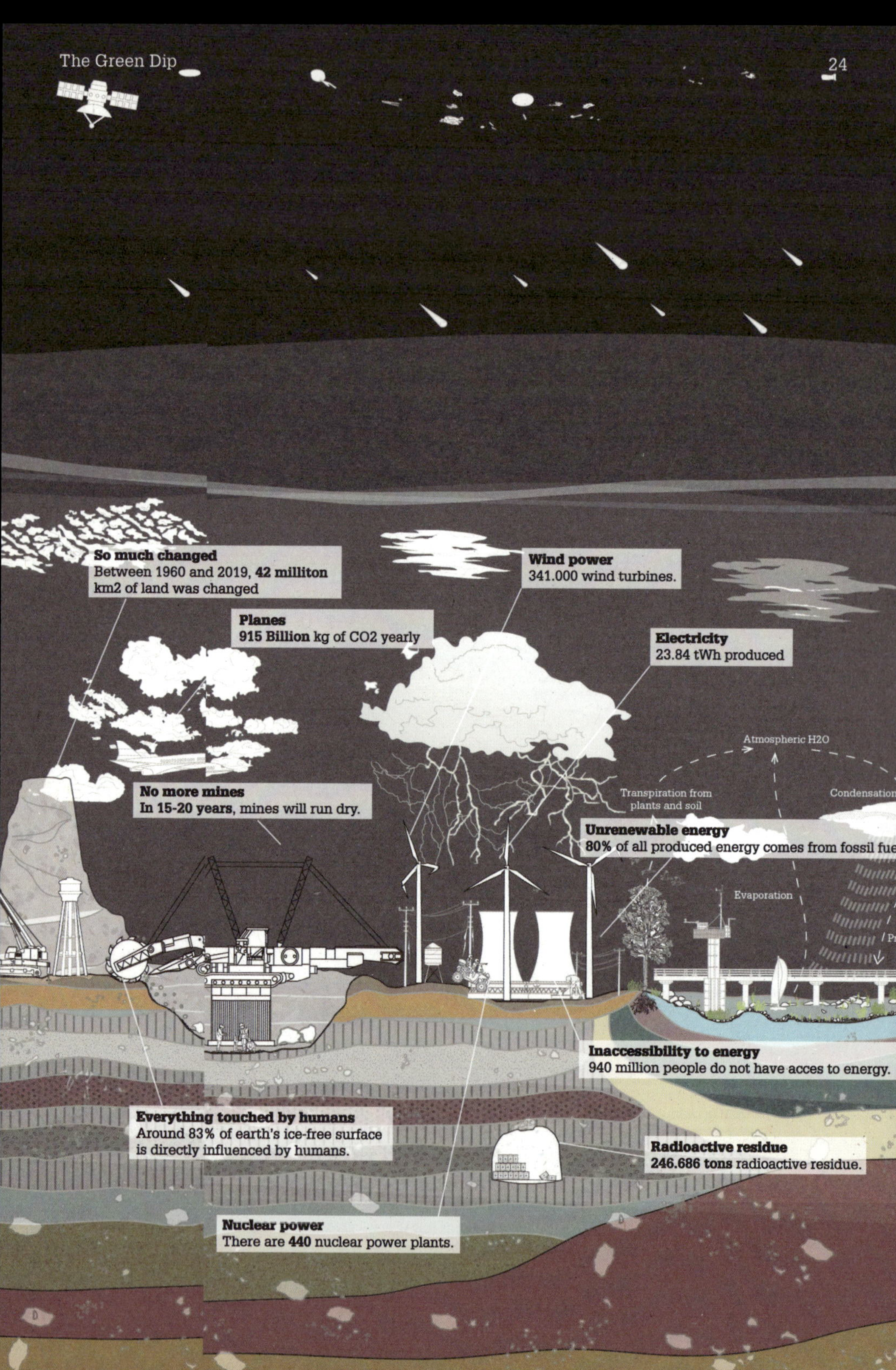

So much changed
Between 1960 and 2019, 42 milliton km2 of land was changed
Wind power
341.000 wind turbines.
Planes
915 Billion kg of CO2 yearly
Electricity
23.84 tWh produced
Atmospheric H2O
Transpiration from plants and soil
Condensation
No more mines
In 15-20 years, mines will run dry.
Unrenewable energy
80% of all produced energy comes from fossil fue
Evaporation
Inaccessibility to energy
940 million people do not have acces to energy.
Everything touched by humans
Around 83% of earth's ice-free surface is directly influenced by humans.
Radioactive residue
246.686 tons radioactive residue.
Nuclear power
There are 440 nuclear power plants.

Food needed
3.7 billion tons food is needed per year to feed everyone.

Cropland
One human needs **0.1 km2** of cropland

Unsustainable agriculture
50% of habitable land on earth or **58.460.000 km2** is used for agriculture.

Inaccessibility to food
957 million people still face hunger every year.

Basic need for cropland is disappearing
13% of all land is cropland or 19.890.000 **km2** of cropland.

Food produced and thrown away
4 billion tons food is produced per year.

Green? Yes, green!

Winy Maas

In 1969, three years before the Club of Rome published *The Limits to Growth*—a report which made dire predictions that startled people around the world—Ian McHarg breathed new life into the vision of a better world. In his book *Design with Nature*, he rekindled hope for a world in which humans and nature could coexist in a healthier relationship.

When we reflect on both publications, it's astounding to see how more than 50 years of scientific, technological, and philosophical progress of our civilisation haven't been able to put an end to the misguided belief in endless growth. This belief has pushed the world to the brink, a situation that demands a paradigm shift in urbanisation.

The Green Dip is the first book in a trilogy, to be followed by *BiodiverCity* and *Biotopia*. This trilogy invites everyone involved in the making of cities to introduce a new relationship between humans and nature, and imagine a genuine entanglement of life between humans and other-than-humans.

The first issue of the trilogy, *The Green Dip*, studies the relation between humans and plants. Here we envision a world where cities—which cover only 1-3 per cent of terrestrial land—are blanketed with forests of plant species from their corresponding biomes, not just for the environmental benefits that could result in a significant planetary temperature reduction but also for the profound emotional rewards that come from greening our cities. This exercise extends beyond the often criticised *greenwashing* to offer a genuine path to better quality of life.

BiodiverCity explores the relationship between humans and animals. It studies how architectural and urban design can facilitate meaningful relationships between humans and other species. It explores innovative ways for animals and humans to live next to each other, seeking new modes of city design that integrate animal life and their natural habitats into our daily environment.

Lastly, *Biotopia* explores the relationship between humans and material. It introduces the concept of a genuinely biological world, supported by a new three-dimensional substrate made from bioengineered materials. This innovative 'soil' enables water management, growth, adaptability, biodiversity, and porosity. It accumulates to form surfaces, walls, floors, columns, pipework, and entire cities, shaping not just our interiors and homes but our cities and, ultimately, our world as well.

The Green Dip re-evaluates our cities' spatial, biological, and metaphorical concepts of nature. It actively considers the development of the city as a living organism where ecological, agricultural, and forestry production are prioritized as a catalyst for development.

The Green Dip extends beyond research and student work; it's a call to action intended to mobilise experts, stakeholders, and the public for collaboration. This collaboration commenced as The Why Factory initiated research with other academic institutions, including IAAC in Barcelona, Spain, and GSAPP in New York, USA. To address the urgent challenges of the climate emergency, we must expand the campaign and the mandate is clear work together, transcending conventional boundaries, to drive transformation.

The Green Dip is an inspirational journey to encourage people to live better. It experiments with advanced planting, food production, ecology, health, and biodiversity, leading to a city where green areas, public space, and production, typically confined to ground level, extend upwards into our buildings. This incorporates architectural elements such as facades, roofs and floors, and construction techniques that facilitate the integration of greenery into our cities.

The Green Dip is an invitation to dream. It brings this vision to life through visualisations of cities worldwide, from Beijing to Singapore, Dubai, Moscow, Kinshasa, Paris, New York, and Sao Paulo. It envisions a world where people, plants, and animals coexist symbiotically. Although some images may evoke a post-apocalyptic scene, resembling a world reclaimed by nature after human absence, we utilize this dystopian imagery—a sort of overgrown apocalypse—to contrast and highlight a utopian vision.

The Green Dip is an ambitious endeavour, but one worth pursuing.

Part 1

What can green do?

Green fashions

Trends and controversies

Integrating vegetation into buildings is not new. It has a long history, demonstrating the enduring connection between flora and fauna, architecture, and the city.

Amid pressing environmental concerns, greening emerges as a valuable solution. Planting is effective, rapid, enhances real estate appeal and serves as a political asset for municipalities. There is a global proliferation of tree-planting initiatives, with cities vying for the title of the greenest and the most verdant.

The vision of a green future is undeniably appealing, inspiring hope and a sense of collective purpose. It resonates with everyone. However, beneath this vision lies a potential for misunderstanding. Will this vision of greenery be the same in every city? Will all these envisioned trees truly thrive in urban settings? How will maintenance be managed? Who stands to benefit from greening and is it genuinely environmentally responsible or a form of greenwashing?

Over the past decade, future-oriented urban projects have notably embraced green imagery. This shift represents a transition from a hyper-technological vision of the future to a more biocentric approach to urban design. Nowadays, designers envision cities as green oases, where skyscrapers evolve into verdant mountains with greenery extending onto every floor.

This chapter explores the underlying questions, advantages, and disadvantages at the heart of the debate surrounding the greening of buildings and cities.

El Oasis. Fernando Higueras, Madrid, Spain, 1972

Planeta Building. Josep Maria Fargas and Enric Tous, Barcelona, Spain, 1978

Bosco Verticale. Stefano Boeri Architetti, Milan, Italy, 2014

One Central Park. Ateliers Jean Nouvel, Sydney, Australia, 2014

Chicland Hotel. VTN Architects, Da Nang, Vietnam, 2020

Urban Farming Office. VTN Architects, Ho Chi Minh, Vietnam, 2022

Green past

In the last decades, there has been a notable surge in projects integrating plants into buildings. The proliferation of such initiatives, coupled with their public appeal and success, has established the greening of buildings as a prominent trend that has effectively influenced policies and urban development.

Les Etoiles. Jean Renaudy, Ivry-sur-Seine, France, 1975

Alterlaa. Harry Glück, Vienna, Austria, 1986

La piece pointue. Atelier Iwona Buczkowska, Blanc-Mesnil, France, 1992

Tower Flower. Édouard François, Paris, France, 2004

Tour de la Biodiversité. Édouard François, M6B2, Paris, France, 2016

Trudeau Vertical Forest. Stefano Boeri Architetti, Eindhoven, The Netherlands, 2021

Affordable green

Due to the associated planting and maintenance costs, social housing rarely incorporates green elements. Nevertheless, a few examples have emerged to demonstrate the feasibility of affordable green housing.

Musée du Quai Branly. Ateliers Jean Nouvel, Patrick Blanc, Paris, France, 2006

Caixa Forum. Herzog & de Meuron, Patrick Blanc, Madrid, Spain, 2008

The Palace Hotel, Gary Grant, London, United Kingdom, 2013

L'Oasis d'Aboukir. Patrick Blanc, Paris, France, 2013

Sportplaza Mercator. VenhoevenCS, Amsterdam, The Netherlands, 2013

Edificio Santalaia. Exacta proyecto total, Bogota, Colombia, 2015

Green facades

Preceded by several successful examples, green facades have become quite fashionable and can now be found in various parts of the world. Although appealing and capable of enhancing a building's thermal performance, they are often expensive and challenging to maintain, particularly if the selection of plants doesn't align with the local biome. Green facades can be realised by either cladding a supporting structure for plant growth or guiding plants to grow directly from the ground.

View of Montecarlo, with green rooftops, Monaco

ACROS Fukuoka. Emilio Ambasz, Fukuoka City, Japan, 1995

Green Roof, Chicago City Hall. William McDonough + Partners,Chicago, United States of America, 2001

Kampung Admiralty. WOHA, Singapore, 2017

Hilldegarden Bunker. Hamburg, Germany, 2018

Kö-Bogen II. Ingenhouven, Dusseldorf, Germany, 2020

Green roofs

From traditional techniques of constructing turf roofs in Scandinavia to the implementation of containers for agriculture on flat rooftops and the planting of trees, green roofs serve as an effective method for insulation, water management, wildlife preservation, and community enhancement. Beyond their aesthetic and environmental benefits, they can also redefine the ownership of rooftops in cities by making them public and accessible.

Chichu Art Museum. Tadao Ando, Japan, 2004

Pool Pavilion. Gluck+, United States of America, 2009

Earth House. BCHO Architects, South Korea, 2009

Shilda Winery. X-architecture, Kakheti, Georgia, 2016

Taoyunju Community Center. Vector Architects, Chongqing, China, 2016

Skamlingsbanken. CEBRA architecture, Denmark, 2021

Green camouflage

Living within a camouflaged crust of greenery not only hides the building from its surroundings but also from nature itself. When a building is guided by its context, the boundaries between architecture and its surroundings blend and merge. Obscuring the demarcations between architecture and landscape brings the significance of the surrounding environment sharply into focus.

Barbican Conservatory. Chamberlin, Powell and Bon, London, United Kingdom, 1976

Biosphere 2. John P. Allen, Arizona, United States of America, 1991

National Botanic Garden of Wales. Foster + Partners, Llanarthney, United Kingdom, 2000

Gardens by the Bay. WilkinsonEyre, Singapore, 2012

Jewel Changi Airport. Moshe Safdie, Singapore, 2019

Tropicalia. Coldefy, France, 2023

Artificially green

A historical example is Biosphere 2, an ambitious 1990s project in the Arizona Desert designed to create an artificial ecosystem. However, the endeavour exposed the difficulty and high costs of maintaining such environments.

Ford Foundation Center for Social Justice, New York City, United States of America, 1967

Naturescape, Kengo Kuma, Milan, Italy, 2013

Ecole Polytechnique Learning Centre, Sou Foujimoto, Saclay, France, 2015

Naman Retreat Pure Spa, MIA Design Studio, Da Nang, Vietnam, 2019

Jonggak Station Solar Garden, James Ramsey, Seoul, South Korea, 2019

Lowline Lab, James Ramsey, New York City, United States of America, 2019

Indoor green

Indoor gardens incorporate vegetation within buildings. Successful examples have demonstrated the added value of such design practices. While indoor gardens need environmental control and maintenance, they also enhance air quality and benefit humans.

1Hotel Paris, Kengo Kuma, Paris, France, 2017

Amata, Triptyque, Sao Paulo, Brazil, 2017

Toronto Tree Tower, Studio Precht, Toronto, Canada, 2017

The Farmhouse, Studio Precht, 2019. Unbuilt

WoHO, Mad Arkitekter, Berlin, Germany, 2021

C6, Fraser and Partners, Perth, Australia, 2023

Green wood

Planting trees on structures adds substantial weight, contributing to increased CO_2 emissions due to the added structural requirements. A potential solution is to use wood structures, a material with a lower carbon footprint than concrete and steel. Wooden structures can offset environmental costs from heavy soil loads and act as carbon sinks, storing carbon over time. Responsible wood sourcing and construction practices are crucial to maximising these benefits.

Cheonggyecheon Restoration. Seoul Development Institute urban design team, Dongmyung Eng, Daelim E&C, Seoul, South Korea, 2005

Madrid Rio. West 8, Fernando Porras-Isla, Burgos-Garrido, Madrid, 2015

BAM Park. Inside Outside and Petra Blaisse, with Simona and Franco Giorgetta, Milan, Italy, 2022

Camden Highline. Oliver O'Brien, London, United Kingdom, 2015

The Highline. Diller Scofidio + Renfro, Field Operations, New York City, United States of America, 2023

Beltline. Atlanta, United States of America, 2023

Green gentrification

The development of urban green has given rise to the concept of green gentrification. Proximity to parks and green areas significantly impacts property value and rents, contributing to urban inequalities. Who truly benefits from urban green initiatives?

Emirates Golf Club, BSBG, Dubai, 1988

Reunion Resort, BMA, Florida, USA, 2007

Godrej Golf Links, BDP, Greater Noida, Delhi, India, 2016

Caitriona, Ambience, Gurgaon, India, 2016

The Camellias Development, Hafeez Contractor, Gurgaon, India, 2021

Serenity Alcaidesa, One Eden, San Roque, Spain, 2022

Green money

Real estate developers increasingly adopt green features as a selling point, catering to urban residents' desire for access to nature. However, such projects often employ superficial greening that overlooks local ecosystems. These developments frequently target luxury markets and exclude the broader community.

New Town, Cytonn, Kenya 2016

Green River, Dar Al Handasah Landscape Architects, Cairo, Egypt, 2019

Makadi Heights, EDSA, Makadi, Egypt, 2021

The Line, Neom, Saudi Arabia, 2021

Desert Rose city, Khatib & Alami, Dubai, 2022

XZERO City, URB, United Arab Emirates, 2022

Green speculation

Recent architectural renders of future cities predominantly depict hyper-green, sustainable, and organic landscapes. While these visuals are alluring, they often present uniformity, integrating the same plants and technological solutions. They also tend to underrepresent human habitation, prompting doubts about their realism.

Tianjin Ecocity, SSTEC, Binhai, China, 2007 Tianjin Ecocity, SSTEC, Binhai, China, 2007

Paris smart city 2050, Vincent Callebaut Architectures, Paris, France, 2015

Paris smart city 2050, Vincent Callebaut Architectures, Paris, France, 2015

Flemington Sustainable City, Tony Owen Partners, Sydney, Australia, 2018

AI generated

AI generated

Green excess

Future urban scenarios depict excessive greenery, even in arid regions. Some new city projects feature more plants than residents, raising questions about the water resources required to maintain such lush environments. The challenge is assessing whether a city's 'greenness' genuinely improves its liveability.

Green assets

Unfolding performances

Plants are invaluable to humans. They provide aesthetic beauty and a range of essential benefits for creating a healthy environment. These advantages are encapsulated as *ecosystem services*: criteria that gauge the direct and indirect benefits of coexisting with vegetation. Plants provide supporting, provisioning, regulating, and cultural benefits. As per these ecosystem services, plants can reduce atmospheric noise and visual pollution, enhance residents' quality of life, support local biodiversity, lower temperatures, promote physical and mental well-being, and foster a sense of community. Plants can reduce energy expenses, aid in stormwater management, prevent erosion, increase property values, build stronger community bonds, contribute to food and nutrition security, and enhance community resilience against extreme weather events.

In essence, vegetation significantly impacts our existence.

The quantification of those ecosystem services plays a central role in environmental policy discussions, letting cities worldwide plan, maintain, and manage urban forests and trees accordingly. Shifting from objective to subjective performance indicators, this chapter compiles a list of benefits. It proposes a direction for measuring how plants can enhance the environment, human well-being, and cities.

As we envision the global implementation of *The Green Dip*, a cascade of transformative effects becomes evident, each with profound implications for our environment, economy, and quality of life.

1 Carbon emission reduction
Imagine a world where urban landscapes are covered with lush vegetation, where trees and plants thrive on rooftops, facades, and open spaces. This transformation has the power to drastically reduce carbon emissions. With urban areas accounting for a significant portion of global emissions, the widespread integration of vegetation can substantially decrease greenhouse gas emissions.

2 Improved air quality
Enveloping cities with green spaces paves the way for improved air quality and healthier lives for urban residents worldwide. Trees and plants act as natural filters, capturing pollutants and releasing oxygen.

3 Flourishing biodiversity
Cities have suppressed biodiversity, but introducing native plants that create habitats for many species reverses this trend. From insects to humans, urban ecosystems thrive.

4 Temperature moderation
Urban heat islands contribute to discomfort and strain on energy resources. An emphasis on greenery offers a natural solution. Trees provide shade, reduce surface temperatures and lower energy consumption for cooling, creating pleasant urban environments for residents.

5 Water management and resilience
Green spaces absorb rainwater, thereby mitigating flooding and relieving drainage systems. By enhancing the permeability of urban surfaces, cities become more resilient and adaptable to changing weather patterns.

6 Economic implications
The widespread application of these suggestions is not merely an ecological endeavour; it also brings economic advantages by reducing energy consumption and its associated costs.

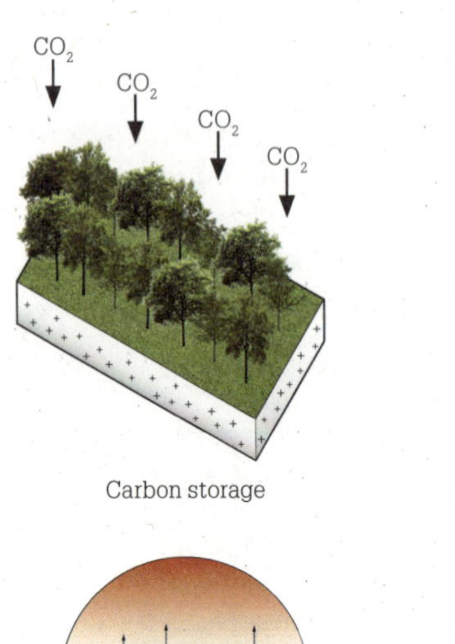

Carbon storage

Biomass production

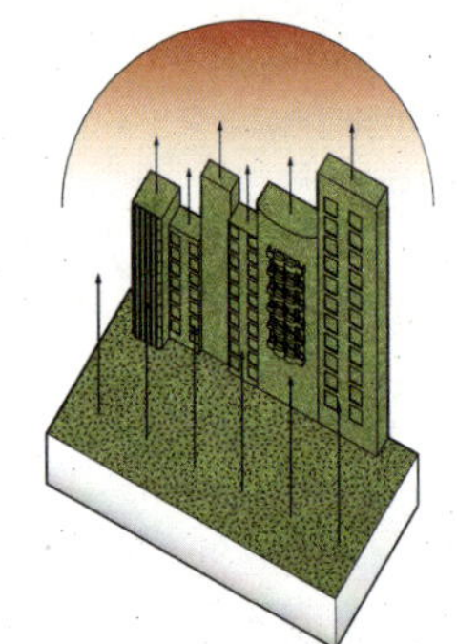

Reduction of urban heat island effect

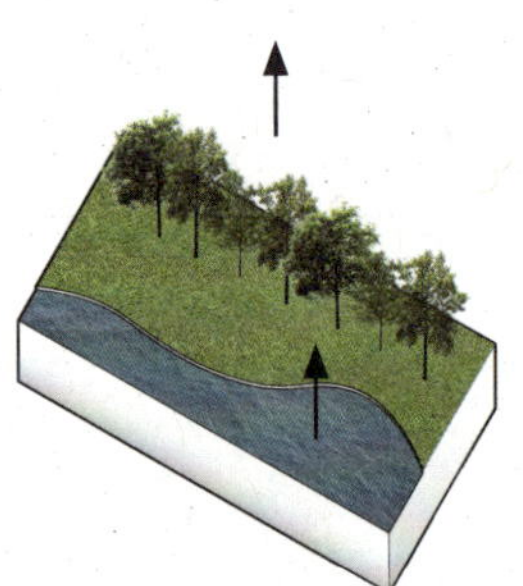

Increased humidity

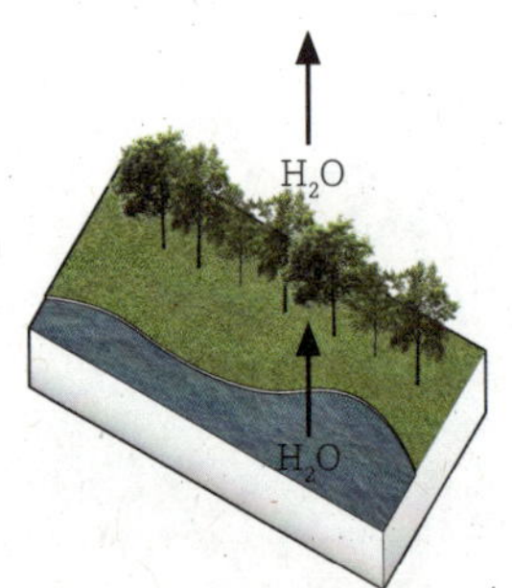

Increased O_2 production

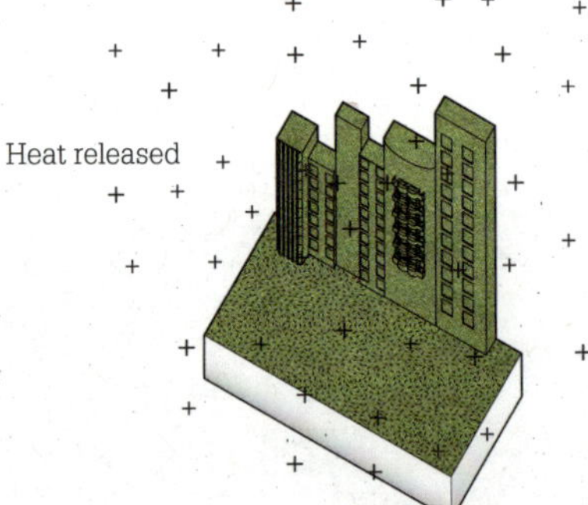

Decreased NO_2 concentration

Greening cities is an important strategy to mitigate climate change and improve air quality, contributing to healthier urban living environments.

Temperature reduction

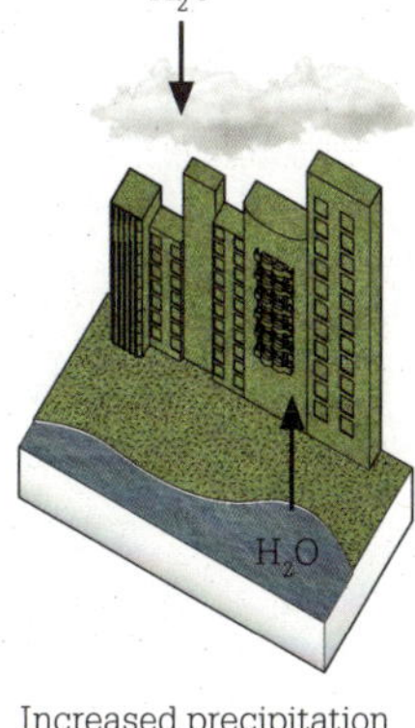

Increased precipitation

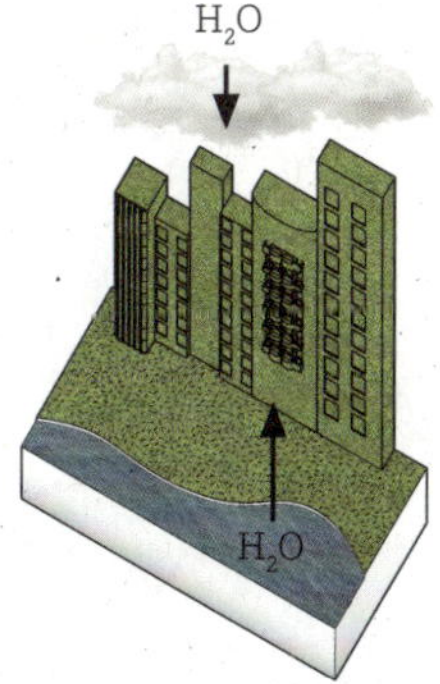

Increased evapotranspiration

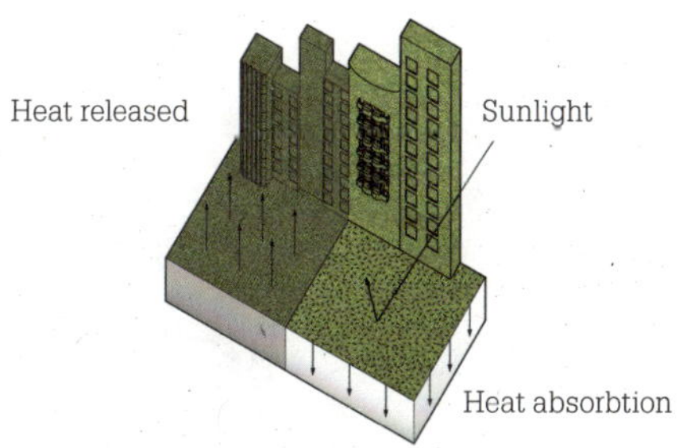

Lower albedo (reflectivity)

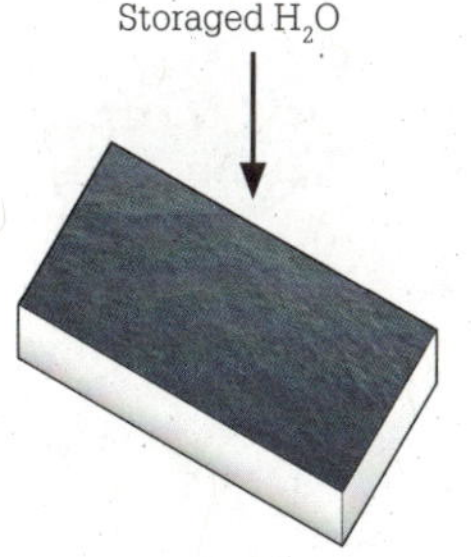

Enhanced water storage capacity

Soil quality enhancement

Plants play a significant role in various aspects such as albedo, biomass, stored carbon, CO_2 absorption, evaporation, water storage, heat island effect, humidity, NO_2, O_2 production, precipitation, and temperature regulation.

Timber structure use

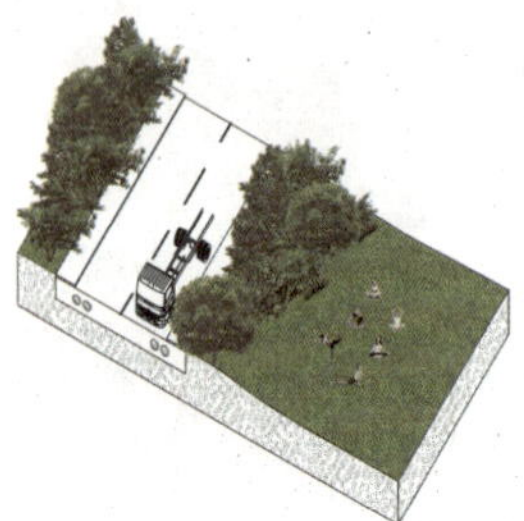

Noise reduction

Improved air quality

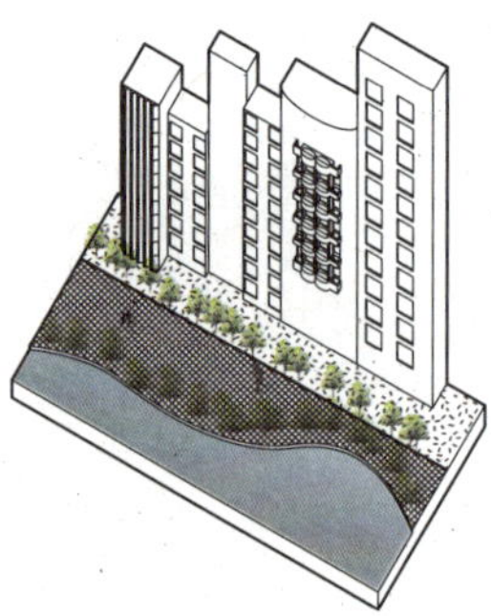

Windbreak function

Efficient water management

Water filtration

Their functionality is diverse. Plants can serve as louvres that provide shadow, natural cooling, and ventilation. They also aid in noise reduction and rainwater collection, and improve the quality of public space.

Shade creation

Light filtration

Camouflage formation

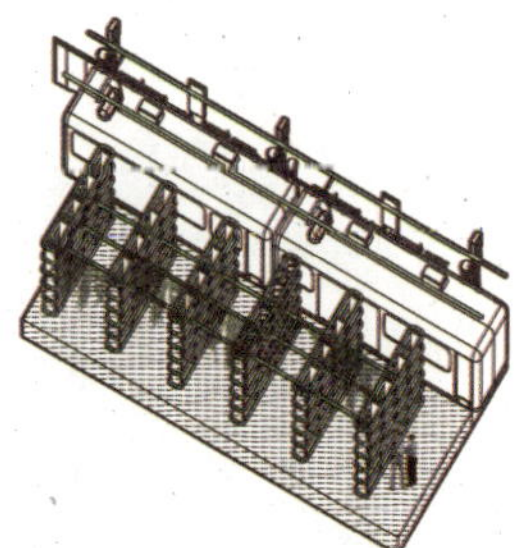

Biofuel generation

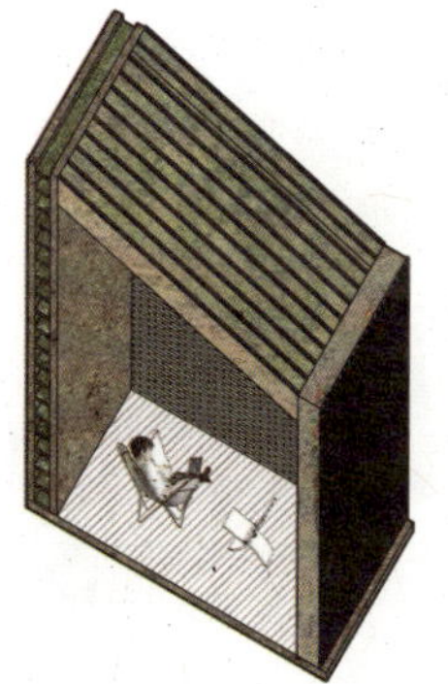

Enhanced thermal performance

Food production

For instance, integrating greenery into buildings can effectively manage wastewater, allow natural light while blocking excessive solar heat gain, reduce noise levels through dense vegetation barriers, and decrease wind speeds with evergreen trees. The shade from trees helps to lower temperatures and energy consumption.

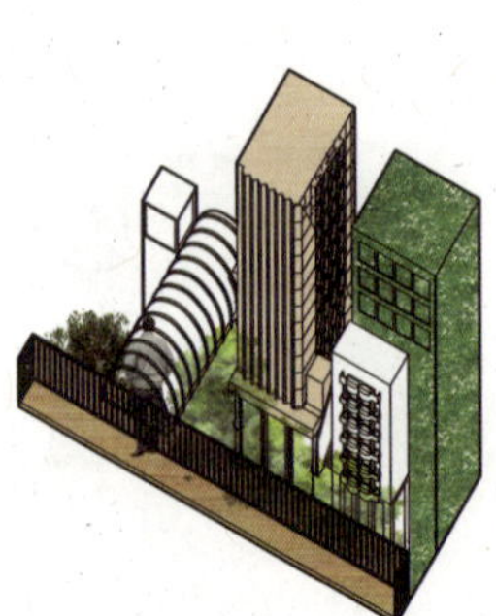

Enhanced views

Support recreational activities and play

Creation of a distinct sense of place

Sense of time progression

Privacy provision

Community enhancement

Green spaces have positive effects on human well-being. Studies indicate that access to green areas can improve physical and mental health by lowering high blood pressure and stress levels. Pregnant women residing near green spaces tend to have fewer premature babies. Aromatic plants such as citrus, lavender, pine, and mint enhance mood, while green areas encourage physical activity among residents.

Additional privacy provision

Improved mental health

Healthier pregnancies

Promotion of physical health

Healthier children

Encouragement of pro-environmental behaviour

Vegetation on buildings creates a sense of intimacy, safety, and freedom. The aesthetic appeal of green spaces influences community satisfaction and interactions. In greener neighbourhoods, residents are more inclined to use shared spaces and engage with neighbours. Native flora establishes a sense of belonging, marking time through seasonality.

If cities were covered with forests

How would it feel?

Forests, encompassing 30 per cent of Earth's land mass, play a fundamental role in supporting life. Yet persistent deforestation threatens this balance. Simultaneously, while urbanised areas occupy only one to three per cent of the planet's land, they are responsible for 50 to 60 per cent of global gas emissions and consume about 75 per cent of global primary energy[1].

Rather than only being responsible for environmental harm, could this urban one to three per cent become a crucial actor in mitigating the climate crisis? *The Green Dip* investigation explores how transforming cities into forests might enhance waste water treatment, improve air quality, mitigate heat island effects and noise pollution, and bolster biodiversity.

The following chapters visualise an extensive greening of cities around the world, raising questions about its implementation and consequences for urban areas and the planet. This is an invitation to imagine cities that resemble and function like forests and to contemplate how far cities are from realising this vision.

Why forests?

Forests provide an array of benefits and ecosystem services. They enhance planetary biodiversity, regulate climate, and act as essential carbon sinks, absorbing roughly 1.5 times the annual emissions of the entire United States.[2] Without forests, there would simply be no life on Earth.

However, over the past 60 years, global forest area has shrunk by 81.7 million hectares, resulting in a more than 60 per cent decline in global forest area per capita. This loss jeopardises the future of biodiversity and affects the lives of 1.6 billion people.

In the past 30 years, the world has lost 10 per cent of its forest area,[3] while the urban population has more than doubled, with 68 per cent of the population expected to live in urban areas by 2050.[4] Urbanized areas have been rapidly expanding, especially in regions such as Shanghai, the Great Bay Area, or West Africa. Urbanization, together with deforestation, are the most visible, irreversible, and rapid alterations in global land coverage.

This rampant urbanisation is responsible for 70 per cent of global CO_2 emissions, 60 per cent of climate emergencies, and up to 80 per cent of the resource consumption that drives deforestation.[5] Life in urban areas depends on intensive agriculture, extensive goods transportation, urban sprawl, and excessive land use—all contributing to environmental degradation.

The urban 1 per cent

Cities are at the frontline of the climate crisis, introducing global urgencies whose consequences necessitate immediate action. Sustainable urbanization is critical to successful development, and cities are the place to act.

Cities are made of predominantly mineral surfaces, making them mostly impermeable and artificialised entities. On the other hand, green areas have demonstrated a positive impact. Parks, boulevards, and gardens act as oases and green lungs and have social, economic, and environmental significance, making them crucial components of the city of the future.

What if cities become the new ground for plants to grow?

How far are cities from realising a Green Dip dream? Faced with the climate crisis and the goal of limiting global warming to 1.5 degrees by 2030 (as stated in the Paris Agreement), some cities have been actively pursuing greening policies, strategies, and pilot projects. *The Green Dip* takes these efforts further by envisioning a comprehensive transformation: what if 1 per cent of urbanised land was 100 per cent green?

Though a series of speculative images produced during a workshop by The Why Factory at IAAC in Barcelona in 2019 as part of the Master of City and Technology programme, this chapter presents visions of cities with 100 per cent tree canopy, located in different regions of the world.

Each city across the globe exists within a unique biome defined by its own fauna and flora. These ecosystems perform differently, and each city's greening impact is different. The most populated biomes are the tropical regions that include densely populated cities in Asia and Africa. Meanwhile, the temperate forests occur in most of Europe and north-eastern America, and the Mediterranean climate prevails in southern Europe, Asia, and large cities in California. This results in the presence of various plant species.

In this initial state of the research, The Why Factory students made a careful selection of plant species, respecting the biomes of each city. From shrubs to trees, these species range from Mediterranean vegetation in Barcelona to tropical forests in Sao Paolo and Kinshasa. The images depict a fusion of cities with their local vegetation, striving to reflect what makes a forest. The results are vivid visions of green cities, where architecture and plants merge and where urbanism becomes landscape.

These visionary images spark a sense of wonder. They aim to raise awareness about the importance of more vegetation in cities, acting as a means of communication to a diverse public, from citizens to policymakers. What kind of architecture and urbanism will arise in this transformed landscape? What materials and products will be required to make plants integral to our cities? What are the essential drivers for greening cities?

Where to start?

Covering cities with vegetation doesn't start from scratch. Cities worldwide have varying land coverage. For instance, Hong Kong's municipality boasts high green coverage (59 per cent), whereas Milan rates notably lower (12 per cent). Datasets provide information about existing green areas and their distribution. This forms a benchmark for assessing the effort needed to transform these cities into complete urban forests.

At the local level, neighbourhoods and districts exhibit differing needs for greening. Underprivileged neighbourhoods often lack vegetation. Some urban centres face substantial expansion and suburbanisation, endangering green land coverage. Some regions qualify as green deserts; some are more polluted than others, some are more exposed to flood risks, and so on.

Some areas also have greater greening potential. They are simply easier to green and require less investment, offer more space for experimentation, or facilitate low-maintenance plant growth. Wastelands, neglected spaces, post-industrial areas, and vacant plots present such opportunities. It is imperative to identify drivers for greening. For instance, identifying heat island locations and initiating planting projects within these specific areas is crucial.

On a territorial scale, cities are part of a larger network of urban areas. They form an interconnected system of urban centres linked by infrastructure. Should this network be entirely enveloped in green, cities might act as natural parks instead of mineral entities. They could become comprehensive biodiversity corridors ensuring continuity throughout the territory instead of generating barriers: an unbroken ecological network.

[1] https://unhabitat.org/topic/urban-energy

[2] Forests around the world are estimated to absorb about 7.6 billion metric tons, acting as a net carbon sink of roughly 1.5 times the annual emissions from the entire United States.

[3] https://www.nature.com/articles/ngeo756

[4] https://www.un.org/development/desa/publications/2018-revision-of-world-urbanization-prospects.html

[5] https://ourworldindata.org/deforestation#:~:text=The%20world%20loses%20almost%20six,this%20occurs%20in%20the%20tropics.

https://news.climate.columbia.edu/2010/02/11/urbanization-deforestation-reforestation/

https://www.nature.com/articles/ngeo756

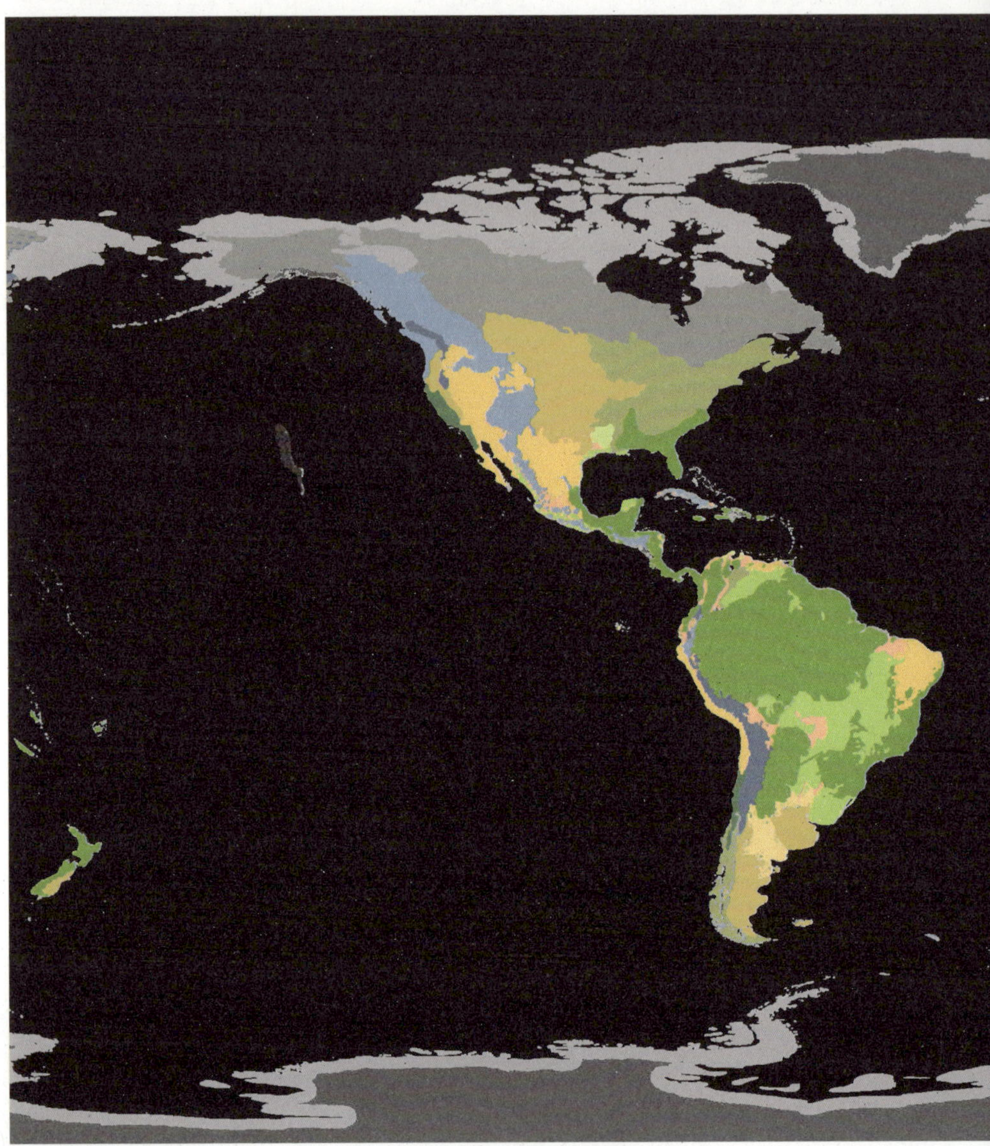

World map of biomes

- Tundra
- Taiga
- Alpine tundra
- Montane forest
- Mediterranean
- Rainforest
- Dry leaf forest
- Semi arid desert
- Arid desert & xeric shrubland
- Dry steppe
- Savanna
- Temperate steppe
- Temperate broadleaf forest
- Monsoon forest

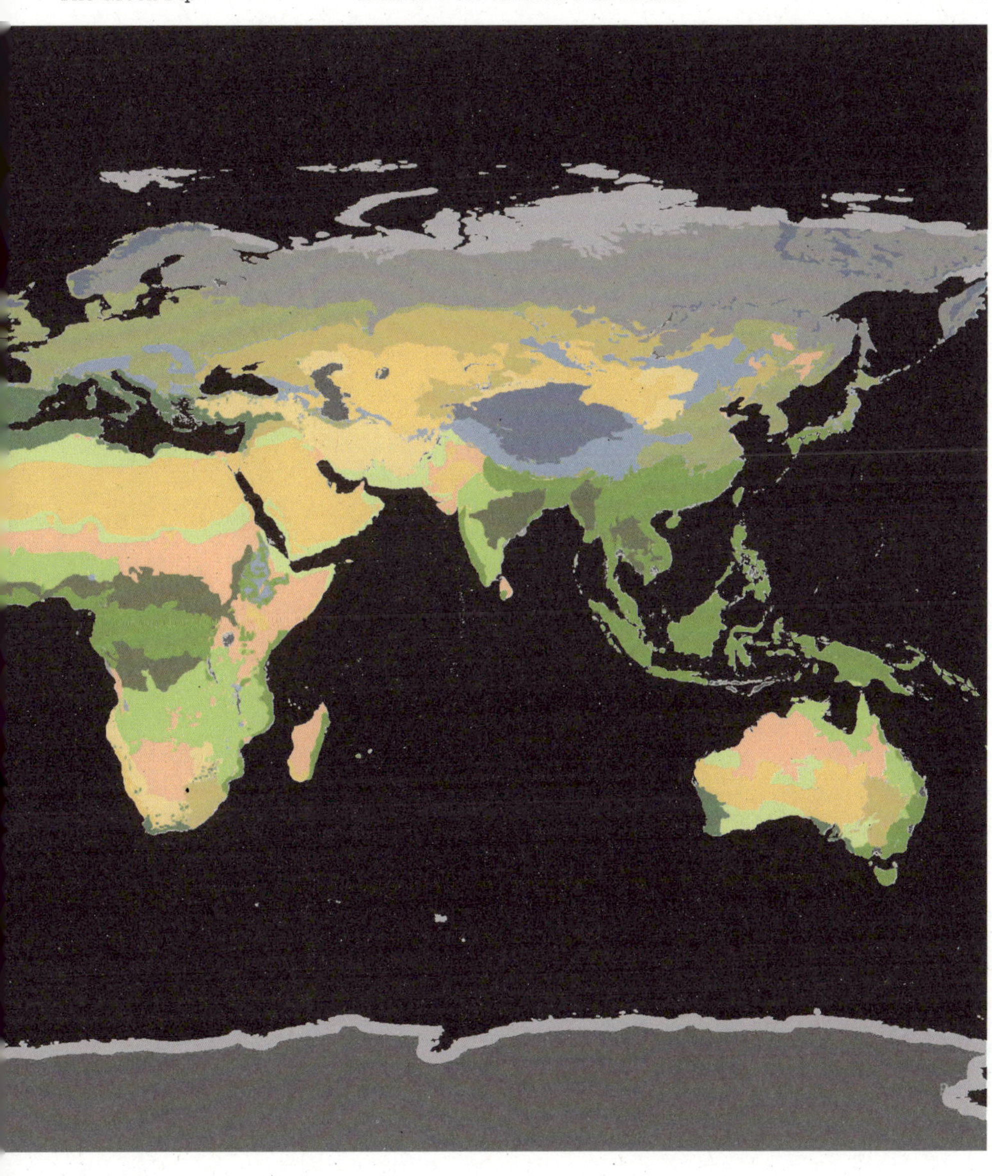

New York

São Paulo

World map of urbanised areas in their respective biomes

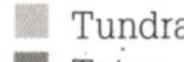

- Tundra
- Taiga
- Alpine tundra
- Montane forest
- Mediterranean
- Rainforest
- Dry leaf forest
- Semi arid desert
- Arid desert & xeric shrubland
- Dry steppe
- Savanna
- Temperate steppe
- Temperate broadleaf forest
- Monsoon forest

St Petersburg
Moscow
Beijing
Milan
rcelona
Dubai
Mumbai
Kinshasa
Hong Kong

Beijing (China)

Biome: Rainforest
From 36 per cent to 100 per cent of green coverage within the municipal administrative boundaries

Hong Kong (China)

Biome: Rainforest
From 59 per cent to 100 per cent of green coverage within the municipal administrative boundaries

Wallcovering
金運来
TAXI

Saint Petersburg (Russia)

Biome: Taiga
From 25 per cent to 100 per cent of green coverage within the municipal administrative boundaries

Kinshasa (DR Congo)

Biome: Rainforest
From 25 per cent to 100 per cent of green coverage within the municipal administrative boundaries

Milan (Italy)

Biome: Mediterranean
From 12 per cent to 100 per cent of green coverage within the municipal administrative boundaries

TORINO

Barcelona (Spain)

Biome: Mediterranean
From 19 per cent to 100 per cent of green coverage within the municipal administrative boundaries

Sao Paulo (Brazil)

Biome: Rainforest
From 30 per cent to 100 per cent of green coverage within the municipal administrative boundaries

Green voices

In conversation with experts

What do experts say about *The Green Dip*?

This chapter compiles three interviews and an essay from various researchers, landscape engineers, and urban ecologists.

From theory to practice, the different viewpoints explore the reasons and methods behind extensively greening the city and highlight genuine concerns. The chapter underscores the role of science in making cities greener, and the potential benefits. It also reveals the need to publicise successful projects, allowing initiatives to take root, emphasising control and maintenance, acknowledging that these transformations take time, and demonstrating the importance of working with data.

Reflecting on *The Green Dip* and providing insights into The Why Factory's research, the experts explore the effectiveness and long-term benefits of integrating vegetation in cities, the metrics behind the growth of plants in urban spaces, and the necessity to advocate for an ecologically conscious approach to urbanisation.

"Time will prove greening works"

Adrien Ravon in conversation with Anna Yudina

Adrien Ravon: What's your first reaction to our research for *The Green Dip*?

Anna Yudina: Regarding the controversy about greenwashing, there is a need to disclose and criticise some approaches that are clearly greenwashing. On the other hand, there is a need to discuss some valid concerns. What are the challenges that are related to the idea of massively greening cities? Not in the sense of why it won't work, but if there are objections that really need consideration, they should be discussed. Architects need to think about this. Greenwashing is one thing. Valid concerns are something else, which implies being optimistic and being able to prove that greening cities works.

AR So, if it is proven that greening cities provides benefits for cities, why is it not happening?

AY Greening cities involves a lot of financial, political, and sociological aspects. People are sometimes not ready to embrace that change.

I'm witnessing that a few projects that received the approval of municipalities are struggling with implementing this greening idea. The Low Line, a project of an underground park testing the ability to bring sunlight underground and to grow plants in a subterranean environment below New York City's Lower East Side, or one of the 'Reinventing Paris' competition winners project of a bio-facade, allowing for cultivating micro-algae by photosynthesis, by XTU architects, in Paris, are two examples. Even though those projects have proven to be functional and provide benefits in different aspects, they are now on hold because no one is ready to take on the financial risk.

AR Most of those projects still have an experimental character. What do you think about the role of design experimentation in the context of greening cities?

AY Real estate development is not an area willing to accept failure. A lot of work should be done by those who are popularising or championing *The Green Dip* concept. It needs to make all the successful examples known and widely publicised. Some projects already gained some proof that it works. There is a need to convince investors in such projects that this is worth a try. The work of Stefano Boeri Architetti already took some steps in convincing stockholders and the public. They went from a luxury project, the Bosco Verticale in Milan, Italy, to a social housing project, the Trudo Vertical Forest, in Eindhoven, the Netherlands. It shows that implementing green in buildings doesn't have to be a luxury if you deal with it properly.

It's a lot about publicising success stories, also on a small scale—then to talk and team up at the level of cities. Some municipalities are more open to these kinds of experiments. Some want to put themselves on the map as being forerunners. It's about gaining support and showing that it has worked on a number of occasions.

AR I understand that there is a need to publicise small-scale experimentation and not only large-scale projects. Is it easier to convince others that small-scale projects can be implemented?

AY I do not think there needs to be a scale distinction. I am interested in how new forms of urban nature, new forms of hybrids between architecture and nature, can be born from different functional requirements. That's what I call *fusion*: trying to understand the urban forms these new hybrids can take. Claudia Pasquero and Marco Poletto from Ecologic Studio have a very interesting way of formulating this: putting trees and plants on buildings is interesting, but what can be done to have them function as a single organism? How can the greening of cities work as a metabolic system?

I also researched the idea of *expansion*. Where can you implement green space if the city is already tightly built? For example, Le Jardin des Fonderies in Nantes, France, by Doazan + Hirschberger, turned a former industrial foundry site of 3,200 m^2 into a park, where plants grow amid the remains of a steel building skeleton. Many of those projects are on a larger scale. But some were also very small-scale projects: for instance, the FLEG Daikanyama, from Taketo Shimohigoshi, in Tokyo, Japan. They just placed some vegetation suspended above the entrance of a green desert neighbourhood. Projects can be different scales. It's just a question of how they respond to the idea of a lack of space for greenery.

I have also developed the idea of *coexistence*, exploring how humans can co-inhabit with flora, as well as *performance* and how to find new architectural forms to implement farming into the cities. This is not small-scale. It's a totally different architectural challenge. For example, the Croton Water Filtration Plant project in New York by Grimshaw gives, on the one hand, a public golf field to the city. On the other hand,

"Depending on your purpose, some challenges may probably be achieved in a better way without using plants. A project could be cheaper, more efficient, and healthier, but without plants. We need to understand how vegetation would be the best way to improve life in cities. It can be an experimental, experiential, or emotional aspect. It's not necessarily always practical."

it finds a way to create a purification landscape that is visible and accessible to the public. This is about performance.

Scale depends on what you are looking for. What kind of functionality are we looking for in a project? It can be very small; it can be very big. No scale should be omitted.

AR So benefits depend on the drivers, then? What do we want to achieve by implementing vegetation in buildings?

AY Depending on your purpose, some challenges may probably be achieved in a better way without using plants. A project could be cheaper, more efficient, and healthier, but without plants. We need to understand how vegetation would be the best way to improve life in cities. It can be an experimental, experiential, or emotional aspect. It's not necessarily always practical. But, of course, it must be justified.

AR Greening cities may not be the solution to the climate crisis, but it can contribute to the absorption of CO_2, mitigate heat island effects, and improve air quality. On the other hand, it can also help to make better architecture and cities. To make more places to meet and interact, and it increases our knowledge about plants. How can you measure this impact?

AY The Australian Pavilion for the World Expo in Milan in 2015, designed by Klaus K. Loenhart from *breathe. austria*, is interesting in that regard. They produced an enclosed forest, which was a reproduction of several layers of alpine forest. This sensory journey increased oxygen production and humidity in a healthy way. It acted as a natural cooling machine in addition to a natural producer. The most interesting part is almost philosophical. When you start living together with nature on such a level, you start reconsidering your relationship with the world and your relationship with the other. That's an interesting way of letting the living into your life. You could interact with it while being in the city and not having to escape to the countryside. It kind of changes your attitude to the world.

Le Jardin des Fonderies, Doazan + Hirschberger, Nantes, France, 2009

Le Jardin des Fonderies, Doazan + Hirschberger, Nantes, France, 2009

AR It seems that there is still a need to convince stakeholders that interacting with the living has an added value. It seems that we need to translate these performances in terms of economic value to prove that it's worth it. Do we need a tool to measure and compare these performances?

AY I think it's very useful for architects and other specialists involved in this set of transformations. It's some kind of revolution of mentality that they are calling upon.

In a way, you need to accept that cities can be completely different. And to achieve this, a lot of things must change on many different levels. People need to become, on one hand, psychologically ready for this idea. On the other hand, you need some facts and figures to support your ideas. There's plenty of research about the fact that vegetation is good for your well-being. There have been research papers that prove how it affects creativity, mental well-being, psychological well-being, and so on. But hard facts are also needed. Both ways are necessary in a coordinated effort to create this shift of mentality.

AR Your motivations for working on the book *Garden City* were to publicise the trends and successes of implementing green in buildings—to prove that it works. What do you think about this trend five years later? What did we learn?

AY When I started the book, the interesting part was to try and see what kind of new experiences of the city and new architectural forms can be born from bringing together nature and architecture. The idea was that we are not pretending even for a second that we can kind of recreate an original forest in the city.

On the other hand, we are so used to having all the benefits that living in a city can bring you. We are not ready to give that up. That doesn't mean that the city is necessarily an unhealthy environment. What can be done, and what can we change to bring back nature into the city? That necessarily means that it will be a new kind of city and a new kind of nature. What kind of hybrid forms and what kind of new experiences of the city will that create? This was the point and the reason for me to write this book, and that's how this idea of new forms of architecture and new forms of nature in the city was born.

If I had to revisit the book five years later, I would look at what is happening to these projects now. Are they happening? Some of the ideas, unfortunately, didn't fly. That's not because they were proven not to be working. Someone still needs to invest in them. It's a very challenging question. Not that I'm pessimistic. But I see that there is still a long way to go.

AR Are time and long-term thinking key issues in those projects?

AY Time and long-term thinking are necessarily integrated because you work with living nature. It needs time to prove that it works, or that it doesn't work, or that it should be dealt with a little bit differently. There should also be some degree of flexibility integrated into projects. It's not about having plan A and plan B but rather being able to adapt the situation to the circumstances. Even though the first option doesn't work, you must find a way to still make it work differently.

Projects can still be alive in very different ways.

AR A building with a lot of trees also implies a series of maintenance costs and it needs water. That also has implications for future generations, who may not be able to afford it. Reversibility and adaptability are important. Are they being considered?

AY In the 90s, Dominique Perrault designed the underground forest for the Bibliothèque Nationale in Paris. Back then, no one believed that this would survive. But now, this beautiful forest is part of the neighbourhood.

In Lille, Gilles Clément designed L'île Derborence. That's an area of 3,500 m^2 of inaccessible nature within the city. The design is to let it grow. So, we can learn from the third landscape, a concept introduced by Clément, inviting us to explore the space neglected by humans and ruled over by natural evolution as an approach to design. How do you allow nature to take over some parts of the building in a controlled way? How can you integrate that into cities? That's an interesting challenge.

AR What's your take on this idea of wilderness in the city? A city where vegetation is not maintained, and we let it grow. Are we ready for this?

AY It has to do with some cultural conditioning. When you compare Asian cities, such as Hong Kong or Taipei in Southeast Asia, with other European cities, they are much more open to somehow negotiating and not letting everything be regulated by the rules provided by official bodies. Somehow, people living in the neighbourhood are used to negotiating different situations. My point is that it's kind of being more open to not regulating everything but letting people negotiate and be more open to a more chaotic and spontaneous expression within the city. Maybe in Europe it's not something we can so easily accept. I don't know how this can be changed. But we need to be less afraid of uncertainty. I'm fantasising, obviously. I'm dreaming and believing in peoples' common sense more than the officials do now. I believe in people's ability to distinguish between bad and good on their own without being told.

Anna Yudina is an author and curator primarily interested in cross-border collaborations and intersecting interests between architecture, design, art, science, and other disciplines. She's the author of *Garden City*, *Supergreen Buildings*, *Urban Skyscapes* and the *New Planted Space*, published in 2017 (Thames & Hudson). The book is a global survey of some of the world's most inventive buildings that bring architecture and horticulture into a sustainable whole.

Breatheaustria, Austrian Pavilion at Expo Milano, Klaus K. Loenhart, Milan, Italy, 2015

Urban ecology lessons for greening the city

Nicholas Pevzner

Design writing is filled with calls to "green the city." Central to the project of *The Green Dip* presented in this book is a reinforcement of the age-old binary in which the city is characterised as "grey," in contrast to the theoretically "green" world outside its bounds. Such binaries are quickly complicated; however, if one looks more closely at the ecosystem processes happening both inside and outside the city, amid all the areas outside of cities that appear green from above, one can find lots of grey bits, as well as many less visible alterations and human intrusions. Conversely, one can find a lot of existing green within city limits. The reality is that many essential natural ecosystem processes exist inside even the densest cities. Beyond the most visible bits of green within the city—the well-tended parks and gardens and tree-lined avenues—there is even more ecosystem activity in the less maintained spaces—in the wooded verges of rail lines and roadways, the scruffy edges of urban waterways, in untended and overgrown backyards, and amid the spontaneous vegetation that colonises vacant, abandoned, or even just temporarily underutilised parcels. Nature being exclusively "out there," outside the city, is an increasingly outdated concept. In fact, the entire field of urban ecology is dedicated to studying and describing how ecosystems inside cities operate and how the whole city operates as an ecosystem.[1]

Urban ecology offers a conceptual framework for approaching the city that doesn't arbitrarily create a binary between natural and constructed systems. By adding social and built systems to the traditional idea of biophysical ecosystems, urban ecology treats humans, our built environment, our infrastructure, our institutions, our culture, our laws, our economies, and our aesthetic preferences all as *part* of urban ecosystems, not outside of them.[2] Redesigning the city as a green oasis is a worthy pursuit. But in asking whether adding more green to the urban environment will produce higher ecological function, we must look at the specifics because not all green is the same.

Plants on buildings: Benefits and tradeoffs

Urban vegetation and urban green spaces can provide a host of ecosystem services,[3] such as water and microclimate regulation, biodiversity support, and cultural services, such as human health and well-being.[4] Yet nuance is needed in where and how this vegetation is added to the urban environment. For example, urban heat island generally decreases with the reduction of paved or built surfaces and the addition of more vegetation. For this reason, many cities have focused on increasing the percentage of urban tree canopy as their primary strategy for reducing daytime temperatures. However, a few scattered trees make little difference to overall heat reduction, while more extensive canopy cover adds up to significant cooling effects.[5] Green roofs and facades are not the same as tree canopy—they can certainly cool the buildings they are on but have a much weaker effect at street level.[6] Yet, as with trees, their overall cooling impact increases the more green roofs a city deploys.

For stormwater regulation, vegetation at ground level or on buildings can reduce the amount of stormwater to some degree through evapotranspiration. Still, the primary mechanism by which green infrastructure provides stormwater benefits is by storing that water in the soil. The higher the soil volume, regardless of vegetation, the more stormwater can be detained there. Rather than being the star player, vegetation, in this case, is a bonus on top of what is essentially a plumbing problem.

For carbon sequestration, the value of adding a veil of vegetation to buildings is less straightforward still. There is a direct trade-off between covering a building in trees and the embodied carbon[7] of the additional structure that this would entail. The carbon that a tree can absorb over its lifetime will rarely exceed the embodied carbon of the extra concrete or steel that it would take to support the weight of the soil that the tree requires to grow. At the same time, that tree will also be paying back the initial carbon debt of all the carbon emissions associated with growing that tree in a commercial nursery, transporting it a long distance to the construction site, and producing all the planting media, drainage layers, inputs, and irrigation needed to sustain it over time.[8]

But what about other vegetation and green space benefits that are harder to quantify? Cultural services like the physical and mental health benefits that everyday access to green space in the city offers have been well-described by an entire canon of public health literature.[9] This access to nearby nature, which can be introduced into even the densest of cities, can bring elements of nature closer to home, offering important value that might supersede that of any other ecosystem services for many people.

The limiting factors for putting vegetation on buildings come down to the same constraints that regulate

"There is a direct trade-off between covering a building in trees and the embodied carbon of the additional structure that this would entail. The carbon that a tree can absorb over its lifetime will rarely exceed the embodied carbon of the extra concrete or steel that it would take to support the weight of the soil that the tree requires to grow."

vegetation elsewhere: soil, water, climate, light, and care. While landscapes on buildings are indeed components of living, functioning ecosystems, their upkeep and longevity require significant long-term labour. From the point of view of resources, trees on buildings need to be given adequate volumes of soil and water. From the point of view of care, it matters whether those trees can self-seed and reproduce on their own or whether they will be reliant on gardeners to install and maintain them—and eventually replace them at the end of their life.

On the other hand, spontaneous vegetation requires minimal tending: aggressive urban-adapted species will seek out the cracks and crevices of urban spaces wherever they can take root and grow. While it can appear informal and unruly and may be less appreciated by some residents,[10] and while it often features a significant percentage of non-native species, spontaneous urban vegetation nevertheless provides important ecosystem services by sequestering carbon, regulating stormwater, and providing cooling and biodiversity value,[11] while introducing a bit of wildness into the urban environment. Even if not universally beloved, these informal, spontaneous wild spaces can carry unique social and emotional benefits, especially for young people.[12]

Different building typologies can offer more or less opportunity for different types of green interventions in cities.[13] From the perspective of available space, the large, wide roofs of industrial buildings offer more potential area than those of tall, skinny residential towers. From the standpoint of providing the necessary soil volume for growing vegetation, a building's structural capacity will limit how deep a soil profile it can physically support. The extent of the soil volume will determine how much these plants on structure will behave more like they would in-ground versus in a pot—with consequences for both their degree of required care and their ecological potential.

Green patches and stepping stones

From the point of view of biodiversity value and ecosystem function, if our goal is to increase the overall

Philadelphia, USA

Philadelphia, USA

vegetation and landscape in the city, we should primarily look not at the surfaces of buildings but at all the space between them. More important than the building's typology in hosting vegetation is the city's urban form—the pattern of open space and how much land remains unbuilt and available for in-ground landscape. Did a city retain large green spaces or fill everything with urban fabric? How much total green space is between the city's many lots and properties? Zoning concepts such as green area ratio (GAR)[14] attempt to regulate and increase the amount of green space on a given parcel, but the same idea can be applied at the scale of the block, the neighbourhood, or the city writ large.

From a landscape ecology perspective, the biggest determinant of how much habitat a green patch in the city provides has to do with how large it is: what is called its species-area relationship (SAR), whereby the larger the patch, the greater the total number of species that it can host.[15] Large parks—defined as those above 50[16] or 200[17] hectares—offer the most ecological value, allowing for a mosaic of habitat types, including enough habitat for area-sensitive species and "urban avoiders" and the potential to adapt to and recover from disturbance. Next, we might look at a patch's habitat structure: how much structural diversity does it have? More structural diversity corresponds with more habitat niches, thus serving a greater species diversity. Does the site have a variety of vegetation heights, branches, perches, cavities, and hiding spaces? Does it contain vegetation that supports the mutual relationships that some native insect and animal species have co-evolved with and that they depend upon for food?[18] Structural diversity can occur at any scale, from a large forest to a small backyard, side lot, or green roof. The most biodiverse green roofs, for instance, are not shallow uniform carpets of non-native sedum but rather contain more diversity in soil depth and materials (including the random pile of bricks or woody debris) and native soils that might contain native seeds—all of which allows for controlled colonisation by a wider mix of plant species.[19] Strategies like these increase the structural complexity of the 3-dimensional urban matrix and make more room for a wider assortment of species.

Beyond the size of a given green space on its own, the degree of connectivity or isolation of a given patch of habitat from other similar patches matters.[20] Taken together, even small bits of high-quality habitat can be stepping stones, helping some species move from one patch of large, high-quality habitat to another. The degree of connectivity depends on the mobility of a species; species that can fly can use a much larger and more dispersed archipelago of habitats than those that can only walk or crawl. Conversely, the degree of isolation depends on how dangerous or inhospitable the intervening space between patches of habitats is to the species in question and how much it acts as a barrier to movement. The size, shape, and likelihood of success of a connectivity intervention will depend on understanding and matching the target species' habitat needs and movement preferences.

Finally, we must recognise that greening the city must be seen within a broader spatial context. Most species population declines are driven by habitat losses outside the city, with agriculture being the primary driver of biodiversity loss globally due to land conversion, increasing farm homogenisation, and the chemical toxicity of industrial agriculture.[21] Fragmentation of large unbroken forest habitats by roads, infrastructure, clearings, or other human interventions also drives global biodiversity loss, with an especially pronounced effect on species that are "interior specialists" that cannot survive in the edge conditions that fragmentation produces.[22] Other species are being harmed by the disappearance of specific habitats fine-tuned by evolution to match those species' needs, such as stopover feeding grounds for migratory shorebirds, which are disappearing due to the combined pressures of coastal development, wetland loss, and sea level rise.[23] To the extent that urban density can alleviate some of the pressure of urban sprawl elsewhere, regardless of whether it is green or grey, then we can look at it as a net benefit for biodiversity—urbanisation as a form of land sparing.[24]

But the design of the city itself still matters. To begin to turn the tide against the biodiversity crisis and create joyful and wondrous pockets of nature accessible to all of the city's residents, an aggressive attitude towards greening the city is required. Can buildings be designed to work together as pieces of a larger habitat mosaic, hosting biodiverse and structurally diverse native gardens fine-tuned to cater to local species of concern? Can they be designed to restitch disconnected fragments of habitat back together at multiple scales and levels, prioritising these green connections as the city's new primary ground plane while perhaps routing people and their vehicles below? Can they become carbon-neutral or carbon-negative in their material sourcing, reducing and even reversing their emissions profiles?[25] Can they celebrate and elucidate the variety, diversity, and interconnection of food webs, ecosystem flows, species, and ecological relationships present on a site at some prior time and aspire to rebuild and maintain this ecological complexity? It is here that the potential of greening the city is the most profound. As the intersecting biodiversity and climate crises increase the urgency of designing better with nature, we need to be operating along all scales and practices—in conservation planning and urban design, as well as landscape and architecture, to create more ecologically functioning, resilient, legible, and delightful cities for humans and non-humans alike.

Nicholas Pevzner is an Assistant Professor in the Department of Landscape Architecture and Regional Planning at the University of Pennsylvania's Weitzman School of Design. His research spans across the topics of urban ecological systems, energy landscapes, and climate policy.

[1] Steward T.A. Pickett, Mary L. Cadenasso, J. Morgan Grove, Charles H. Nilon, Richard V. Pouyat, Wayne C. Zipperer, and Robert Costanza. "Urban Ecological Systems: Linking Terrestrial Ecological, Physical, and Socioeconomic Components of Metropolitan Areas." *Annual Review of Ecology and Systematics* 32 (2001): 127-157.

[2] Steward T.A. Pickett and J. Morgan Grove. "Urban ecosystems: What would Tansley do?." *Urban Ecosystems* 12 (2009): 1-8.

[3] Ecosystem services have been defined as "the benefits human populations derive, directly or indirectly, from ecosystem functions" by Costanza et al. (1997), and are divided into four main types: Provisioning Services that supply human populations with fresh water, wood and fibre, fuel, or food either directly or through the service of pollination; Regulating Services that regulate climate, flood, disease, and water quality; Cultural Services that offer people with recreation, educational experiences, aesthetic experiences, or spiritual enrichment; and Supporting Services like nutrient cycling, soil formation, biodiversity, and primary production that are necessary for supporting all the other ecosystem services.
See: Robert Costanza, Ralph d'Arge, Rudolf De Groot, Stephen Farber, Monica Grasso, Bruce Hannon, Karin Limburg et al. "The value of the world's ecosystem services and natural capital." *Nature* 387, no. 6630 (1997): 253-260.

[4] Thomas Elmqvist, Heikki Setälä, S. N. Handel, Sander van der Ploeg, James Aronson, James Nelson Blignaut, Erik Gómez-Baggethun, D. J. Nowak, Jakub Kronenberg, and Rudolf de Groot. "Benefits of restoring ecosystem services in urban areas." *Current opinion in environmental sustainability* 14 (2015): 101-108.

[6] Carly D. Ziter, Eric J. Pedersen, Christopher J. Kucharik, and Monica G. Turner. "Scale-dependent interactions between tree canopy cover and impervious surfaces reduce daytime urban heat during summer." *Proceedings of the National Academy of Sciences* 116, no. 15 (2019): 7575-7580. Francis, Lotte Fjendbo Møller, and Marina Bergen Jensen. "Benefits of green roofs: A systematic review of the evidence for three ecosystem services." *Urban forestry & urban greening* 28 (2017): 167-176.

[7] Embodied carbon is defined as the carbon emissions associated with the manufacturing, transportation, installation, maintenance, and disposal of a project's building materials. See: Carbon Leadership Forum. "Embodied Carbon 101." (Seattle: Carbon Leadership Forum, 2020). https://carbonleadershipforum.org/embodied-carbon-101/

[8] Dewayne L. Ingram, Charles R. Hall, and Joshua Knight. "Understanding carbon footprint in production and use of landscape plants." *HortTechnology* 29, no. 1 (2019): 6-10.

[9] Rod Matsuoka, and William Sullivan. "Urban nature: Human psychological and community health." In: Ian Douglas, David Goode, Mike Houck, and Rusong Wang (eds.) *The Routledge handbook of urban ecology* (London and New York: Routledge, 2010): 408-423.

[10] Gonzalo de la Fuente de Val. "The Effect of Spontaneous Wild Vegetation on Landscape Preferences in Urban Green Spaces." *Urban Forestry & Urban Greening* 81 (2023) 127863.

[11] Ingo Kowarik. "Urban biodiversity, ecosystems and the city. Insights from 50 years of the Berlin School of urban ecology." *Landscape and Urban Planning* 240 (2023): 104877.

[12] Hugh R. Stanford, Georgia E. Garrard, Holly Kirk, and Joe Hurley. "A social-ecological framework for identifying and governing informal greenspaces in cities." *Landscape and Urban Planning* 221 (2022): 104378.

[13] Robert I. McDonald, Myla F. J. Aronson, Timothy Beatley, Erin Beller, Micaela Bazo, Robin Grossinger, Kelsey Jessup, Andressa V. Mansur, José Antonio Puppim de Oliveira, Stephanie Panlasigui, Joe Burg, Nicholas Pevzner, Danielle Shanahan, Lauren Stoneburner, Andrew Rudd, Erica Spotswood. "Denser and greener cities: Green interventions to achieve both urban density and nature," *People and Nature* vol. 5, Issue 1 (February 2023).

[14] Melissa Keeley. "The Green Area Ratio: an urban site sustainability metric." *Journal of environmental planning and management* 54, no. 7 (2011): 937-958.

[15] This species area relationship, where the number of species rises along a curve as the area of a given landscape patch increases, has been observed in countless studies across all kinds of taxa, from insects, to birds, plants, and mammals. It has been called "one of community ecology's few genuine laws" by Thomas W. Schoener (1976). See: Thomas W. Schoener. "The

species-area relation within archipelagos: models and evidence from island land birds." In 16th international ornithological congress, 629-642. 1976.

[16] The San Francisco Estuary Institute defines green areas 130 acres (52.6 hectares) in size as "Regional Biodiversity Hubs." See: Erica Spotswood, Robin Grossinger, Steve Hagerty, Micaela Bazo, Matthew Benjamin, Erin Beller, Letitia Grenier, Ruth Askevold. *Making Nature's City.* SFEI Contribution No. 947. (Richmond, CA: San Francisco Estuary Institute, 2019). https://www.sfei.org/documents/making-natures-city

[17] Ecological designer and planner Nina-Marie Lister defines "Large Parks" as those larger than 500 acres (202 hectares). See: Nina-Marie Lister. "Sustainable large parks: ecological design or designer ecology." In: Julia Czerniak, George Hargreaves, and John Beardsley (eds.). *Large parks.* (New York: Princeton Architectural Press, 2007): 35-57.

[18] Examples of plant-insect or plant-animal mutualisms might be based on trading pollen for pollination services by bees, or trading edible berries for seed dispersal by birds, for example. See: Steven N. Handel. "The role of plant-animal mutualisms in the design and restoration of natural communities." In: Krystyna M. Urbanska, Nigel R. Webb, and Peter J. Edwards (eds.) *Restoration ecology and sustainable development* (Cambridge: Cambridge University Press, 1997): 111-132.

[19] Nigel Dunnett. "Ruderal green roofs." In: Richard K. Sutton (ed). *Green roof ecosystems.* (Lincoln, Nebrasca: Springer, 2015): 233-255.

[20] The relationship of the degree of isolation between patches on how many species could survive on a given patch was demonstrated by MacArthur and Wilson in their experiments in the Florida Keys, which confirmed the theory of island biogeography. See: Robert H. MacArthur and Edward O. Wilson. *The theory of island biogeography.* (Princeton: Princeton University Press, 2001).

[21] Tim G. Benton, Carling Bieg, Helen Harwatt, Roshan Pudasaini, and Laura Wellesley. "Food system impacts on biodiversity loss: Three levers for food system transformation in support of nature." Chatham House, London (Research Paper), February 2021. https://www.unep.org/resources/publication/food-system-impacts-biodiversity-loss

[22] Nick M. Haddad, Lars A. Brudvig, Jean Clobert, Kendi F. Davies, Andrew Gonzalez, Robert D. Holt, Thomas E. Lovejoy et al. "Habitat fragmentation and its lasting impact on Earth's ecosystems." *Science advances* 1, no. 2 (2015): e1500052.

[23] North American Bird Conservation Initiative. "The State of the Birds, United States of America, 2022." (Washington, DC: North American Bird Conservation Initiative, 2022). https://www.stateofthebirds.org/2022/wp-content/uploads/2022/10/state-of-the-birds-2022-spreads.pdf

[24] Masashi Soga, Yuichi Yamaura, Shinsuke Koike, and Kevin J. Gaston. "Land sharing vs. land sparing: does the compact city reconcile urban development and biodiversity conservation?." *Journal of Applied Ecology* 51, no. 5 (2014): 1378-1386.

[25] There are many avenues to reducing the carbon intensity of building materials, as well as electrifying buildings to eliminate their on-site fossil emissions. While there are very few carbon-negative building materials currently available, the use of climate-smart wood products and agricultural waste products in bio-based building materials offer one such pathway: locking up biogenic carbon that would have returned to the atmosphere through decomposition in long-lived building materials instead. See: Stephanie Carlisle and Nicholas Pevzner. "The Thin Thread of Carbon." In: Space Caviar (ed.) *Non-Extractive Architecture, Volume 1: On Designing Without Depletion* (London: Sternberg Press, 2021).

Philadelphia street, USA

"Tiles out, plants in!"

Adrien Ravon in conversation with Marco Roos

Adrien Ravon: Naturalis Biodiversity Center is the Netherlands national research institute for biodiversity, dedicated to describing, understanding, and preserving biodiversity. What's your research at Naturalis focusing on?

Marco Roos: I have a special interest in the floristic aspects of urbanisation. My research revolves around projects that range from industrial design for green roof walks, pavement plants, and spontaneous plant growth in cities to urban biodiversity corridors. I also collaborate with some architecture offices, providing feedback on the biodiversity aspects of their projects and how they can enhance the biodiversity components of their designs.

AR Have the collaborations and exchanges between architects and urban ecologists evolved over the past decades?

MR My experience covers the last five years, and I must admit that I'm somewhat disappointed with the new buildings in the Bioscience Park in Leiden, where we provided advice on improving biodiversity five years ago. The new buildings are exceptionally sterile, constructed mainly from steel, glass, and concrete. They offer no opportunities for spontaneous colonisation of plants and animals. The reality often doesn't align with the architects' visualisations, which tend to present idyllic summer sceneries.

Some architects genuinely desire to gain knowledge of urban ecology, but financial constraints play a significant role. Implementing a green roof, for instance, necessitates more planting, which comes at a cost.

AR It's puzzling that we still need to prove the value of biodiversity. Many people remain unconvinced about the benefits of incorporating plants into buildings and are more focused on the drawbacks.

MR The benefits of biodiversity are long term, while the drawbacks tend to be short term. This poses a challenge to us.

As a botanist, it strikes me how biodiversity is often perceived. Biodiversity is commonly understood as coexisting with animals: plants are often taken for granted, seen as mere substrates for animals. We need to consider how to coexist with other living organisms.

In *The Green Dip*, the term "forest" is used when, in reality, it's merely about planting trees. Simply planting many trees doesn't create a forest. A forest represents the climax stage of a succession of ecological cycles, moving from pioneer or disturbed vegetation towards a woody, tree-dominated habitat. A forest is an intricate combination of soil development, the surrounding biome, microorganisms, and the plant species that settle in. Many factors contribute to forming a forest.

I often lecture about rewilding cities, focusing on creating autonomous and spontaneous vegetation, not just individual plants. Real vegetation establishes itself through colonisation and natural successions, shaped by the interaction of soil development and plant growth. This concept is central to my vision of a genuinely nature-inclusive city.

Architectural projects often emphasise ecosystem functions but overlook specific tree species. Ecologically, the species used and how they are introduced into an ecosystem are crucial. The source of these species, which should ideally be from the local vicinity, impacts biodiversity. Biodiversity is about genes, species, and habitats, with genes often being neglected. Nowadays, there's a trend towards introducing cultivated plants, which can disrupt natural biodiversity patterns.

From a design perspective, it's about designing ecological processes rather than striving for a predetermined final product. A building should serve as a starting point for natural colonisation.

AR Does "spontaneous" mean "not maintained"?

MR Spontaneous doesn't solely refer to the absence of maintenance. By introducing species, you provide a head start for newcomers. However, these natural colonisers need more time to establish themselves, but do so organically. There is a risk that repeated planting and sowing might be necessary because the initial placement of plants is often incorrect.

There's a saying in the Netherlands: "Tiles out, plants in." My view is that if you remove tiles, plants will naturally follow. That's the autonomy and the spontaneity of plant growth.

Control primarily lies in maintenance. The choice of whether to allow high vegetation, encourage succession toward a forest, or maintain a herbaceous landscape depends on the preferred maintenance regime. The emphasis should not solely be on the forest; open vegetation is often crucial for insects, flower diversity, and providing open soil for nesting. The mowing regime directs the fundamental ecological direction. A sustainable urban vegetation strategy necessitates considering the full complexity of the ecosystem, encompassing soils, species composition, herbivores, pollinators, and more. This comprehensive perspective, instead of focusing on individual species, is crucial.

We tend to grow trees in the city, often in locations unsuitable for their growth. Consequently, various arrangements are required. Nevertheless, these trees often have minimal mycorrhizal connections to the soil, leading to a high maintenance demand. Approximately 80% of the carbon fixed by trees is stored in the organic component of the soil, not in the tree itself. When the trees are removed, the carbon is released into the atmosphere, while the soil remains a stable climate buffer. However, the urban soil is often meagre.

To promote a genuinely nature-inclusive city, we should establish new soil types on buildings, such as emulating Mediterranean rock landscapes. This approach involves a mix of shrubs and trees that are less vulnerable to extreme weather conditions (draughts, floods...). It's not about creating a luxurious forest but rather mimicking rocky landscapes where microorganisms can interact with plant roots, allowing the development of a comprehensive ecosystem.

AR Would introducing species and processes from the Mediterranean biome to cities like Paris or Rotterdam be more suitable?

MR While I'm not entirely against introducing helpful species, most plant species migrate naturally due to human activities, such as travelling by train, adhering to car tyres, or hitching rides on planes. There are already numerous Mediterranean elements in Northern European cities. Allow the processes to start with pioneers but offer limited assistance though occasional seeding of select species, then observe how spontaneous colonisation develops. Indigenous species have ample potential if we allow them to establish naturally. This requires courage.

Some ecologists argue that we cannot afford to lose trees in the city, advocating for digital monitoring and artificial methods to maintain tree health. However, if a location is unsuitable for trees to grow, we should consider allowing shrubby or herbaceous vegetation to take root. An herbaceous ecosystem can accumulate carbon in the soil when it remains undisturbed, which is essential for climate buffering.

AR It seems that there's a dichotomy between cities and nature, or cities and countryside, opposing these two environments. But cities are often much more biodiverse than certain parts of the countryside, especially in the Netherlands. Is that really the case?

MR Amsterdam is proud of having so many species within its municipality. It's a mosaic of different biotypes. The area is quite fragmented.

Another point is that most cities resemble each other. When you visit London, Berlin or Amsterdam, urban biodiversity is quite similar. The specific biodiversity of the surrounding and original landscape is disappearing on a larger scale. Urbanisation globally standardises flora, creating a similar biome and mosaic.

Leiden Bio Science Park, Leiden, Netherlands

Leiden Bio Science Park, Leiden, Netherlands

“Simply planting many trees doesn’t create a forest. A forest represents the climax stage of a succession of ecological cycles, moving from pioneer or disturbed vegetation towards a woody, tree-dominated habitat. A forest is an intricate combination of soil development, the surrounding biome, microorganisms, and the plant species that settle in. Many factors contribute to forming a forest.”

At the local scale, in the Netherlands, agricultural land is almost sterile. From the farmers’ perspective, any additional animals or plants come at the cost of their yield, so they tend to reduce biodiversity. Transforming agricultural land into an integrated urban environment with ample space for local habitats would be an improvement. But building in natural sites always results in a loss. The typical forest or swamp would be under pressure, leading to increased stress factors.

In the Netherlands, about two-thirds of our land is agricultural, while 20% is urbanised with cities and their infrastructure, including main roads and railroads. Less than 14% is what we classify as nature, including cultivated nature like tree plantations. The city landscape is the second largest landscape after the agricultural landscape. Our nature sites are lagging behind.

AR So, cities and networks of cities have great potential to connect and improve biodiversity on a larger scale?

MR We need to pursue that. The urban landscape in the Netherlands comprises 20% of urbanisation. China’s coastal zone faces even worse challenges. Cities dominate many areas worldwide, and we must also consider urban sprawl.

This perception affects how people view nature. Today’s population, including farmers, predominantly views life from an urban perspective and manages our environment as such. We must shift toward a more nature-based perspective, beginning with the autonomous and spontaneous settlement of organisms. We often accept this for bees, butterflies, and birds, but not for plants. Every organism seeks its ideal climate, food, safety, and reproduction conditions. If we fail to provide these for certain organisms, they will not come, reproduce or flourish. We must take care of these settlement factors to foster large plant populations in the city instead of trying to eliminate them.

AR There is an understanding and conviction that we need to act to make cities better places to live. We know that green spaces hold value. Why are we not doing enough to green our cities?

MR There is a social and psychological reason for this. Many people view unmanaged plant growth as chaotic and feel that it affects their sense of safety. Allowing street plants to grow spontaneously may make an area appear neglected, which is often linked to social status.

Street plants are essential for soil life, insects, pollinators, and birds. For instance, sparrows feed on the seeds of street plants, contributing to a broader biome. If a street is used, plants won't grow. Additionally, people appreciate butterflies but may inadvertently destroy caterpillars. They do not realise that by eliminating the caterpillars, butterflies also disappear, along with many other species. The trend for neatly manicured lawns has led to the loss of various species.

AR It's clear that we have much work to do, not only in the way we design our cities but in how we inhabit them.

MR We must build with ecological processes in mind. A building should offer spaces for spontaneous plant settlements. Some plants may fail, while others thrive. Predicting the outcomes is challenging because of variable weather conditions, including dry spells, wet spells, prevailing winds, and peak winds. You can't predict what will happen. Designing more ruin-like buildings, which offer numerous opportunities for spontaneous settlement, can be advantageous. This is where local plant life can thrive.

AR So, we must sometimes embrace the possibility of failure. Is that the case?

MR In nature, a 95% loss is affordable. This is how plant populations should be organised. There needs to be some degree of loss, allowing the best adapted to survive.

Everything starts with the soil. We should consider how to utilise the indigenous soil, the soil that's present, to align with the geomorphology and hydrology of the area. When designing above ground, starting from the soil and creating space for roots is worthwhile.

AR So, essentially, no more pots?

MR Pots are primarily decorative. They contain only one plant and have a very limited microbiome. Plant growth heavily relies on interactions with mycorrhiza and other components of the soil biome, as well as water and nutrients. Potted plants often require frequent replacement. When plants are connected, a soil ecosystem begins to develop.

AR Do you view buildings as extensions of the soil, then?

MR When we think of novel ecosystems in the city, rooftop systems could be a promising area for further development. These systems often consist of just a five-centimetre substrate layer. In the Netherlands, we have these wildlife bridges that cross main roads. They have become ecosystems in themselves, autonomously vegetated. This concept is also applicable to buildings.

If we connect novel ecosystems in the city with the soil level and surrounding areas, they will soon be inhabited by numerous species and continue to evolve.

In ruins, we can observe this happening. It is also possible in new buildings. By connecting them, people can traverse from one rooftop to another, creating a genuine real urban network. We can achieve much if we take incremental steps, moving from street level to at least a significant portion of rooftops.

Marco Roos has a background in tropical botany and, in the past decade, has specialised as a biologist focusing on urban biodiversity. He imparts his expertise to students through teaching, during field trips, and supervising internship projects. Furthermore, he collaborates with municipal and other authorities to advocate for biodiversity in the urban ecosystem.

Leiden Bio Science Park, Leiden, Netherlands

"Green makes a difference"

Javier Arpa Fernández and Adrien Ravon in conversation with Wim Beining and Sander de Klerk

Javier Arpa Fernández: Could you explain what Ebben does?

Wim Beining: Ebben is a family company that started 165 years ago. They were one of the first nurseries in The Netherlands to work with multi-stemmed trees. Now, Ebben is one of the largest nurseries globally, growing 1,250 species, mainly multi-stemmed. Multi-stemmed trees are especially vital because they are quite stable. They have a very low centre of gravity and therefore can be used on roof gardens, where winds are usually stronger than at ground level.

JAF Where are your nurseries?

WB Our nurseries are in the Netherlands, in Kuik. Ebben owns 170 different parcels, which together comprise five hundred hectares.

JAF Can you grow everything in Kuik, or are you limited by climate constraints?

WB The plots are near a river. Over hundreds of years, the river changed its path, so we have a wide variety of soils. Some are sandy, others with clay, which means you can grow a great variety of plants and trees.

Sander de Klerk: All the big nurseries in Europe are along rivers because of the variety of soils. We have light, poor soils where pine trees grow, and we have very hard soils, and all the varieties in between.

JAF What was your initial impression when you saw our research on The Green Dip?

WB A *Green Dip* of all world cities like the one you propose in your research depends very much on the local climate

“While there's an initial resource investment in materials and the carbon footprint associated with construction, the long-term environmental benefits of having trees in urban environments tend to outweigh these concerns.”

and climate change. For instance, certain regions of the Netherlands, Germany, and Belgium share similar climates that accommodate only specific trees and plants. These same plants wouldn't thrive in the southern regions. However, due to climate adaptation, these plants are beginning to thrive further north. We anticipate that in the next 10, 20, or 30 years, native trees and plants in the Netherlands won't thrive as they currently do. The maintenance of these native species will likely become quite expensive.

Now, consider the east of Europe, where some species can endure extreme weather conditions down to −20 degrees Celsius. However, we no longer experience such frigid temperatures in the Netherlands. Conversely, if you look at a place like Greece, you'll find many trees that also grow successfully in the Netherlands. In fact, at Ebben, we have cultivated at least a hundred species of trees from the Mediterranean, and they thrive here. Why? Because we no longer experience extreme temperatures, such as −10, −15, and −20 degrees Celsius.

Sometimes, we introduce species from North America that haven't previously been cultivated in the Netherlands. We allow them to grow for 10, 20, or 30 years to determine whether any of these species can adapt to the local climatic conditions. If they can, it means we have a new tree variety in the Netherlands. However, it's worth noting that the same tree grown in the Netherlands and in North America can be remarkably different.

JAF You have been working with different municipalities and architects. Why do you think cities and architecture are asking nurseries to bring trees to them?

WB There are several reasons for this growing interest. Trees offer several advantages. They provide shade and contribute to cooling the environment. For instance, a building with a glass façade surrounded by tall trees, about 20 m high, located at 1.5 m from the facade, can reduce indoor temperatures by as much as 6 degrees Celsius during the summer. At our headquarters, for example, which is surrounded by trees, we've even eliminated echoes. We have also developed a roof garden with trees reaching up to ten metres in height. People love going there to sit and relax. Having trees to see and walk under is extremely important for people's health and well-being. Trees have a positive impact on the overall climate.

For example, the Platanus trees planted along the Coolsingel avenue in Rotterdam, which are both 20 m high and 20 m wide, help break the wind coming from the coast as it moves over the Maas River. This significantly improves the experience of walking, sitting on terraces, and other activities along the Coolsingel. These contributions have a meaningful impact on the people living in these areas. Greenery truly makes a significant difference. Our clients increasingly recognise the added value of trees, but it is an evolving process.

SdK In the summer, a car parked in direct sunlight can become like an oven, with temperatures inside reaching 40 or 50 degrees Celsius within a few hours. However, this doesn't happen when there are trees providing shade. Shade from trees is crucial for people's comfort and safety.

JAF Is it necessary for a city to have buildings covered by greenery? How complicated is it to implement vegetation on a building versus on a sidewalk or garden?

WB Building greenery is indeed necessary, and it has numerous advantages. We often create roof gardens to provide people with spaces to relax and enjoy. Trees on rooftops significantly impact environmental conditions such as wind and temperature. Roofs can become excessively hot, reaching up to 80 degrees Celsius in the summer and plummeting to -20 degrees Celsius in winter. Installing roof gardens can help mitigate those fluctuations.

Waterproofing on rooftops is a critical consideration. Walking on the roof can cause leaks. Roof gardens, on the other hand, can extend the life span of the waterproofing layer. It usually takes 20 to 30 years before repairs are needed without a garden, but with a roof garden, this lifespan can be extended to 40, 50, or even 60 years, resulting in significant cost savings.

Furthermore, some roof gardens incorporate sports facilities. The greenery on the roofs also shade streets and facades, offering several functional benefits. Roof gardens absorb nitrates, improve oxygen levels, and reduce particulate matter.

In terms of urban design, the layout of trees in streets and alongside facades plays a crucial role. We often plant two rows of large trees, and the way the crowns grow together can help mitigate pollution. This is particularly effective near roadways where the wind can't easily disperse pollution. Planting a single row of trees in smaller streets is sufficient because the wind can blow pollutants away. Choosing which side to plant the trees is carefully studied, considering the sun's angle. Green facades can be installed on the other side of the street to further improve air quality. This thoughtful planning also benefits temperature regulation, as the shade provided by trees prevents heat from escaping, helping maintain a more stable temperature.

It is important to highlight the importance of biodiversity, encompassing not just the trees but the entire ecosystem. For instance, 15 years ago, in the Netherlands, many streets had one tree species. However, this approach has evolved. Today, different tree species are mixed within streets. This biodiversity benefits pollinators like bees. For instance, by planting trees that bloom at various times throughout the summer, bees have a continuous source of food.

Additionally, a diversity of tree species can reduce the risk of diseases. Diseases can spread rapidly when just one tree species is planted along

Depot Boijmans van Beuningen, MVRDV, Rotterdam, 2020

Depot Boijmans van Beuningen, MVRDV, Rotterdam, 2020

a street. Introducing three or four different species can significantly curtail the spread of diseases because the responsible insects are less likely to feed on multiple tree species in one location. Natural forests tend to have fewer disease issues as they've evolved to coexist. It's when we artificially plant trees in a monotonous manner that diseases become more problematic. Diverse planting schemes can help mitigate these risks and result in healthier trees.

Considering the entire biodiversity web is vital to creating sustainable and resilient urban green spaces.

AR If I understand correctly, we need to consider plants as a design device that has impacts on the environment, society, and the economy simultaneously. Do these interlinkages make projects more successful?

SdK You have summarised it well. There is indeed a growing discussion around these aspects in the context of urban design. Some trees excel in terms of climate adaptation and air quality, but they may not contribute significantly to biodiversity. It is essential to evaluate if local insects can access the nectar from these trees, sustain themselves on them, and if they offer suitable nesting sites for birds. A successful project should aim to provide multiple benefits. Trees and greenery should be multifaceted, addressing environmental, social, and economic concerns, and supporting local ecosystems.

JAF What we propose to do with *The Green Dip* is to turn the entire city into a forest. How easy is it to turn a city into a forest?

WB From a tree-centric perspective, converting a city into a forest is an excellent approach.

For example, when you plant a solitary tree on a rooftop, it's exposed to strong winds from all directions. However, by planting trees closer together, potentially with some lower shrubs, you create the forest-like environment that you envision. Each tree helps protect its neighbours from the wind and excessive sun. This collective system promotes tree health and optimal growth.

The critical factor here is ensuring you have the right amount and type of substrate. Substrate refers to the growing medium or soil on rooftops or in urban environments. It plays a vital role in tree growth. You need about 60 cm of substrate for multi-stem trees on a rooftop. But for much taller trees, you'd require a clump of substrate about 1.20 m deep. There are specific guidelines for the required substrate volume based on the tree height. In the case of large trees, you'd need at least 40 m^3 of soil per tree. It's important to note that soil can be quite heavy, typically weighing around 1,350 kg per m^3. Proper substrate management is essential to support urban forestation projects.

JAF When I think about the significant amount of soil needed to place a tree on top of a building, I am a bit concerned about the resources and carbon emissions associated with this. Does this weight factor somehow counteract the environmental benefits of having trees in cities?

SdK I understand your apprehension. Indeed, weight constraints can pose challenges in these projects. The weight of the soil and other materials used to support trees on buildings can be substantial.

While there's an initial resource investment in materials and the carbon footprint associated with construction, the long-term environmental benefits of having trees in urban environments tend to outweigh these concerns. Urban trees provide numerous advantages, including air purification, temperature regulation, shade, and improved aesthetics. These benefits can contribute to a healthier and more sustainable urban environment.

Moreover, efforts are being made to reduce the weight of rooftop garden systems, such as using lighter substrate materials and innovative designs to mitigate the environmental impact and resource use. So, while weight is a consideration, the overall benefits of urban greening projects remain quite valuable.

Wim Beining graduated as a landscape architect. He has been working at Boomkwekerij Ebben nursery for the past ten years. He has been an advisor on roof gardens, green facades, parks, and squares. At 66 years old, that is what he wants to do: advise architects and landscape architects.

Sander de Klerk has an international background in gardening and landscape architecture. He works at Ebben, which he considers an ambitious tree nursery where many ideas can be developed. It's not just about growing and selling trees; Ebben's innovative projects and technical advice for vegetation combined with sales are his greatest interest.

Ebben tree nursery, Cuijk, Netherlands

Part 2

How to green?

The Green-Maker

A tool for greening the city

The need for more green spaces is driving some cities to develop urban reforestation policies. These policies include the allocation of dedicated spaces for urban forests, the identification of streets suitable for green corridors, the transformation of schoolyards into green oases, the dissemination of manuals for citizens on how to green rooftops or walls, or the participation of residents in greening public spaces.

Despite these initiatives, there can be resistance from municipalities, policymakers, developers, and residents due to financial or political risks. It is necessary to provide evidence of the value of greening cities in environmental, societal, and economic terms. Successful examples can help promote these benefits, but quantifying them is essential. Tools are needed to debunk controversies, raise awareness, and reveal the impacts of greening cities.

The Green-Maker addresses this need by speculating on a generic tool for cities. The Green-Maker, when realised, would offer a combination of expertise in buildings and flora to offer a systematic method for implementing large-scale urban forest scenarios while measuring its local impacts.

Why a tool?

The green transition represents a significant challenge for the coming decades. While many cities are actively involved in greening, they face challenges in providing concrete evidence of its benefits and value. *The Green Dip* can sometimes seem superficial, expensive to maintain, or merely a form of real estate branding—and for these reasons, it needs a quantitative approach. The Green-Maker is a proposal for a software designed to fulfil this need, functioning simultaneously as a visualisation and assessment tool. Additionally, it integrates a game engine, enabling the visualisation and experiential exploration of various urban forestation scenarios.

The Green-Maker can test, measure, and assess greening strategies, including those related to greening rooftops, sidewalks, balconies, and facades. It also enables the comparison of vegetation implementation in different cities, considering their unique urban forms and biomes, and measures their respective impacts.

The Why Factory has a rich history of developing custom digital tools. The Green-Maker joins a growing list of digital tools created by the Why Factory, such as House Maker, Village Maker, The Generator, Porocity Maker, Planet Maker, Biome Maker, (w)Ego Game, and Green City Calculator, among others. These tools are consolidated in what's known as The Controller, a library of scripts and software components that form an evolving series of urban software. The endeavour aims to store knowledge on theoretical models for future cities.

Developing custom digital tools allows for self-evaluation of designs and data-informed decision making. The Why Factory's tools fall into three categories: analysis, generation, and optimisation. Each design option generated is analysed and compared based on a set of criteria, fostering the development of a form of data-driven design. These digital tools play a crucial role in communicating research findings to various stakeholders and a broader audience, making a vision of the future city tangible.

Developing digital tools with students is integral to the Why Factory's methodology. It is a design process, emphasising a systematic breakdown of problems into parts: a step-by-step approach to data-driven design and design with systematic thinking.

A step-by-step manual

The Green-Maker is conceived for storing, exchanging, and integrating knowledge pertaining to architecture, the city, and plant life. The Green-Maker compiles the knowledge generated from the collaboration of experts from various fields—botanists, epidemiologists, environmental psychologists, meteorologists, engineers, architects, real estate professionals, economists, policy analysts, and citizens—fostering an approach that transcends disciplinary boundaries.

The ability to simulate and generate visions, coupled with relevant data, can facilitate awareness-raising, provide evidence, and offer valuable decision-making support.

Comparative analysis of policies can unveil the interrelations between various impacts. Urban greening initiatives affect climate, the value of building stock, urban agriculture, and the circular economy. They also influence well-being, communities, and public health.

The Green-Maker represents a crucial step toward understanding the interrelationships between the environmental, societal, and economic impacts of urban greening projects and policies.

1 City fabric and urban forms
Begin by selecting a specific piece of city fabric.

2 Mapping flora
Acquire relevant environmental information corresponding to the specific biome in which the location is situated. This ensures that only native plants are employed for each site.

3 Library of plants
Tailored to each biome, a recommended selection of native plants is provided. Each plant entry includes information about the required soil type and water consumption. This database offers additional details about what they need and what they give—total weight, maximum height, oxygen production, and CO_2 absorption.

4 Building with flora
Select architectural components that will act as containers for plants, ranging from various types of pots to mesh or balconies. The tool offers an extensive collection of design solutions suitable for integrating greenery across different sections of a building, facilitating the incorporation of grasses, shrubs, and trees onto any building surface.

5 Greening strategy
Implement the selected plants across rooftops, facades, balconies, courtyards, and more. A selection of nine distinct strategies can be applied, enabling the testing of various scenarios for immersing towers, interiors, and city blocks in green.

6 Green performances
Conduct evaluations before and after the green transformation, measuring environmental impacts. This involves comprehensive environmental analyses that consider factors such as humidity, daylight, and sunlight exposure.

7 Dip city in green
Progress to visualisation and experience. Transition from a two-dimensional depiction of land coverage to a three-dimensional perspective. This entails a dynamic three-dimensional simulation portraying a city entirely enveloped by a forest.

Key features of The Green-Maker:

- Visualisation tool
  The Green-Maker is a visualisation tool that assists in testing and optimising designs for implementing green elements in buildings.

- Systematic evaluation
  It offers a step-by-step evaluation of green projects' successes and actual benefits in urban environments.

- Overview for decision makers
  The tool provides an overview of the journey towards achieving the desired Green Dip, allowing decision-makers to take informed action.

The Green-Maker is an invitation to work towards bridging the gap between the vision of greener cities and the practical steps needed to realise them. By quantifying the environmental, societal, and economic benefits of urban greening it offers a compelling case for cities to embrace and invest in greening.

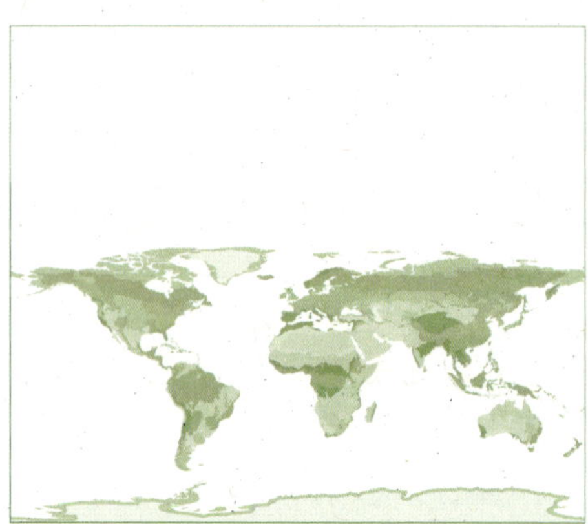

1. Mapping flora

4. Building with flora

7. Perform environmental analysis

2. Library of plants

3. Greening strategy

5. Apply on the chosen city

6. Select stategy

8. Perform solar analysis

9. Dip city in green

Mapping flora

A world of biomes

Cities worldwide are increasingly homogenising their flora despite having different native plant populations. The Green-Maker introduces a new perspective on *The Green Dip*: the biome approach. Biomes represent macro-ecosystems. Depending on the classification method, the Earth boasts more than 846 ecoregions[1] nested within 7 or 14 biomes. Biomes characterise the biosphere according to climatic criteria such as precipitation and temperature, the nature of the soils, latitude, altitude, and the fauna and flora that inhabit them.

Since the beginning of the twentieth century, several attempts have been made to classify the geographical distribution of those biomes. The following classification outlines a world map of 14 biomes: tundra, taiga, Alpine tundra, montane forest, Mediterranean, rainforest, dry leaf forest, semi-arid desert, arid desert and xeric shrub land, dry steppe, savanna, temperate steppe, temperate broadleaf forest, and monsoon forest. Each terrestrial biome possesses unique characteristics, from land coverage to average temperature and annual precipitation. They sustain human populations, plants, and various species in different manners.

Some biomes are expanding and shrinking due to rapid urbanisation and climate crises. For instance, projections indicate that the subtropical biome will expand by 29.5 per cent by 2100[2], significantly impacting nearby cities and their ecosystems.

The Green-Maker facilitates categorising an extensive plant collection based on their native biomes. Examining the world through the lens of biomes and their associated flora—rather than on the basis of administrative boundaries—invites us to consider our planet as a natural and evolving entity.

A world of biomes

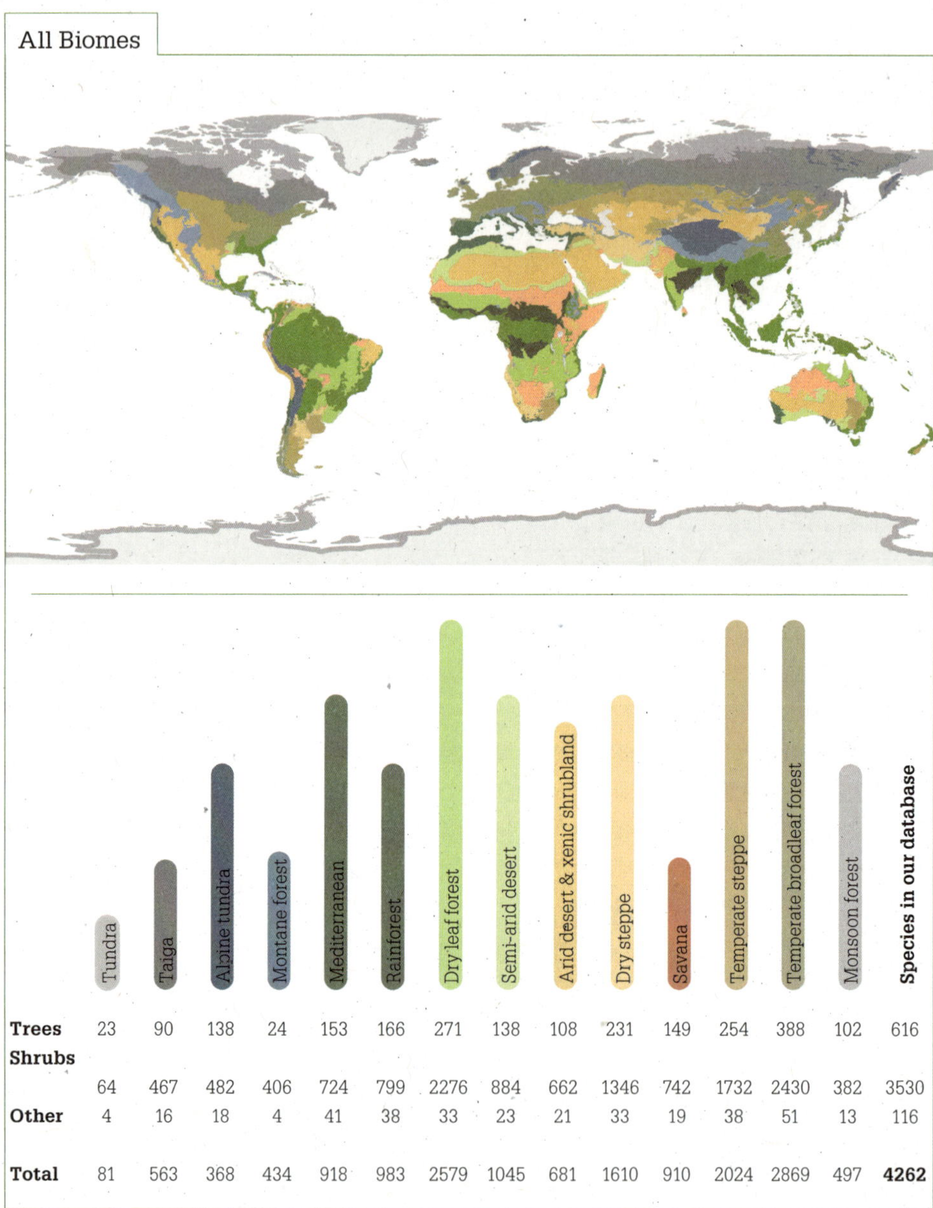

	Tundra	Taiga	Alpine tundra	Montane forest	Mediterranean	Rainforest	Dry leaf forest	Semi-arid desert	Arid desert & xenic shrubland	Dry steppe	Savana	Temperate steppe	Temperate broadleaf forest	Monsoon forest	**Species in our database**
Trees	23	90	138	24	153	166	271	138	108	231	149	254	388	102	616
Shrubs	64	467	482	406	724	799	2276	884	662	1346	742	1732	2430	382	3530
Other	4	16	18	4	41	38	33	23	21	33	19	38	51	13	116
Total	81	563	368	434	918	983	2579	1045	681	1610	910	2024	2869	497	**4262**

Cities span a wide range of biomes, with the most populated areas situated in tropical regions in Asia and Africa. Due to the climate crisis, these eco-regions and their respective flora, fauna, and human communities are undergoing transformation.

A world of biomes

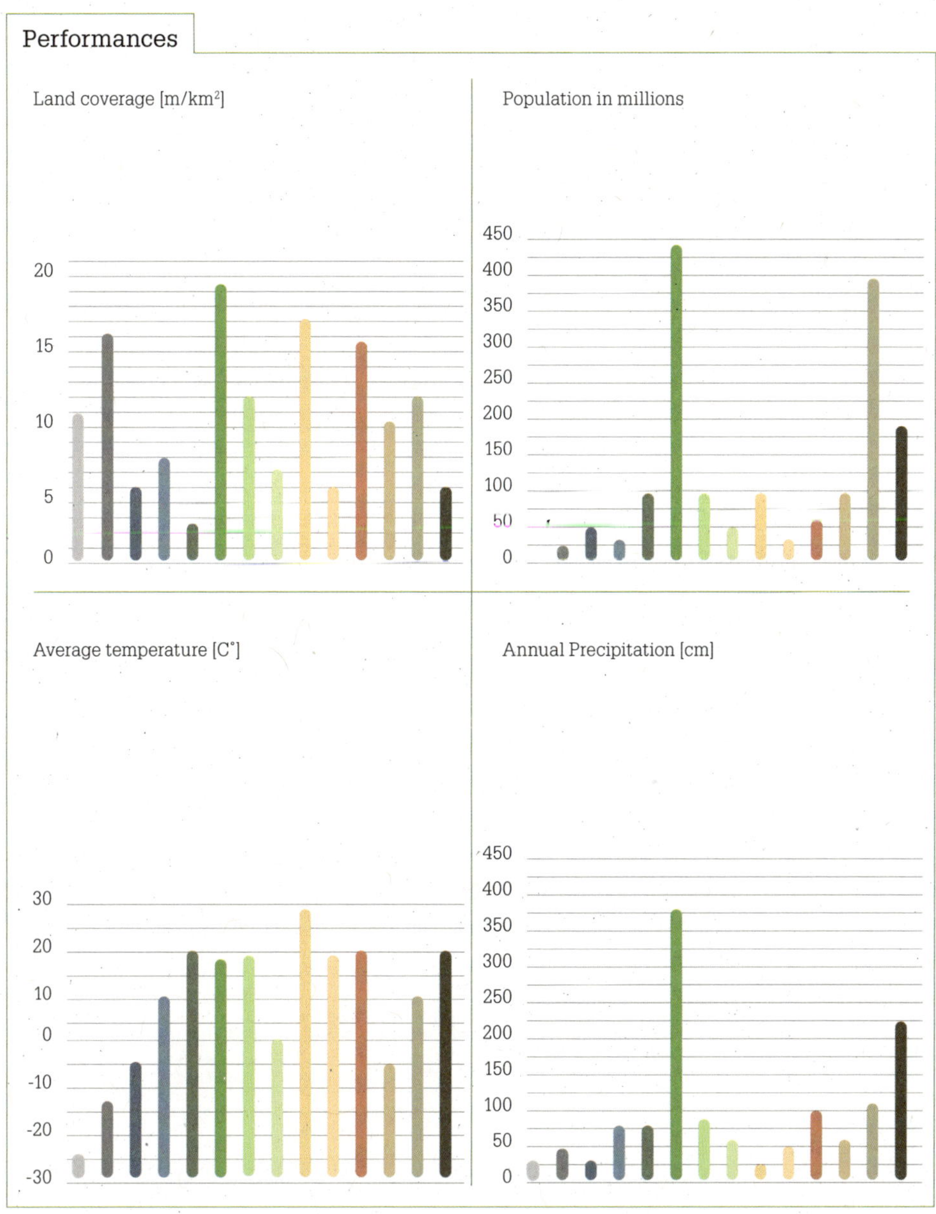

In the Green-Maker, biomes are defined by factors such as land coverage, population, average temperature, and annual precipitation. Each biome also possesses unique flora. These maps reveal the vulnerability of cities and biomes, emphasising the need for improved habitat protection, restoration, or conservation strategies.

A world of biomes

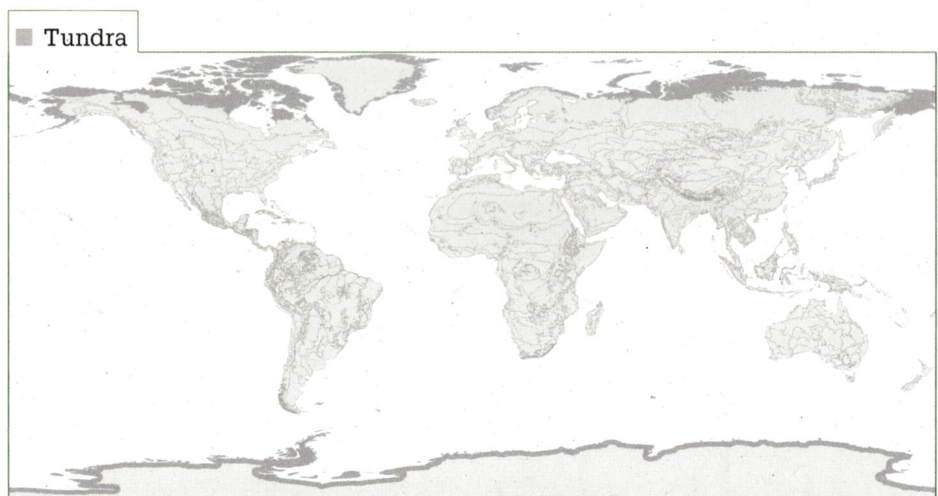

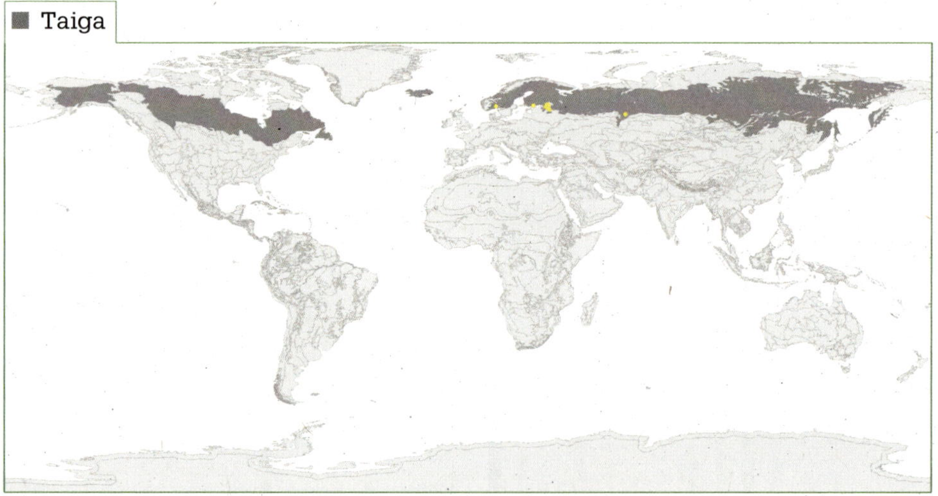

The tundra is the least populated biome, and the coldest, with temperatures ranging from -34 to -6 degrees Celsius. Its vegetation consists of shrubs, grasses, and mosses, and it lacks trees. The taiga is one of the largest land biomes, primarily characterised by coniferous, evergreen trees.

A world of biomes

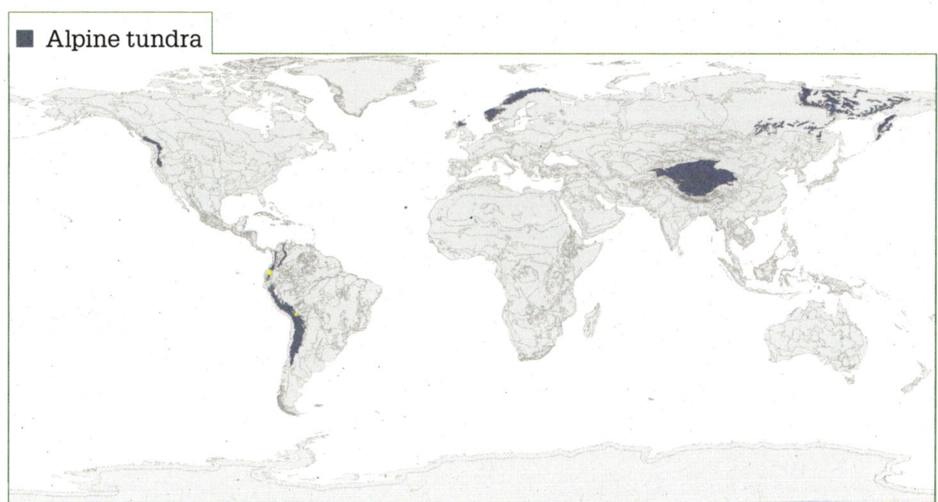

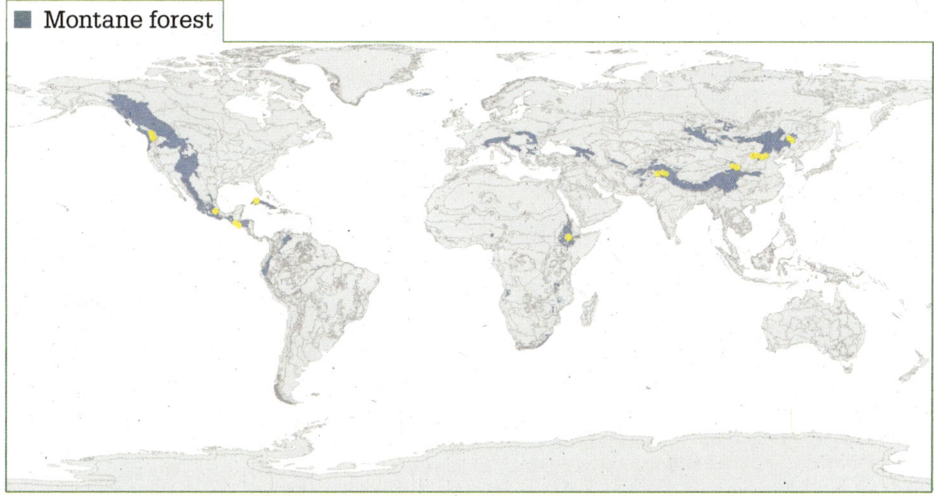

The Alpine tundra lacks trees due to its high elevation and strong winds. Montane forests are characterised by altitudes above 1,000 meters, low temperatures, and high precipitation.

A world of biomes

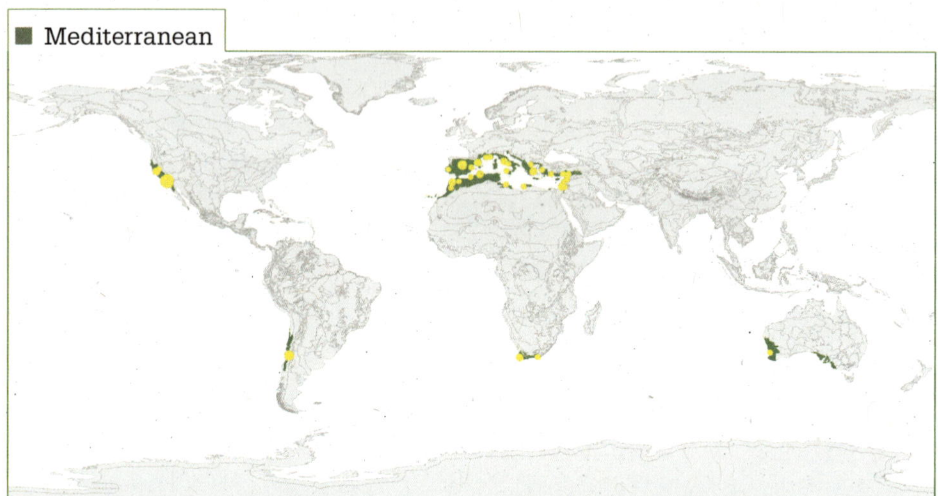

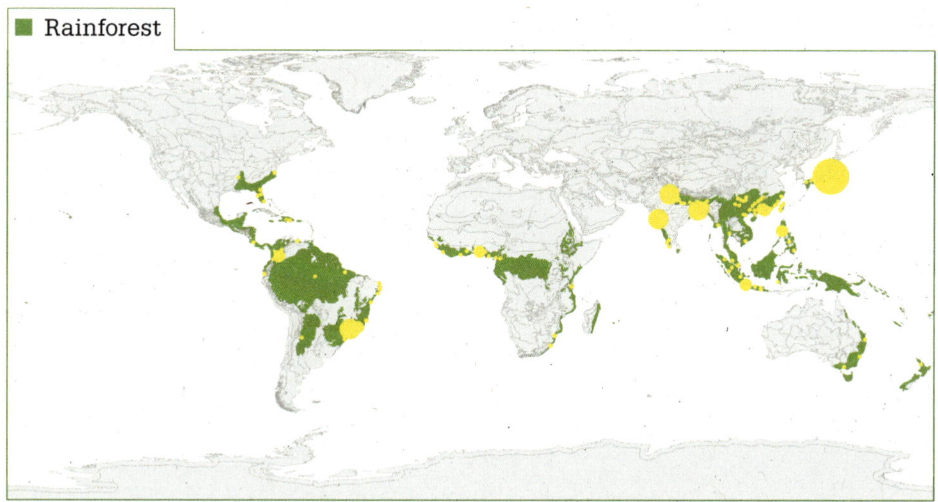

The Mediterranean biome experiences a temperate climate, dry summers, and wet winters. Rainforests are distinguished by a closed and continuous tree canopy and high humidity. It is the largest biome by area and the most populated.

A world of biomes

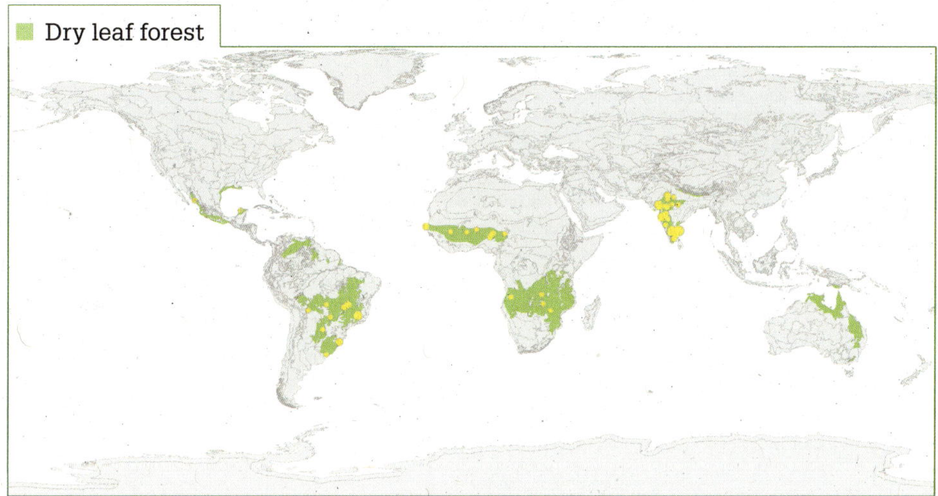

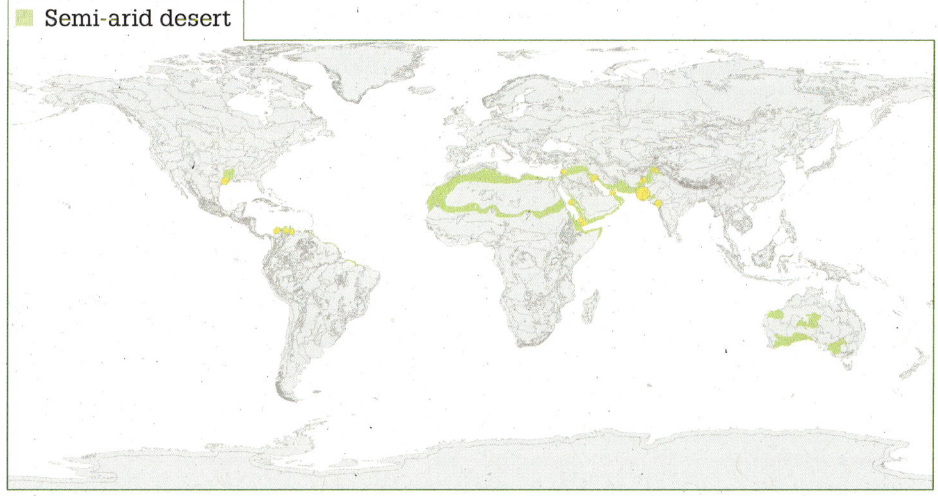

Dry leaf forests feature tall trees that shed their leaves during the dry winter and spring months. Semi-arid deserts receive minimal precipitation, with scattered vegetation consisting of small-leaved shrubs, trees, and desert grass.

A world of biomes

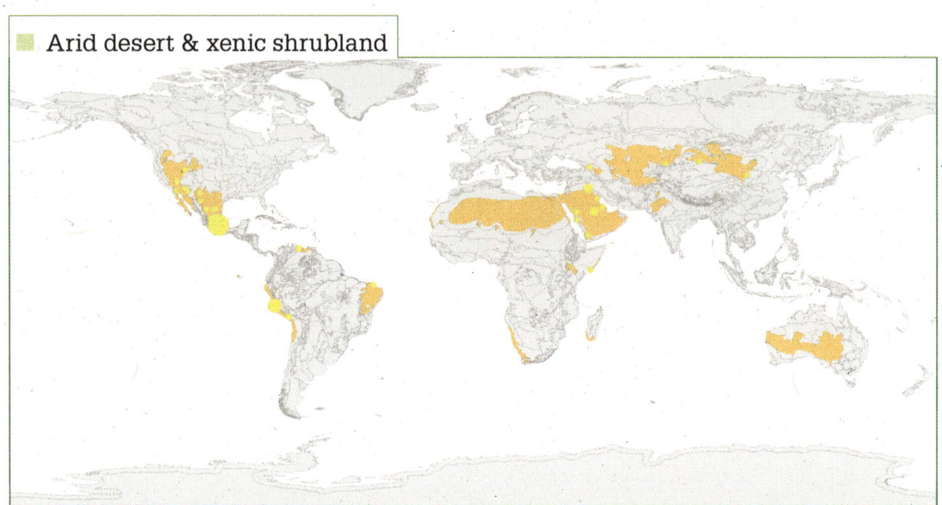

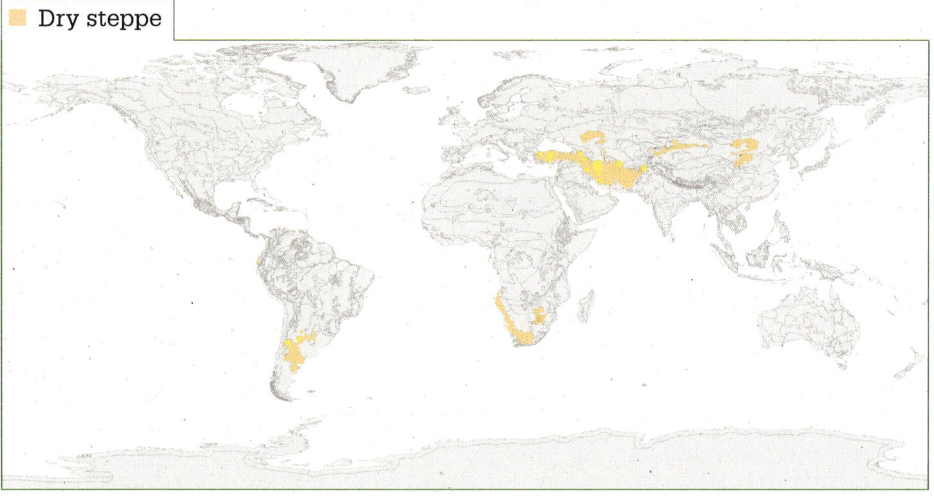

Arid deserts are warm and dry. Most arid deserts are situated near the equator due to the abundant daylight in these regions. The Sahara Desert is an example of an arid desert in Africa. For its part, a steppe is a dry, grassy plain occurring in temperate climates, located between tropical and polar regions of the world.

A world of biomes

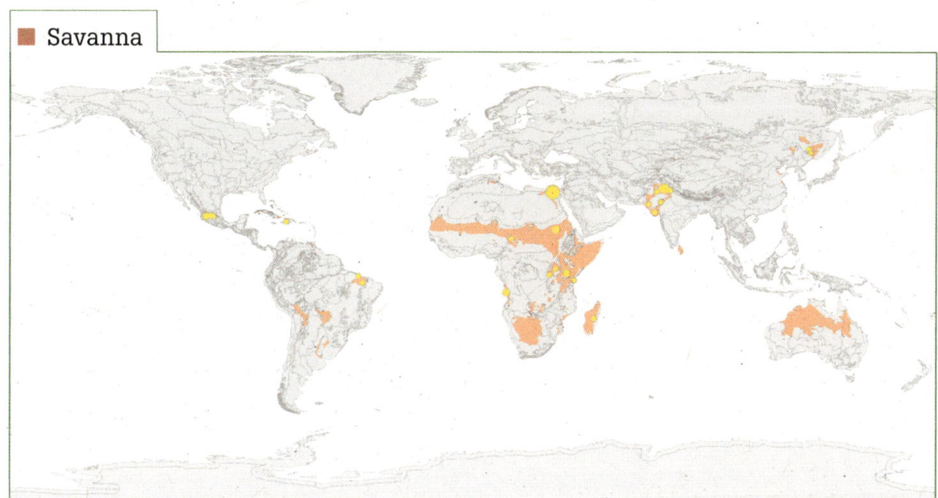

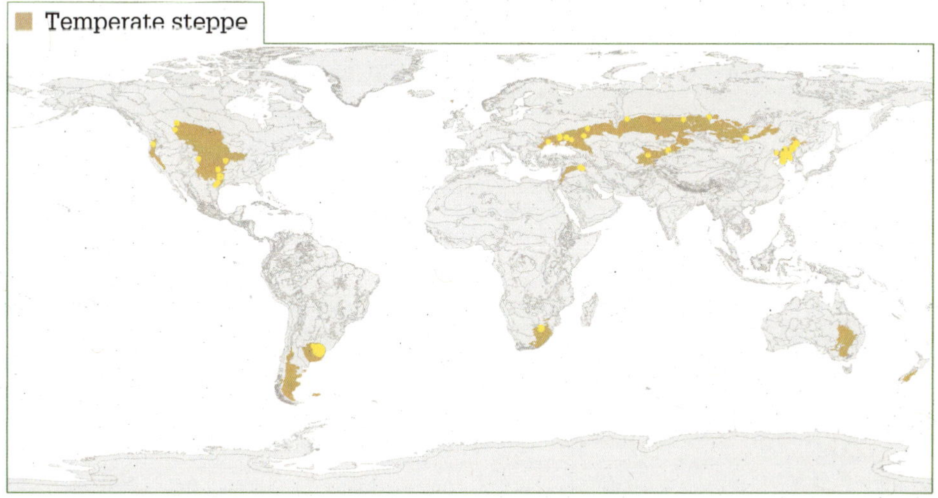

The savanna biome is characterised by extensive grass cover and scattered trees. It acts as a transitional grassland biome between a forest and a desert.

A world of biomes

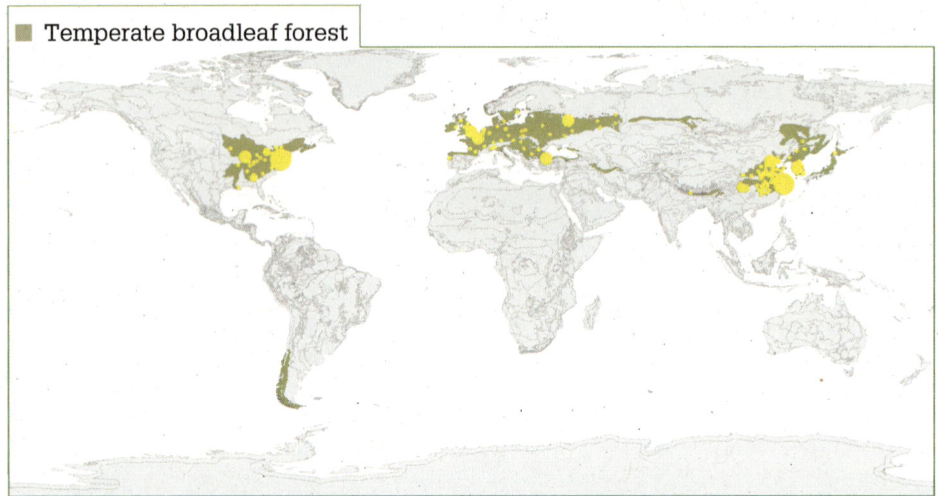

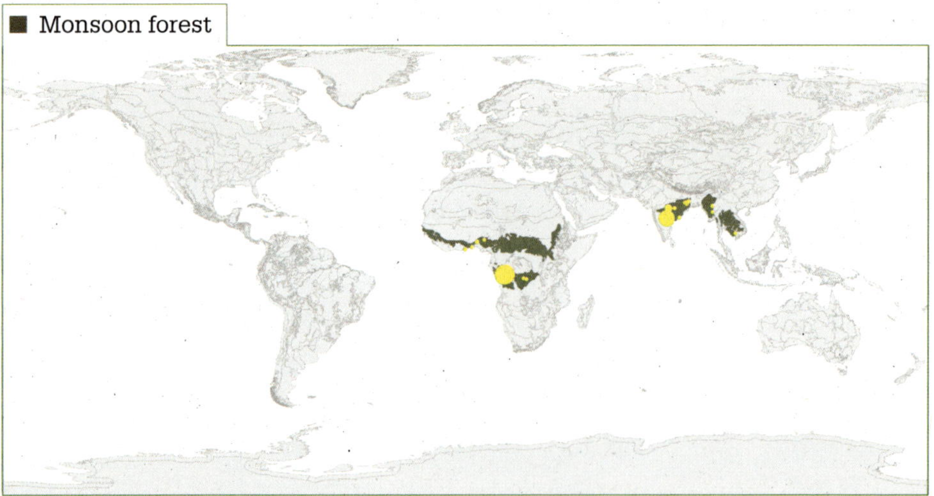

Temperate broadleaf forests thrive through four distinct seasons, offering extended, warm growing periods. Abundant in moisture due to leaf fall, they typically possess rich soils.

Monsoon forests, typical of tropical regions, experience alternating wet and dry seasons along with extreme temperature variations. These forests boast trees reaching up to 50 metres and feature a continuous, enclosed canopy that shades the forest floor.

[1] htttps://ecoregions.appspot.com/
[2] https://academic.oup.com/bioscience/article/67/6/534/3102935?login=true
[3] https://academic.oup.com/icesjms/article/68/6/986/697199

Library of plants

A design database

Each biome has its specific associated flora, and plants exhibit unique qualities and requirements within each biome. Plants need specific types of soil, water, or levels of daylight. They thrive in different parts of the world and at different altitudes. Plants also have their own characteristics, structures, scents, colours, and appearances. They may also have medical properties. This diversity is what contributes to the beauty and richness of vegetation.

There are more than 320,000 species of plants in the world, with approximately 70,000 tree species. Initially considered a branch of medicine, botany became an independent discipline, starting with the classification of plants and the study of their properties and further evolving towards the definition of a standard system of organising flora by family, genus, and species.

From sixteenth-century herbariums displaying annotated dried specimens pressed between two sheets of paper to the evolution of scanning techniques and three-dimensional modelling of trees, plant databases have become more detailed, more precise, and better accessible.

Today, computer-aided design (CAD) libraries of plants are integrated into three-dimensional modelling software used by designers. However, despite their widespread use in architectural renderings, the plants in those libraries are often used merely as decorative elements, with little consideration for their properties or performance.

This chapter proposes a design database of plants produced by architecture students, understanding them as fundamental building components, with a deep understanding of their characteristics. The following catalogue is a step towards a—future—informed user manual on building with plants, listing fundamental properties that the design profession must consider when incorporating them into buildings – a sort of green 'Neufert'[1], effectively serving as a bridge between architects and the knowledge of botanists. Additionally, envisioning a 'library of plants', akin to an 'Ikea of plants', would further democratise access to a diverse array of plant species and their functional attributes, making them readily available for architects and designers to integrate into their projects.

[1] The book *Architect's Data*, by Ernst Neufert, more commonly referred to as Neufert, contains all the necessary information to design and execute works of architecture. The book serves as an essential reference for the preliminary design and planning of building projects. Organized by building type, the volume provides core information for establishing the framework of detailed design. With over 6,200 diagrams offering insights into spatial requirements, the book includes dimensioned illustrations, plans, sections, site layouts, and design details.

Index of flora

Species

Abelia floribunda

Abelia triflora

Abelia x edward gouche

Abies alba

Abies pinsapo

Abutilon cannington carol

Acacia bayleyan

Acacia decurrens

Acacia farnesiana

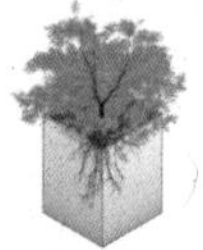

Acacia floribunda

Acanthus mollis

Acer buergerianum

Acer colchium rubrum

Acer negundo variegatum

Acer palmatum corallinum

Acer platanoides

Acer rubrum

Adiantum aleuticum

Aegagropila linnaei

Aesculuc hippocastanum

The Green-Maker showcases a catalogue of 4,326 plants, initially sorted by their scientific names.

Index of flora

Species

Aesculus x carnea

Albizia julibrissin

Alianthus altissima

Aralia elata

Arbutus unedo

Athyrium niponicum

Atripux halimus

Bambusa ventricosa

Bauhinia candicans

Anubias gigantea

Butia capitata

Buddleja davidii

Bryophyta

Brachychiton populneus

Bougainvillea hybrida

Berberis thunbergii

Berberis buxifolia nana

Cabomba caroliniana

Callistemon citrinus

Calocedrus decurrens

It demonstrates the diversity of plants inhabiting various ecosystems.

Index of flora

Species

Camellia japonica

Carex morrowii

Catalpa bignonioides

Cedrus atlantica

Citrus aurantium

Choisya ternata

Chamaerops humilis

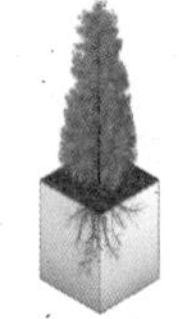
Chamaecyparis lawsoniana

Cercis siliquastrum

Celtis australis

Cedrus libani

Cedrus deodora

Citrus lemon

Cleistocactus strausii

Clematis macropetala

Cornus kousa

Coronilla valentina glauca

Cortaderia selloana

Corylus avellana

Corylus maxima purpurea

This index illustrates the most prevalent plants in each of the world's biomes.

Index of flora

Species

Cupressocyparis x leylandii

Cryptomeria japonica

Crataegus monogyna

Crassula arborescens

Cotoneaster lacteus

Cotoneaster horizontalis

Cotinus coggygria

Cycas revoluta

Cyperus involucratus

Dodonea viscosa purpurea

Duranta repens

Echinocactus grusonii

Eleagnus angustifolia

Fraxinus excelsior

Forsynthia x intermedia

Ficus carica

Feijoa sellowina

Fatsia japonica

Eunymus japonicus

Erybotria japonica

Index of flora

Index of flora for Temperate broadleaf forests

Plants can also be organised by biome, occurrence, family, or type.

Index of flora

Species

>

Abelia floribunda

Abelia triflora

Abelia x edward gouche

Abies alba

Abies pinsapo

Abutilon cannington carol

Acacia bayleyan

Acacia decurrens

Acacia farnesiana

Acacia floribunda

Acanthus mollis

Acer buergerianum

Acer colchium rubrum

Acer negundo variegatum

Acer palmatum corallinum

Acer platanoides

Acer rubrum

Adiantum aleuticum

Aegagropila linnaei

Aesculuc hippocastanum

Index of flora for arid deserts and xeric shrublands

Index of flora

Glossy abelia

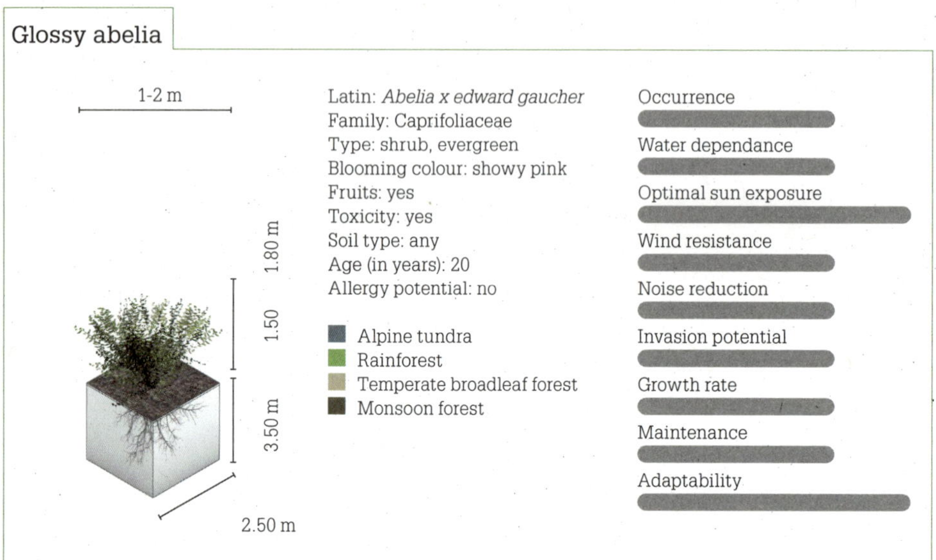

Wine Grape

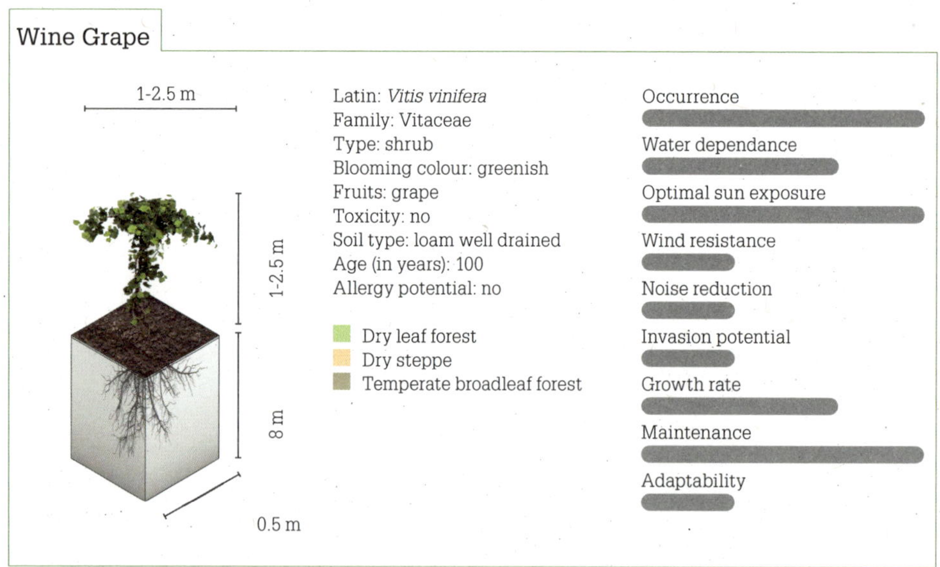

The Green-Maker provides detailed information about the plants' dimensions, blooming periods, colours, fruits, toxicity, soil requirements, age, allergenic potential, water needs, optimal sunlight exposure, wind resistance, noise reduction, invasion potential, growth rate, maintenance, and adaptability.

Index of flora

Silver fir

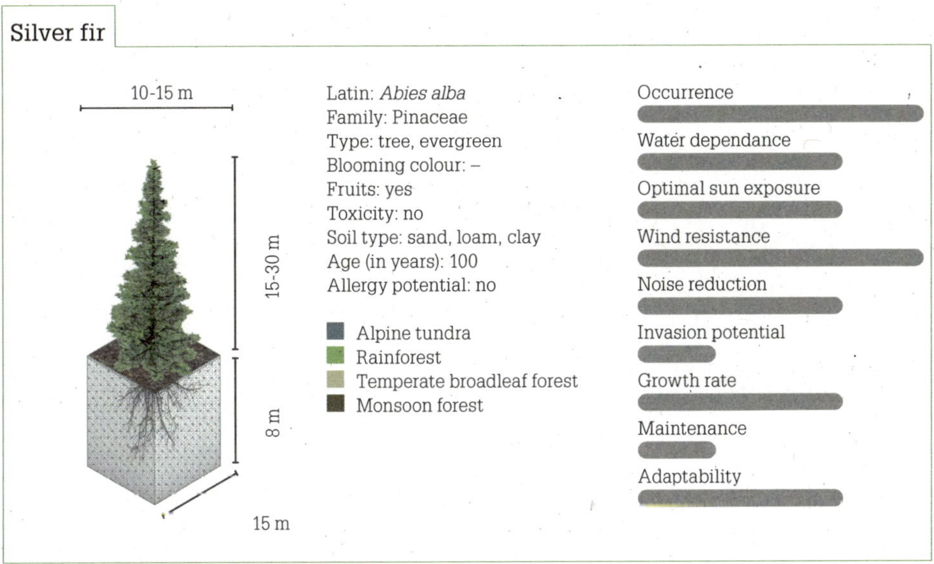

Latin: *Abies alba*
Family: Pinaceae
Type: tree, evergreen
Blooming colour: –
Fruits: yes
Toxicity: no
Soil type: sand, loam, clay
Age (in years): 100
Allergy potential: no

- Alpine tundra
- Rainforest
- Temperate broadleaf forest
- Monsoon forest

Occurrence
Water dependance
Optimal sun exposure
Wind resistance
Noise reduction
Invasion potential
Growth rate
Maintenance
Adaptability

Spanish fir

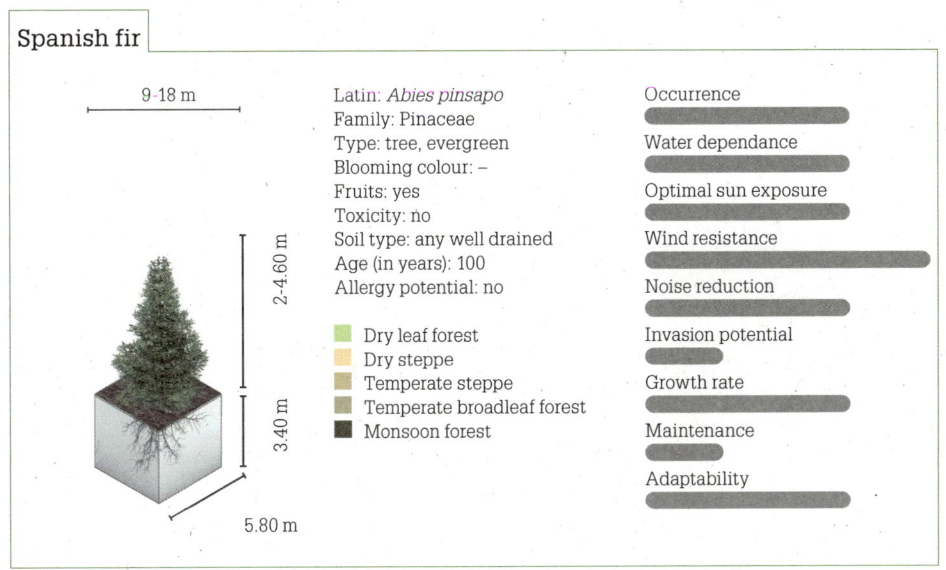

Latin: *Abies pinsapo*
Family: Pinaceae
Type: tree, evergreen
Blooming colour: –
Fruits: yes
Toxicity: no
Soil type: any well drained
Age (in years): 100
Allergy potential: no

- Dry leaf forest
- Dry steppe
- Temperate steppe
- Temperate broadleaf forest
- Monsoon forest

Occurrence
Water dependance
Optimal sun exposure
Wind resistance
Noise reduction
Invasion potential
Growth rate
Maintenance
Adaptability

Index of flora

Cootamundra wattle

2-4 m

3-10 m

3.5 m

Latin: *Acacia baileyana*
Family: Legumes
Type: tree
Blooming colour: yellow
Fruits: yes
Toxicity: no
Soil type: any
Age (in years): 50
Allergy potential: yes

- Rainforest
- Semi arid desert
- Arid desert & xeric shrubland
- Dry steppe
- Temperate steppe
- Temperate broadleaf forest
- Monsoon forest

Occurrence
Water dependance
Optimal sun exposure
Wind resistance
Noise reduction
Invasion potential
Growth rate
Maintenance
Adaptability

Wattle

1.5-3 m

4-8 m

10 m

Latin: *Acacia decurrens*
Family: Legumes
Type: tree
Blooming colour: yellow
Fruits: yes
Toxicity: yes
Soil type: sand, loam, deep depths
Age (in years): 50
Allergy potential: yes

- Dry leaf forest
- Arid desert & xeric shrubland
- Dry steppe
- Savanna
- Temperate steppe
- Temperate broadleaf forest

Occurrence
Water dependance
Optimal sun exposure
Wind resistance
Noise reduction
Invasion potential
Growth rate
Maintenance
Adaptability

Index of flora

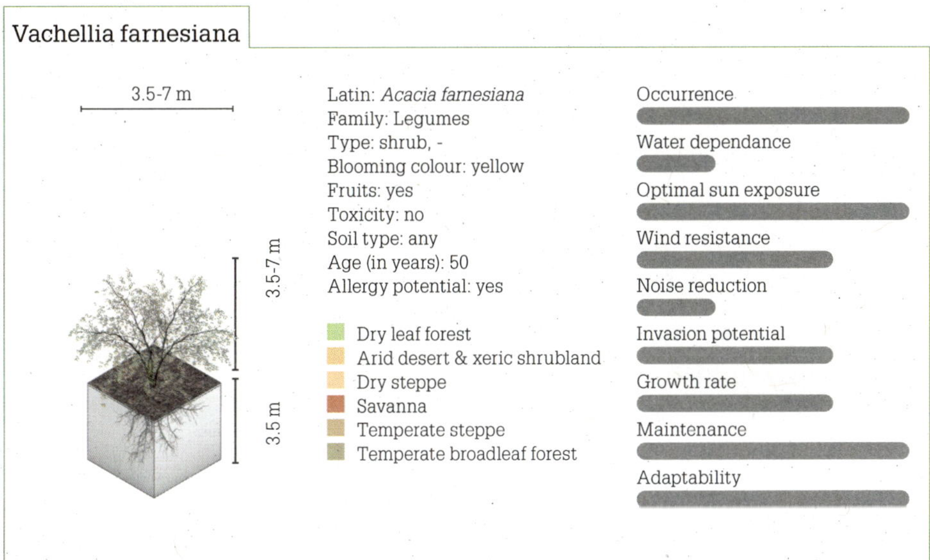

Vachellia farnesiana

Latin: *Acacia farnesiana*
Family: Legumes
Type: shrub, -
Blooming colour: yellow
Fruits: yes
Toxicity: no
Soil type: any
Age (in years): 50
Allergy potential: yes

- Dry leaf forest
- Arid desert & xeric shrubland
- Dry steppe
- Savanna
- Temperate steppe
- Temperate broadleaf forest

Occurrence
Water dependance
Optimal sun exposure
Wind resistance
Noise reduction
Invasion potential
Growth rate
Maintenance
Adaptability

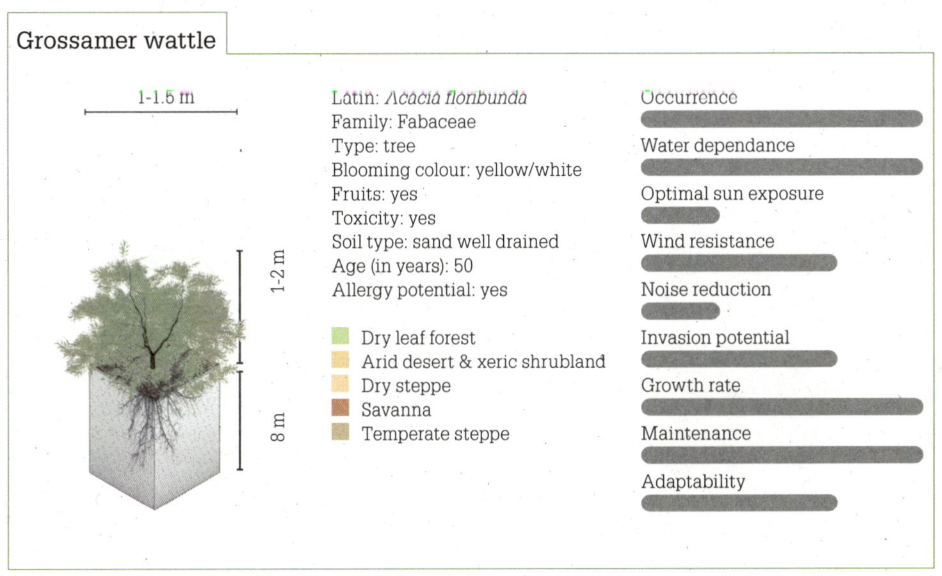

Grossamer wattle

Latin: *Acacia floribunda*
Family: Fabaceae
Type: tree
Blooming colour: yellow/white
Fruits: yes
Toxicity: yes
Soil type: sand well drained
Age (in years): 50
Allergy potential: yes

- Dry leaf forest
- Arid desert & xeric shrubland
- Dry steppe
- Savanna
- Temperate steppe

Occurrence
Water dependance
Optimal sun exposure
Wind resistance
Noise reduction
Invasion potential
Growth rate
Maintenance
Adaptability

Index of flora

Breeches sea dock bearsfoot

Latin: *Acanthus mollis*
Family: Acanthaceae
Type: herb, decidious
Blooming colour: white/pink
Fruits: yes
Toxicity: yes
Soil type: any
Age (in years): 10
Allergy potential: no

- Dry leaf forest
- Dry steppe
- Temperate steppe
- Temperate broadleaf forest
- Monsoon forest

Occurrence
Water dependance
Optimal sun exposure
Wind resistance
Noise reduction
Invasion potential
Growth rate
Maintenance
Adaptability

Trident three-thoothed maple

Latin: *Acer buergerianum*
Family: Sapindaceae
Type: tree, decidious
Blooming colour:
Fruits: no
Toxicity: no
Soil type: well drained
Age (in years): 150
Allergy potential: no

- Alpine tundra
- Mediterranean
- Rainforest
- Dry leaf forest
- Dry steppe
- Temperate steppe
- Temperate broadleaf forest
- Monsoon forest

Occurrence
Water dependance
Optimal sun exposure
Wind resistance
Noise reduction
Invasion potential
Growth rate
Maintenance
Adaptability

Index of flora

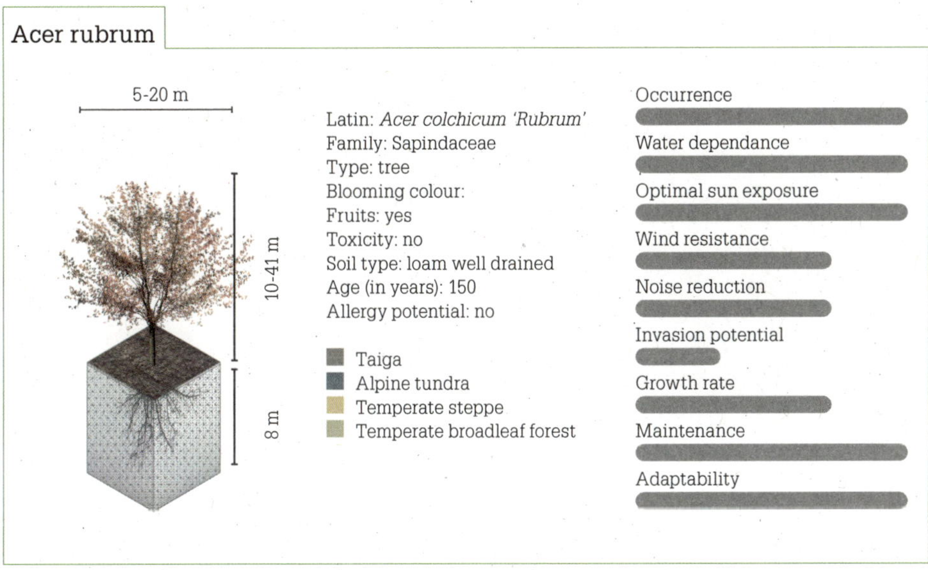

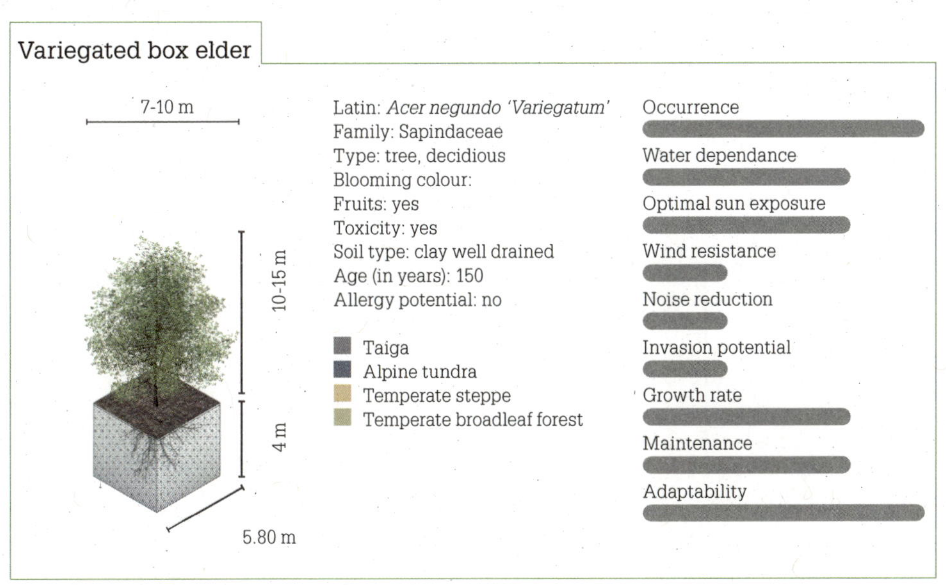

Index of flora

Red-leaf Japanese maple

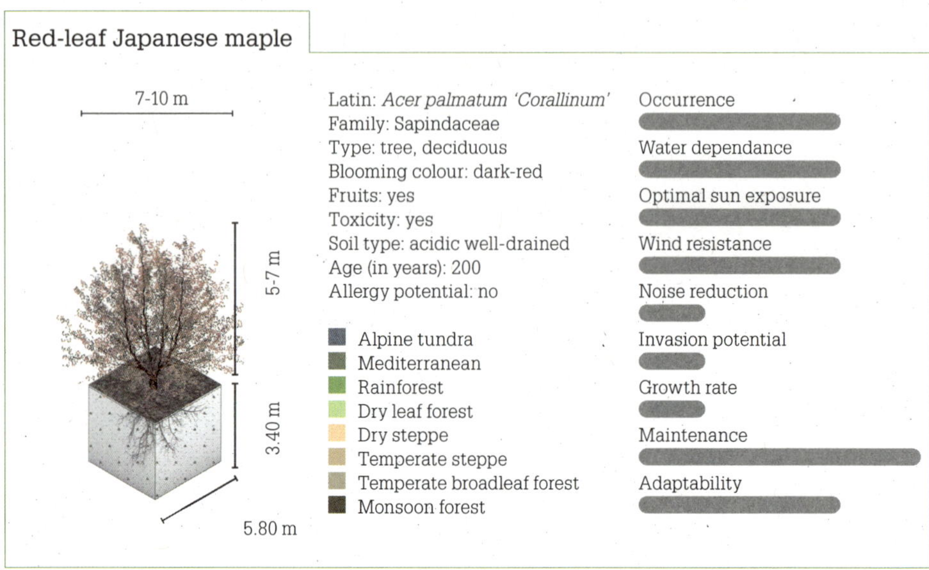

Latin: *Acer palmatum 'Corallinum'*
Family: Sapindaceae
Type: tree, deciduous
Blooming colour: dark-red
Fruits: yes
Toxicity: yes
Soil type: acidic well-drained
Age (in years): 200
Allergy potential: no

- Alpine tundra
- Mediterranean
- Rainforest
- Dry leaf forest
- Dry steppe
- Temperate steppe
- Temperate broadleaf forest
- Monsoon forest

Occurrence
Water dependance
Optimal sun exposure
Wind resistance
Noise reduction
Invasion potential
Growth rate
Maintenance
Adaptability

Norway maple

10-15 m
22-30 m
4.50 m
5.80 m

Latin: *Acer platanoides*
Family: Sapindaceae
Type: tree, deciduous
Blooming colour:
Fruits: yes
Toxicity: yes
Soil type: well-drained
Age (in years): 150
Allergy potential: no

- Taiga
- Alpine tundra
- Mediterranean
- Temperate steppe
- Temperate broadleaf forest

Occurrence
Water dependance
Optimal sun exposure
Wind resistance
Noise reduction
Invasion potential
Growth rate
Maintenance
Adaptability

Index of flora

Red maple

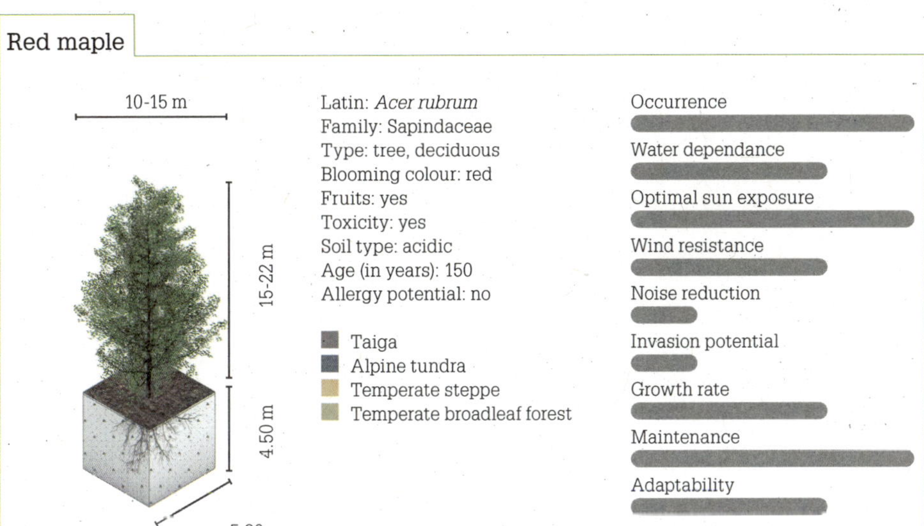

Latin: *Acer rubrum*
Family: Sapindaceae
Type: tree, deciduous
Blooming colour: red
Fruits: yes
Toxicity: yes
Soil type: acidic
Age (in years): 150
Allergy potential: no

- Taiga
- Alpine tundra
- Temperate steppe
- Temperate broadleaf forest

Occurrence
Water dependance
Optimal sun exposure
Wind resistance
Noise reduction
Invasion potential
Growth rate
Maintenance
Adaptability

Western maidenhair fern

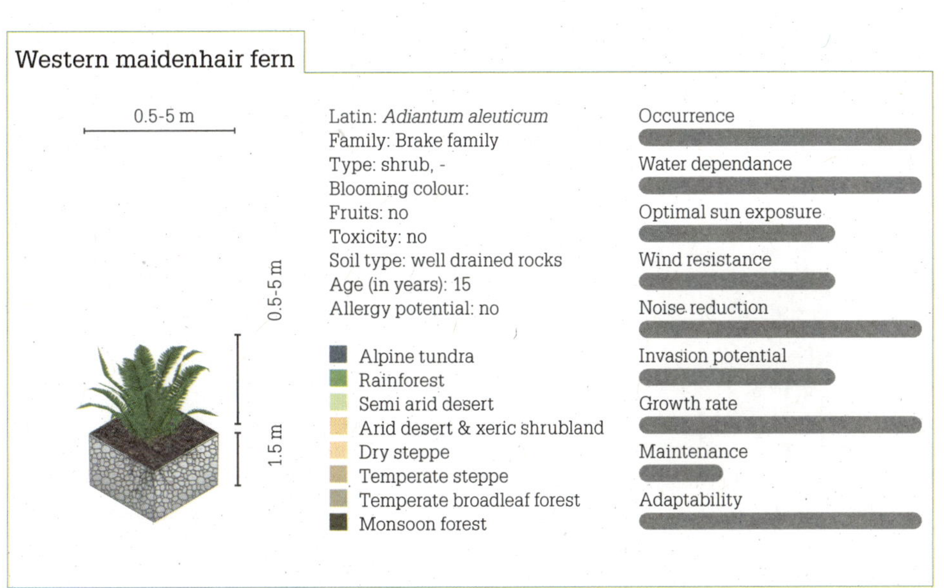

Latin: *Adiantum aleuticum*
Family: Brake family
Type: shrub, -
Blooming colour:
Fruits: no
Toxicity: no
Soil type: well drained rocks
Age (in years): 15
Allergy potential: no

- Alpine tundra
- Rainforest
- Semi arid desert
- Arid desert & xeric shrubland
- Dry steppe
- Temperate steppe
- Temperate broadleaf forest
- Monsoon forest

Occurrence
Water dependance
Optimal sun exposure
Wind resistance
Noise reduction
Invasion potential
Growth rate
Maintenance
Adaptability

Index of flora

Moss balls

Latin: *Aegagropila linnaei*
Family: Cladophoraceae
Type: moss, -
Blooming colour:
Fruits: no
Toxicity: yes
Soil type: water
Age (in years): 15
Allergy potential: no

- Alpine tundra
- Rainforest
- Semi arid desert
- Arid desert & xeric shrubland
- Dry steppe
- Temperate steppe
- Temperate broadleaf forest
- Monsoon forest

Occurrence
Water dependance
Optimal sun exposure
Wind resistance
Noise reduction
Invasion potential
Growth rate
Maintenance
Adaptability

Common horse chestnut

Latin: *Aesculus hippocastanum*
Family: Sapindaceae
Type: tree, deciduous
Blooming colour: white
Fruits: yes
Toxicity: yes
Soil type: well-drained
Age (in years): 100
Allergy potential: yes

- Alpine tundra
- Mediterranean
- Temperate broadleaf forest

Occurrence
Water dependance
Optimal sun exposure
Wind resistance
Noise reduction
Invasion potential
Growth rate
Maintenance
Adaptability

Index of flora

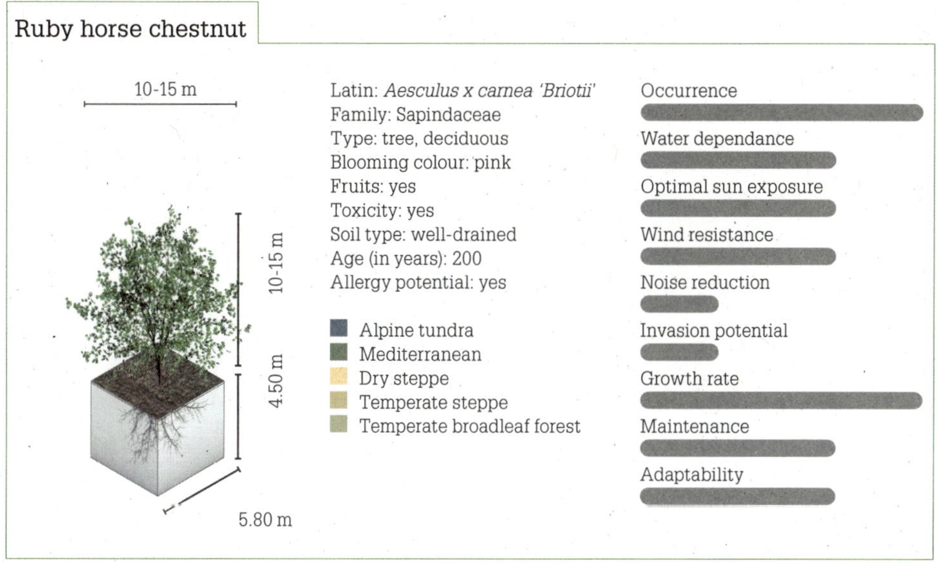

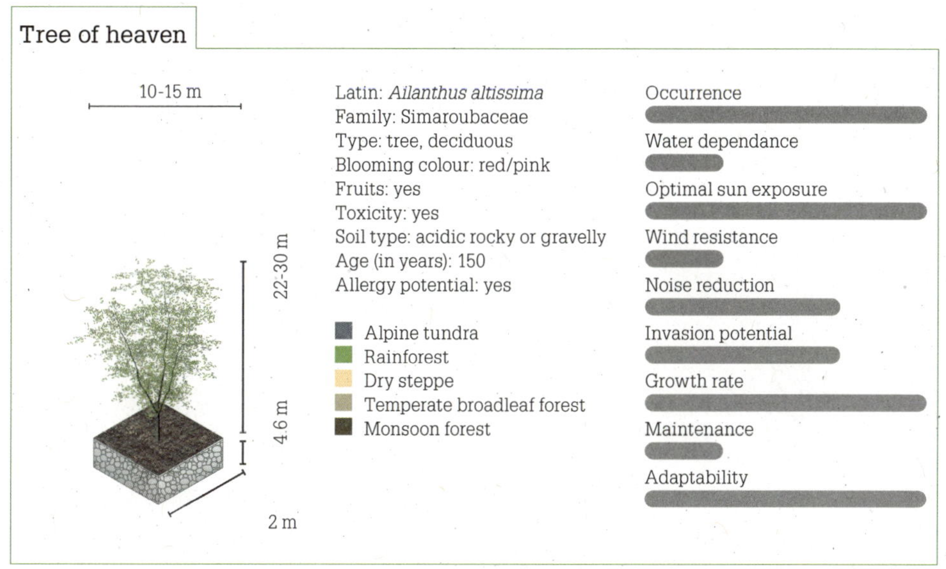

Index of flora

Persian silk tree

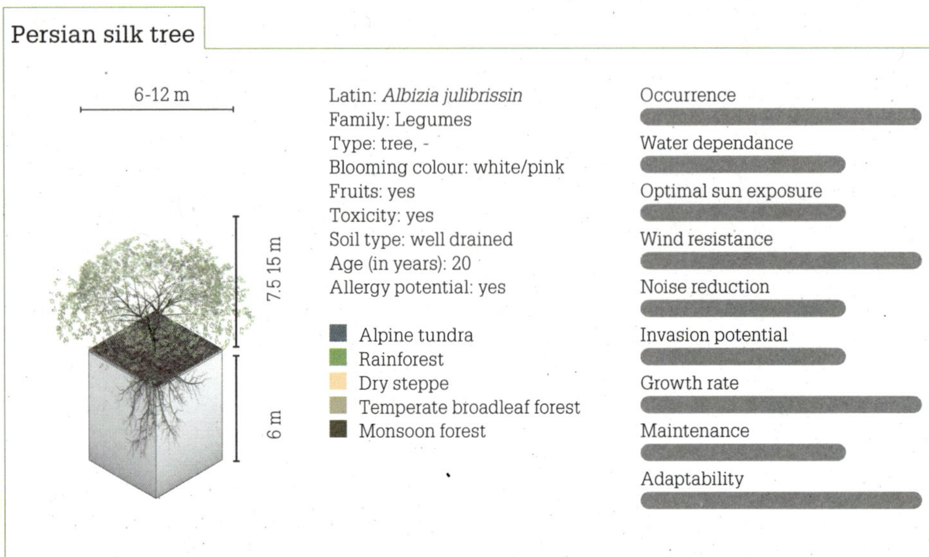

Latin: *Albizia julibrissin*
Family: Legumes
Type: tree, -
Blooming colour: white/pink
Fruits: yes
Toxicity: yes
Soil type: well drained
Age (in years): 20
Allergy potential: yes

- Alpine tundra
- Rainforest
- Dry steppe
- Temperate broadleaf forest
- Monsoon forest

Occurrence
Water dependance
Optimal sun exposure
Wind resistance
Noise reduction
Invasion potential
Growth rate
Maintenance
Adaptability

Strawberry tree

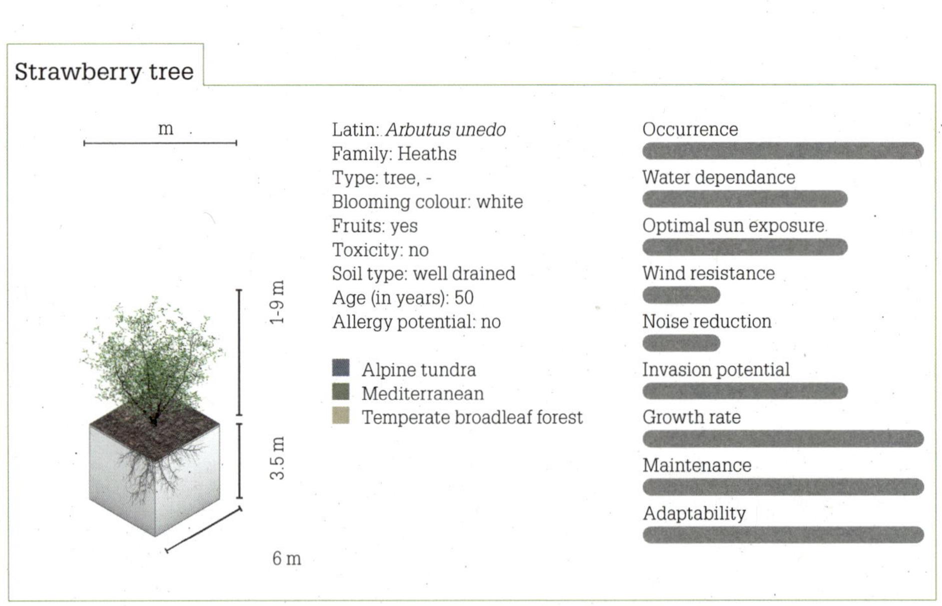

Latin: *Arbutus unedo*
Family: Heaths
Type: tree, -
Blooming colour: white
Fruits: yes
Toxicity: no
Soil type: well drained
Age (in years): 50
Allergy potential: no

- Alpine tundra
- Mediterranean
- Temperate broadleaf forest

Occurrence
Water dependance
Optimal sun exposure
Wind resistance
Noise reduction
Invasion potential
Growth rate
Maintenance
Adaptability

Index of flora

Chinese angelica-tree

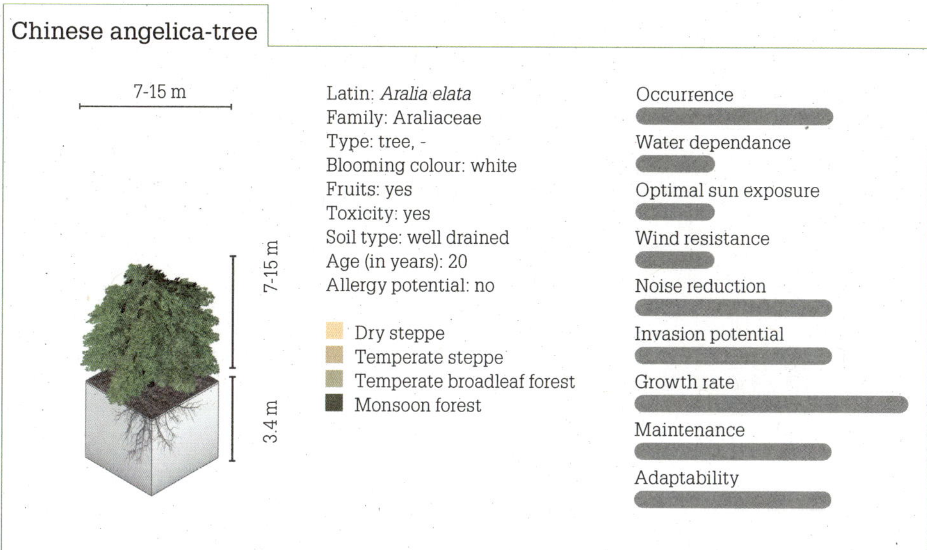

Latin: *Aralia elata*
Family: Araliaceae
Type: tree, -
Blooming colour: white
Fruits: yes
Toxicity: yes
Soil type: well drained
Age (in years): 20
Allergy potential: no

- Dry steppe
- Temperate steppe
- Temperate broadleaf forest
- Monsoon forest

Occurrence
Water dependance
Optimal sun exposure
Wind resistance
Noise reduction
Invasion potential
Growth rate
Maintenance
Adaptability

Giant anubias

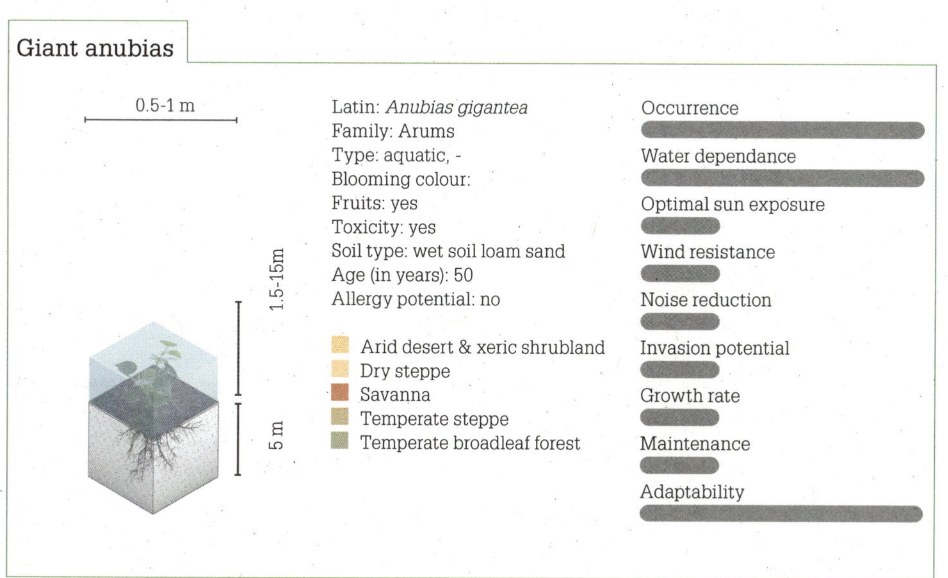

Latin: *Anubias gigantea*
Family: Arums
Type: aquatic, -
Blooming colour:
Fruits: yes
Toxicity: yes
Soil type: wet soil loam sand
Age (in years): 50
Allergy potential: no

- Arid desert & xeric shrubland
- Dry steppe
- Savanna
- Temperate steppe
- Temperate broadleaf forest

Occurrence
Water dependance
Optimal sun exposure
Wind resistance
Noise reduction
Invasion potential
Growth rate
Maintenance
Adaptability

Index of flora

Ghost fern

3-7 m

3-7 m

1.5 m

Latin: *Athyrium niponicum*
Family: Dryopteridaceae
Type: shrub, -
Blooming colour:
Fruits: no
Toxicity: no
Soil type: well drained rocks
Age (in years): 80
Allergy potential: no

- Temperate broadleaf forest

Occurrence
Water dependance
Optimal sun exposure
Wind resistance
Noise reduction
Invasion potential
Growth rate
Maintenance
Adaptability

Japanese laurel

1.5-3 m

1.5-3 m

3.5 m

Latin: *Aucuba japonica*
Family: Dogwoods
Type: shrub, -
Blooming colour:
Fruits: yes
Toxicity: yes
Soil type: any
Age (in years): 10
Allergy potential: no

- Alpine tundra
- Mediterranean
- Rainforest
- Dry steppe
- Temperate steppe
- Temperate broadleaf forest
- Monsoon forest

Occurrence
Water dependance
Optimal sun exposure
Wind resistance
Noise reduction
Invasion potential
Growth rate
Maintenance
Adaptability

Index of flora

Buddha bamboo

Latin: *Bambusa ventricosa*
Family: Grasses
Type: tree, -
Blooming colour:
Fruits: no
Toxicity: no
Soil type: well drained
Age (in years): 50
Allergy potential: no

- Alpine tundra
- Mediterranean
- Rainforest
- Dry steppe
- Temperate steppe
- Temperate broadleaf forest
- Monsoon forest

Occurrence
Water dependance
Optimal sun exposure
Wind resistance
Noise reduction
Invasion potential
Growth rate
Maintenance
Adaptability

Orchid tree

Latin: *Bauhinia candicans*
Family:Legumes
Type: tree
Blooming colour: pink/white
Fruits: yes
Toxicity: yes
Soil type: well drained
Age (in years): 5
Allergy potential: yes

- Alpine tundra
- Mediterranean
- Rainforest
- Dry steppe
- Temperate steppe
- Temperate broadleaf forest
- Monsoon forest

Occurrence
Water dependance
Optimal sun exposure
Wind resistance
Noise reduction
Invasion potential
Growth rate
Maintenance
Adaptability

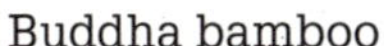

Index of flora

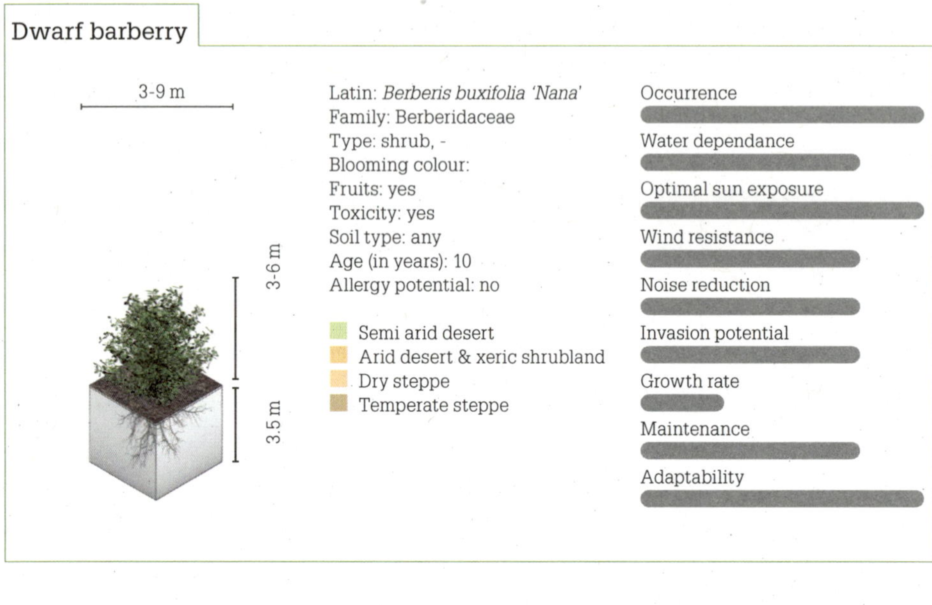

Dwarf barberry

3-9 m

3-6 m

3.5 m

Latin: *Berberis buxifolia 'Nana'*
Family: Berberidaceae
Type: shrub, -
Blooming colour:
Fruits: yes
Toxicity: yes
Soil type: any
Age (in years): 10
Allergy potential: no

- Semi arid desert
- Arid desert & xeric shrubland
- Dry steppe
- Temperate steppe

Occurrence
Water dependance
Optimal sun exposure
Wind resistance
Noise reduction
Invasion potential
Growth rate
Maintenance
Adaptability

Japanese barberry

1-2 m

1-2 m

3.5 m

Latin: *Berberis thunbergii*
Family: Berberidaceae
Type: shrub, -
Blooming colour:
Fruits: yes
Toxicity: yes
Soil type: any
Age (in years): 20
Allergy potential: no

- Temperate broadleaf forest

Occurrence
Water dependance
Optimal sun exposure
Wind resistance
Noise reduction
Invasion potential
Growth rate
Maintenance
Adaptability

Index of flora

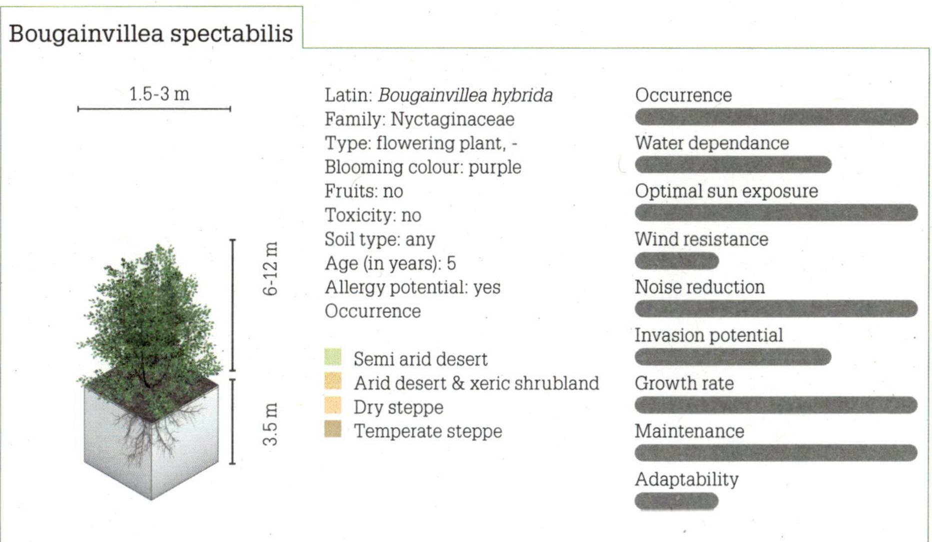

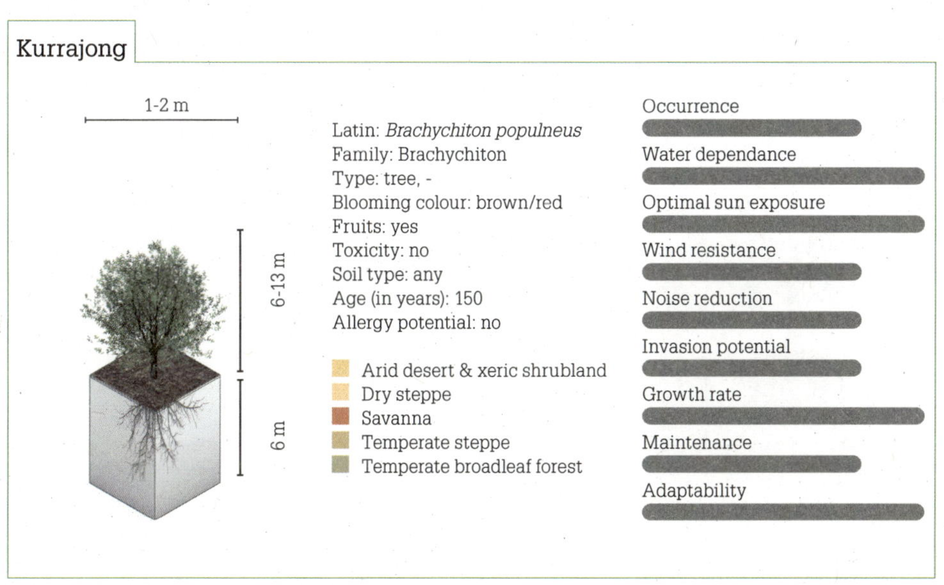

Index of flora

Moss

Latin: *Bryophyta*
Family: Embryophytes
Type: shrub, -
Blooming colour:
Fruits: no
Toxicity: no
Soil type: rocks bare soil
Age (in years): 10
Allergy potential: no

Occurrence
Water dependance
Optimal sun exposure
Wind resistance
Noise reduction
Invasion potential
Growth rate
Maintenance
Adaptability

Jelly palm

Latin: *Butia capitata*
Family: Palm trees
Type: tree, palm
Blooming colour: yellow
Fruits: yes
Toxicity: no
Soil type: sand, loam well drained
Age (in years): 80
Allergy potential: no

Semi arid desert
Arid desert & xeric shrubland
Dry steppe
Temperate steppe

Occurrence
Water dependance
Optimal sun exposure
Wind resistance
Noise reduction
Invasion potential
Growth rate
Maintenance
Adaptability

Index of flora

Butterlfy-bush

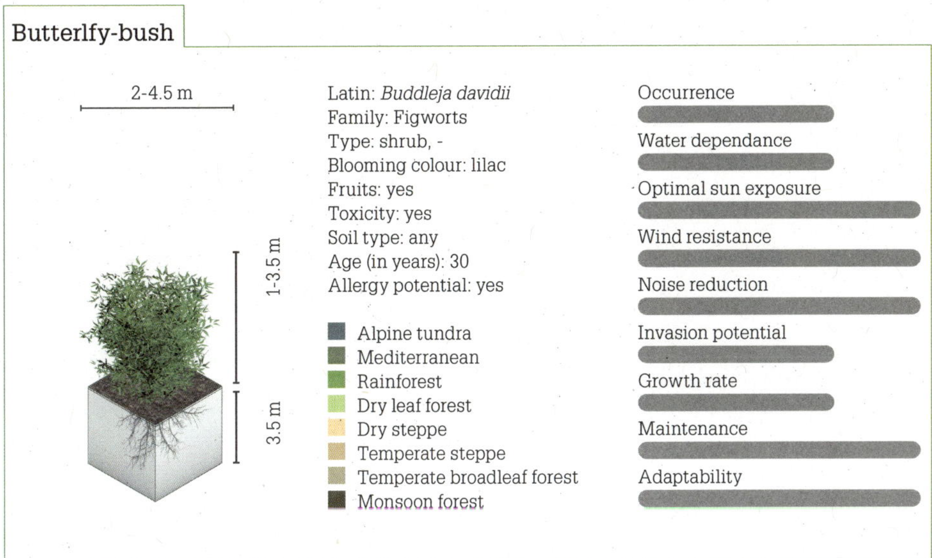

Latin: *Buddleja davidii*
Family: Figworts
Type: shrub, -
Blooming colour: lilac
Fruits: yes
Toxicity: yes
Soil type: any
Age (in years): 30
Allergy potential: yes

- Alpine tundra
- Mediterranean
- Rainforest
- Dry leaf forest
- Dry steppe
- Temperate steppe
- Temperate broadleaf forest
- Monsoon forest

Occurrence
Water dependance
Optimal sun exposure
Wind resistance
Noise reduction
Invasion potential
Growth rate
Maintenance
Adaptability

Boxwood

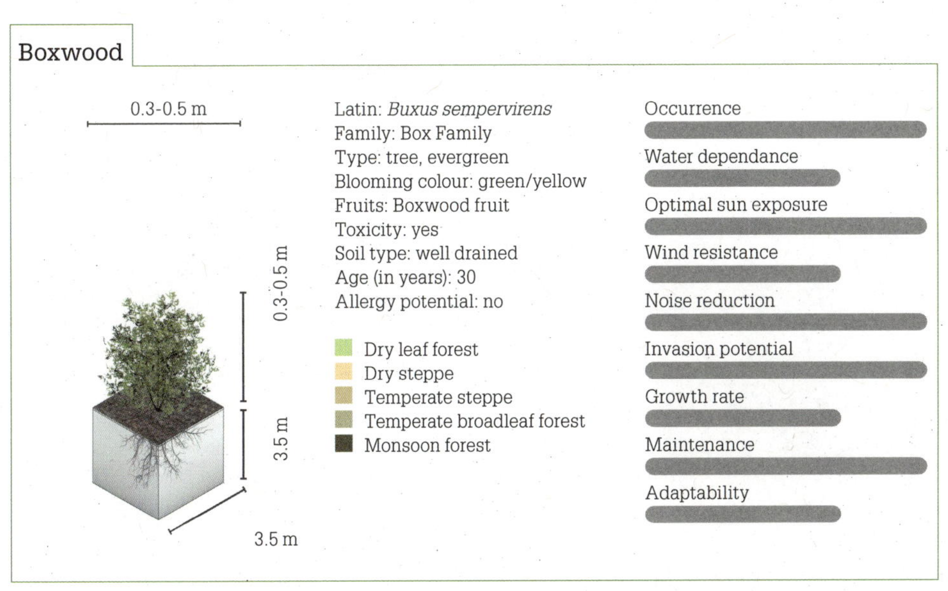

Latin: *Buxus sempervirens*
Family: Box Family
Type: tree, evergreen
Blooming colour: green/yellow
Fruits: Boxwood fruit
Toxicity: yes
Soil type: well drained
Age (in years): 30
Allergy potential: no

- Dry leaf forest
- Dry steppe
- Temperate steppe
- Temperate broadleaf forest
- Monsoon forest

Occurrence
Water dependance
Optimal sun exposure
Wind resistance
Noise reduction
Invasion potential
Growth rate
Maintenance
Adaptability

Index of flora

Carolina water shield

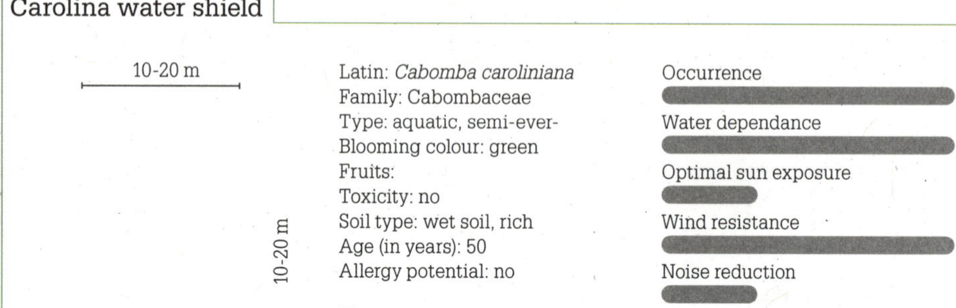

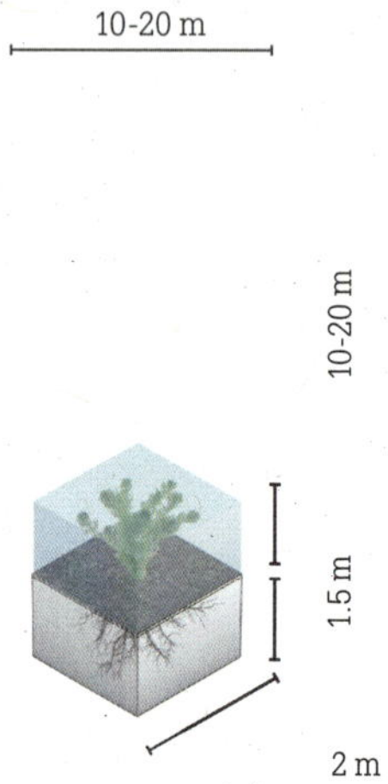

10-20 m

10-20 m

1.5 m

2 m

Latin: *Cabomba caroliniana*
Family: Cabombaceae
Type: aquatic, semi-ever-
Blooming colour: green
Fruits:
Toxicity: no
Soil type: wet soil, rich
Age (in years): 50
Allergy potential: no

- Alpine tundra
- Rainforest
- Semi arid desert
- Arid desert & xeric shrubland
- Dry steppe
- Temperate steppe
- Temperate broadleaf forest
- Monsoon forest

Occurrence
Water dependance
Optimal sun exposure
Wind resistance
Noise reduction
Invasion potential
Growth rate
Maintenance
Adaptability

Lemon bottlebrush

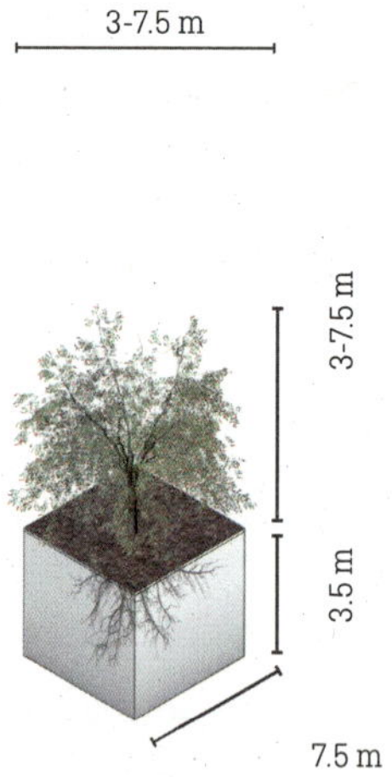

3-7.5 m

3-7.5 m

3.5 m

7.5 m

Latin: *Callistemon citrinus*
Family: Myrtle family
Type: shrub, evergreen
Blooming colour: red
Fruits: berry
Toxicity: yes
Soil type: any
Age (in years): 40
Allergy potential: yes

- Dry leaf forest
- Arid desert & xeric shrubland
- Dry steppe
- Savanna
- Temperate steppe
- Temperate broadleaf forest

Occurrence
Water dependance
Optimal sun exposure
Wind resistance
Noise reduction
Invasion potential
Growth rate
Maintenance
Adaptability

Index of flora

Japanese camellia

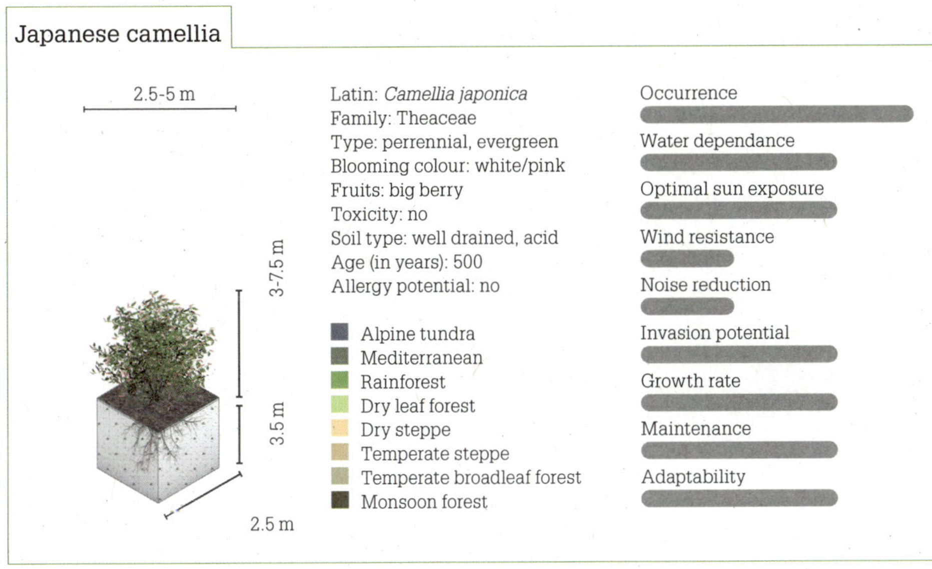

Latin: *Camellia japonica*
Family: Theaceae
Type: perrennial, evergreen
Blooming colour: white/pink
Fruits: big berry
Toxicity: no
Soil type: well drained, acid
Age (in years): 500
Allergy potential: no

California incense-cedar

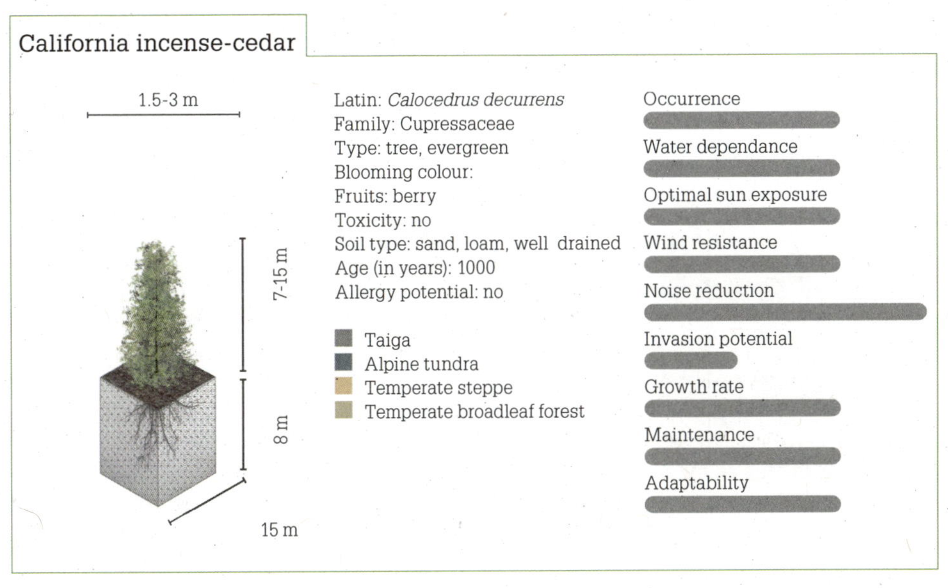

Latin: *Calocedrus decurrens*
Family: Cupressaceae
Type: tree, evergreen
Blooming colour:
Fruits: berry
Toxicity: no
Soil type: sand, loam, well drained
Age (in years): 1000
Allergy potential: no

Index of flora

Japanese sedge

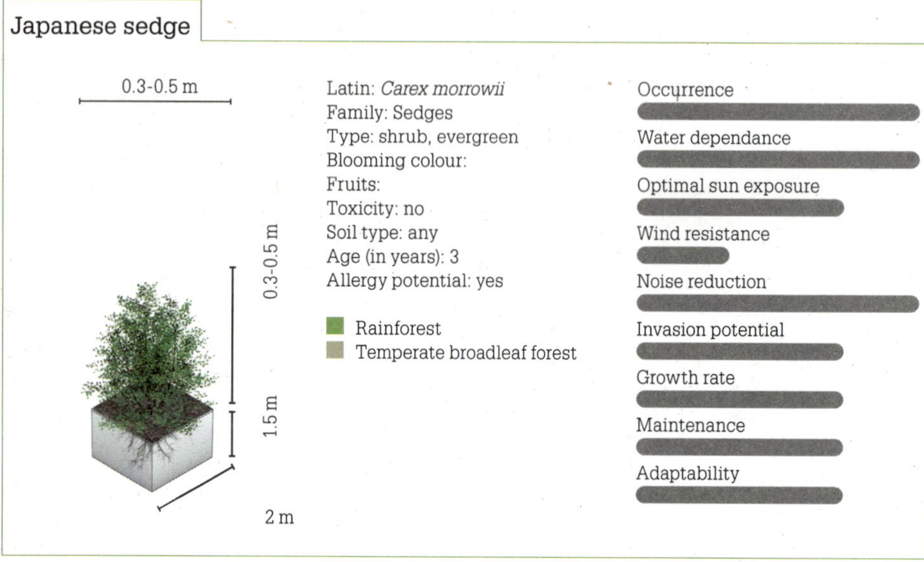

Latin: *Carex morrowii*
Family: Sedges
Type: shrub, evergreen
Blooming colour:
Fruits:
Toxicity: no
Soil type: any
Age (in years): 3
Allergy potential: yes

- Rainforest
- Temperate broadleaf forest

River she-oak

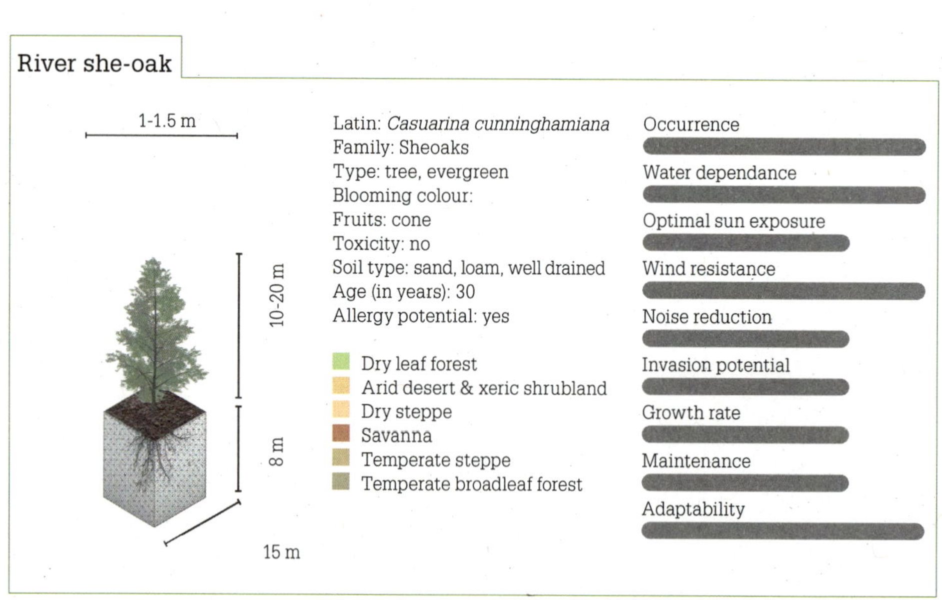

Latin: *Casuarina cunninghamiana*
Family: Sheoaks
Type: tree, evergreen
Blooming colour:
Fruits: cone
Toxicity: no
Soil type: sand, loam, well drained
Age (in years): 30
Allergy potential: yes

- Dry leaf forest
- Arid desert & xeric shrubland
- Dry steppe
- Savanna
- Temperate steppe
- Temperate broadleaf forest

Index of flora

Cigartree

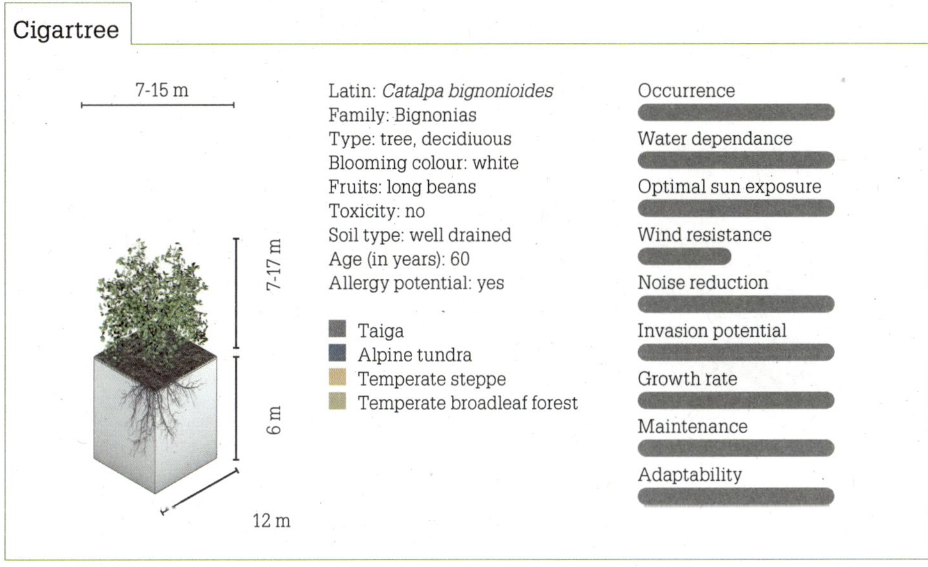

Latin: *Catalpa bignonioides*
Family: Bignonias
Type: tree, decidiuous
Blooming colour: white
Fruits: long beans
Toxicity: no
Soil type: well drained
Age (in years): 60
Allergy potential: yes

- Taiga
- Alpine tundra
- Temperate steppe
- Temperate broadleaf forest

Occurrence
Water dependance
Optimal sun exposure
Wind resistance
Noise reduction
Invasion potential
Growth rate
Maintenance
Adaptability

Atlas cedar

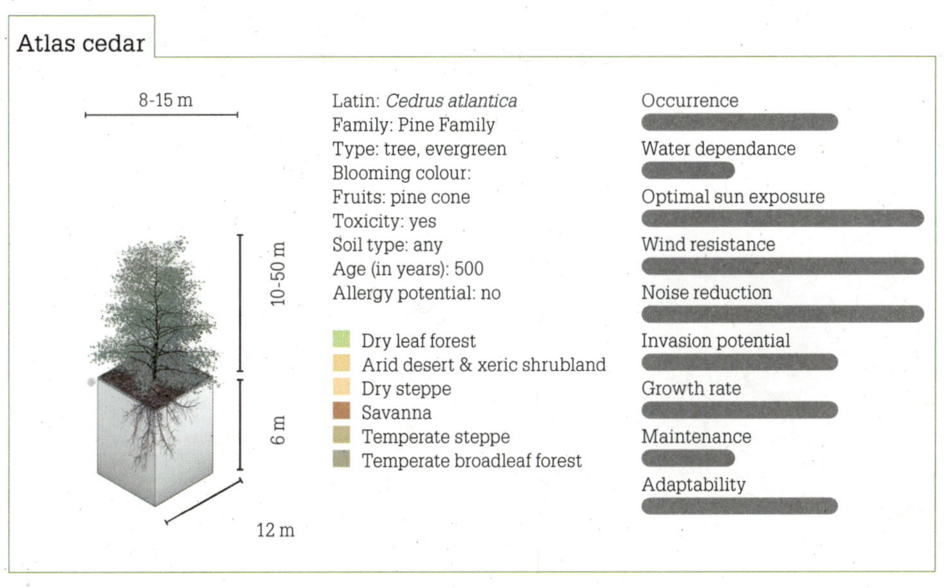

Latin: *Cedrus atlantica*
Family: Pine Family
Type: tree, evergreen
Blooming colour:
Fruits: pine cone
Toxicity: yes
Soil type: any
Age (in years): 500
Allergy potential: no

- Dry leaf forest
- Arid desert & xeric shrubland
- Dry steppe
- Savanna
- Temperate steppe
- Temperate broadleaf forest

Occurrence
Water dependance
Optimal sun exposure
Wind resistance
Noise reduction
Invasion potential
Growth rate
Maintenance
Adaptability

Index of flora

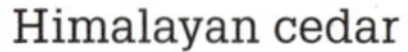

Himalayan cedar

Latin: *Cedrus deodara*
Family: Pine Family
Type: tree, evergreen
Blooming colour:
Fruits: pine cone
Toxicity: no
Soil type: acid
Age (in years): 600
Allergy potential: no

- Alpine tundra
- Rainforest
- Dry leaf forest
- Dry steppe
- Temperate broadleaf forest
- Monsoon forest

Occurrence
Water dependance
Optimal sun exposure
Wind resistance
Noise reduction
Invasion potential
Growth rate
Maintenance
Adaptability

Cedar of Lebanon

Latin: *Cedrus libani*
Family: Pine Family
Type: tree, evergreen
Blooming colour: white
Fruits: pine cone
Toxicity: no
Soil type: any
Age (in years): 300
Allergy potential: no

- Dry leaf forest
- Dry steppe
- Temperate steppe
- Temperate broadleaf forest
- Monsoon forest

Occurrence
Water dependance
Optimal sun exposure
Wind resistance
Noise reduction
Invasion potential
Growth rate
Maintenance
Adaptability

Index of flora

Mediterranean hackberry

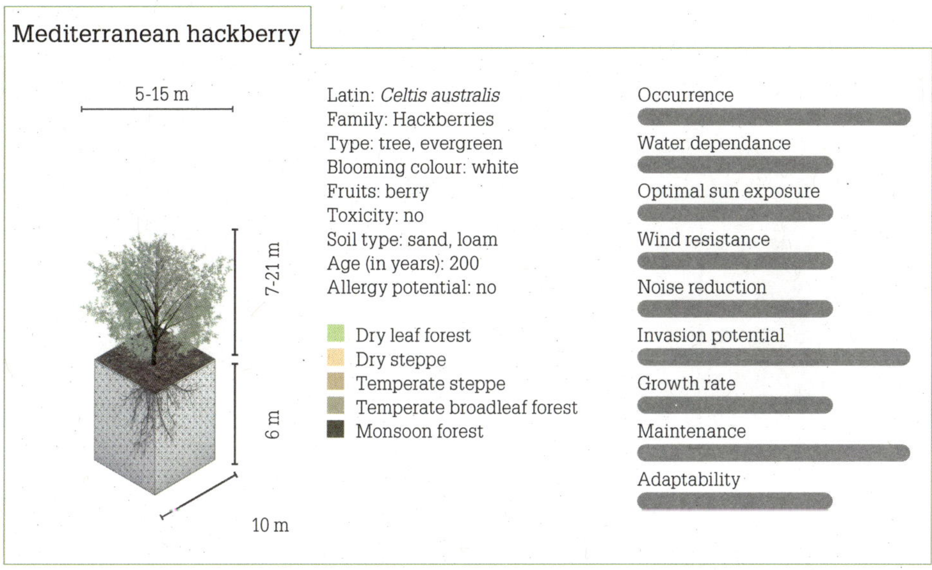

Latin: *Celtis australis*
Family: Hackberries
Type: tree, evergreen
Blooming colour: white
Fruits: berry
Toxicity: no
Soil type: sand, loam
Age (in years): 200
Allergy potential: no

- Dry leaf forest
- Dry steppe
- Temperate steppe
- Temperate broadleaf forest
- Monsoon forest

Judas tree

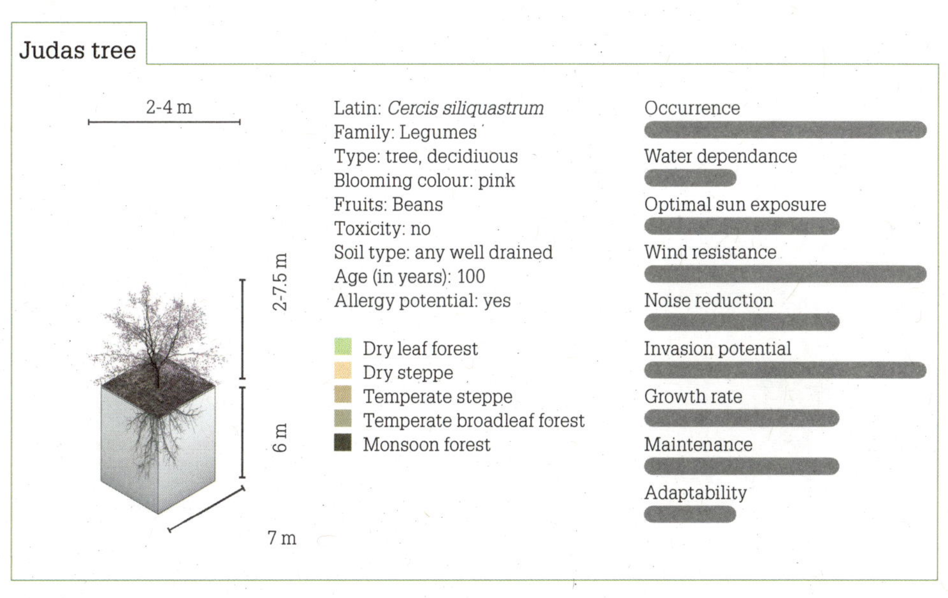

Latin: *Cercis siliquastrum*
Family: Legumes
Type: tree, decidiuous
Blooming colour: pink
Fruits: Beans
Toxicity: no
Soil type: any well drained
Age (in years): 100
Allergy potential: yes

- Dry leaf forest
- Dry steppe
- Temperate steppe
- Temperate broadleaf forest
- Monsoon forest

Index of flora

Lawson's cypress

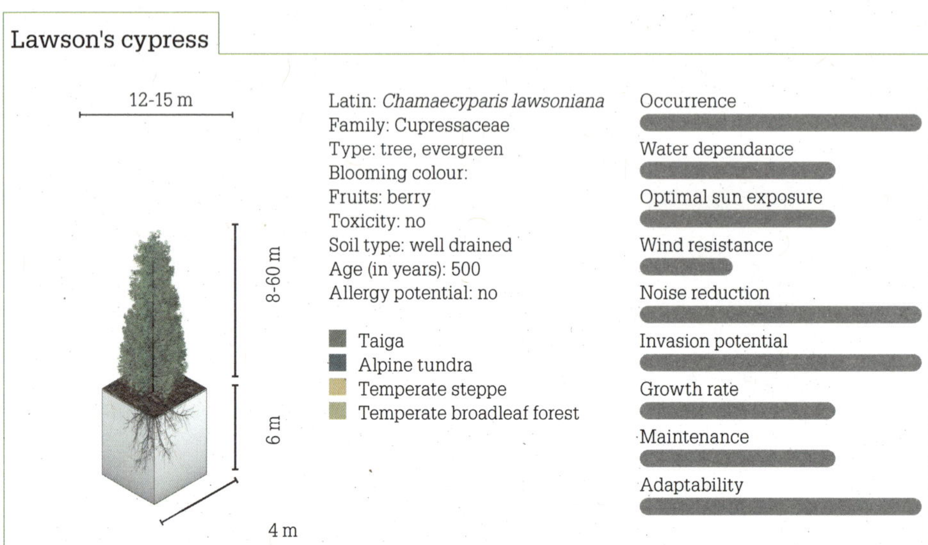

Latin: *Chamaecyparis lawsoniana*
Family: Cupressaceae
Type: tree, evergreen
Blooming colour:
Fruits: berry
Toxicity: no
Soil type: well drained
Age (in years): 500
Allergy potential: no

- Taiga
- Alpine tundra
- Temperate steppe
- Temperate broadleaf forest

Occurrence
Water dependance
Optimal sun exposure
Wind resistance
Noise reduction
Invasion potential
Growth rate
Maintenance
Adaptability

Mediterranean fan palm

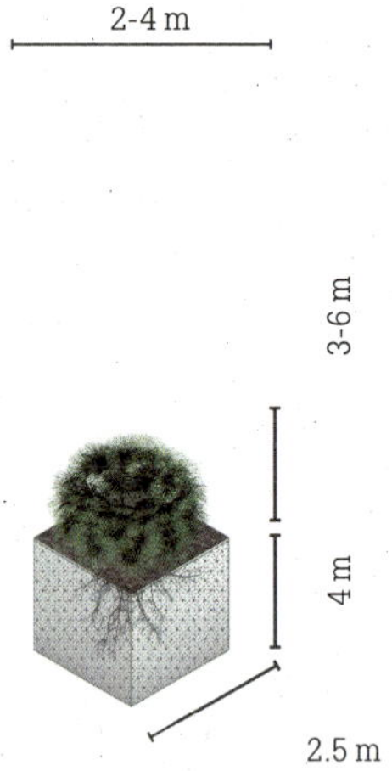

2-4 m
3-6 m
4 m
2.5 m

Latin: *Chamaerops humilis*
Family: Palm trees
Type: tree, evergreen
Blooming colour:
Fruits: berry
Toxicity: no
Soil type: sand, loam
Age (in years): 90
Allergy potential: no

- Dry leaf forest
- Dry steppe
- Temperate steppe
- Temperate broadleaf forest
- Monsoon forest

Occurrence
Water dependance
Optimal sun exposure
Wind resistance
Noise reduction
Invasion potential
Growth rate
Maintenance
Adaptability

Index of flora

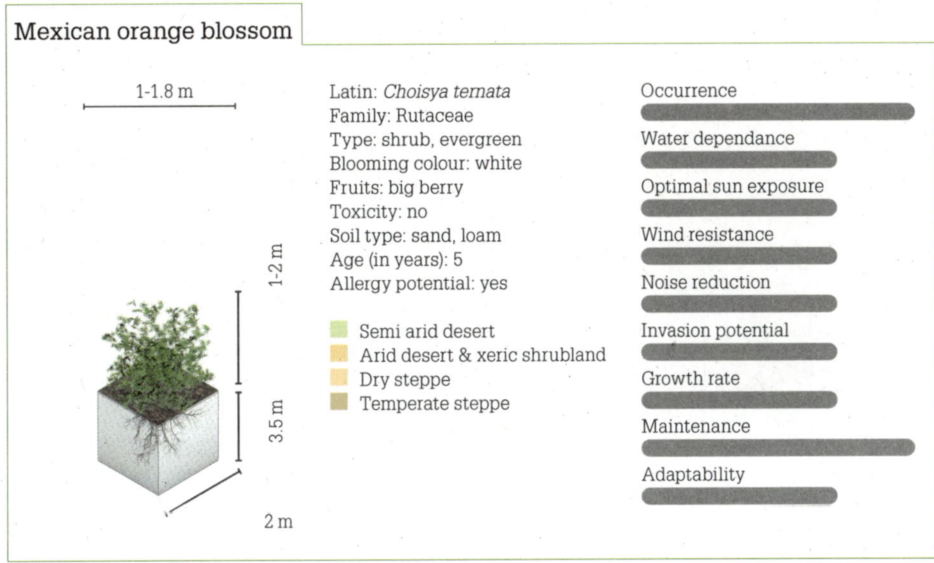

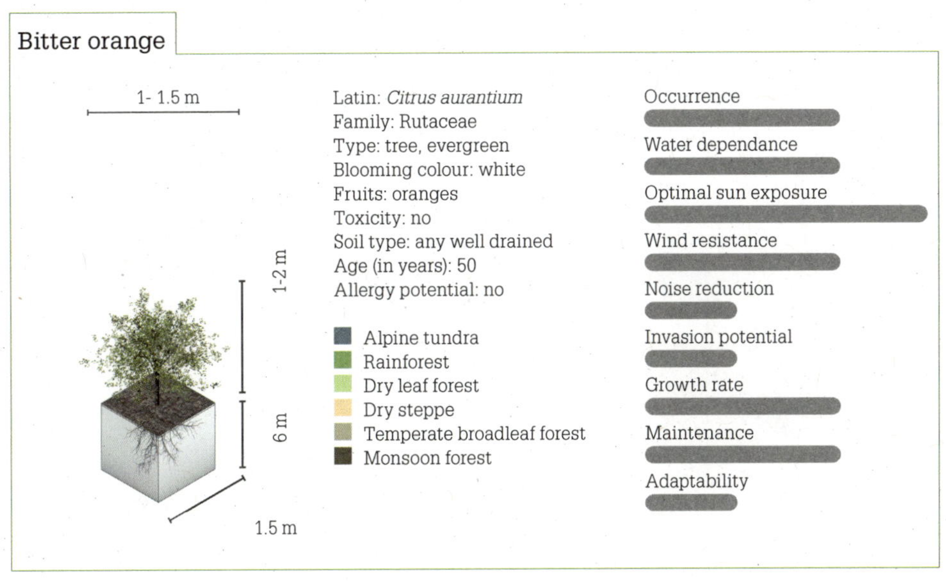

Index of flora

Lemon

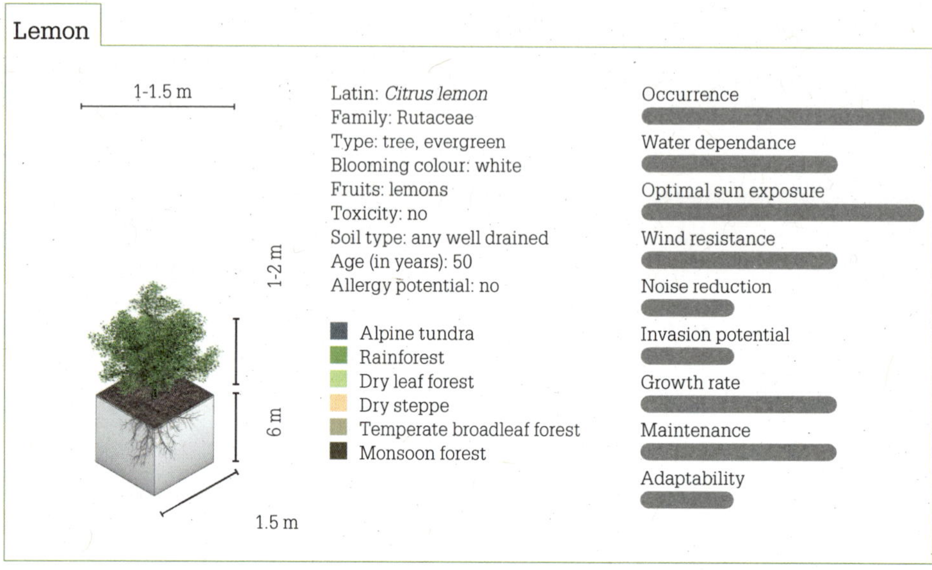

Latin: *Citrus lemon*
Family: Rutaceae
Type: tree, evergreen
Blooming colour: white
Fruits: lemons
Toxicity: no
Soil type: any well drained
Age (in years): 50
Allergy potential: no

- Alpine tundra
- Rainforest
- Dry leaf forest
- Dry steppe
- Temperate broadleaf forest
- Monsoon forest

Silver torch

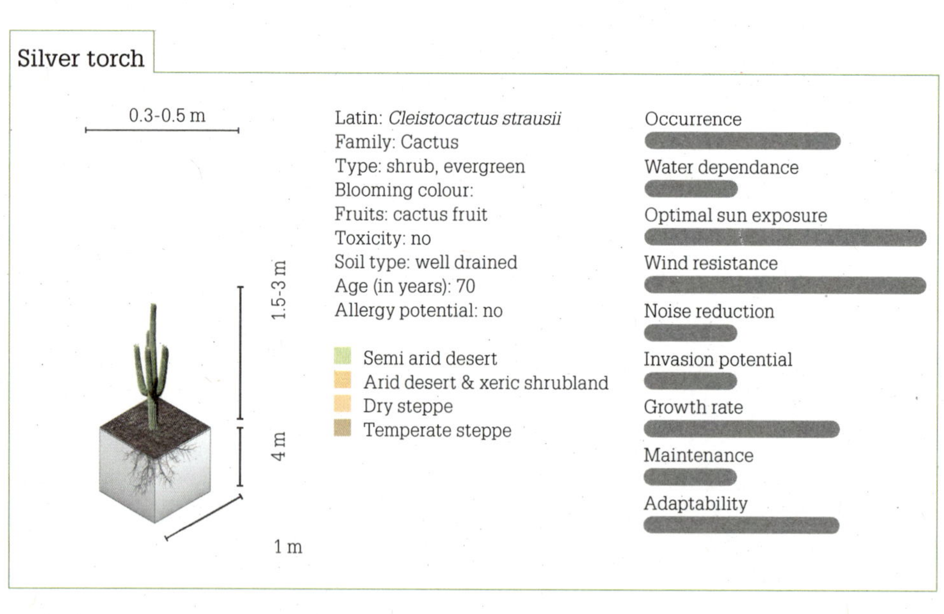

Latin: *Cleistocactus strausii*
Family: Cactus
Type: shrub, evergreen
Blooming colour:
Fruits: cactus fruit
Toxicity: no
Soil type: well drained
Age (in years): 70
Allergy potential: no

- Semi arid desert
- Arid desert & xeric shrubland
- Dry steppe
- Temperate steppe

Index of flora

Downy clematis

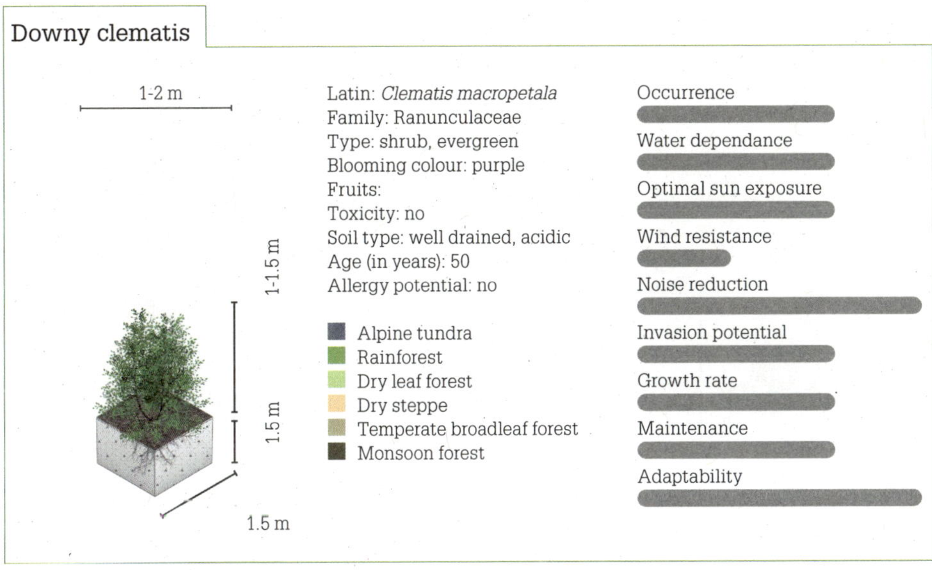

Latin: *Clematis macropetala*
Family: Ranunculaceae
Type: shrub, evergreen
Blooming colour: purple
Fruits:
Toxicity: no
Soil type: well drained, acidic
Age (in years): 50
Allergy potential: no

Kousa

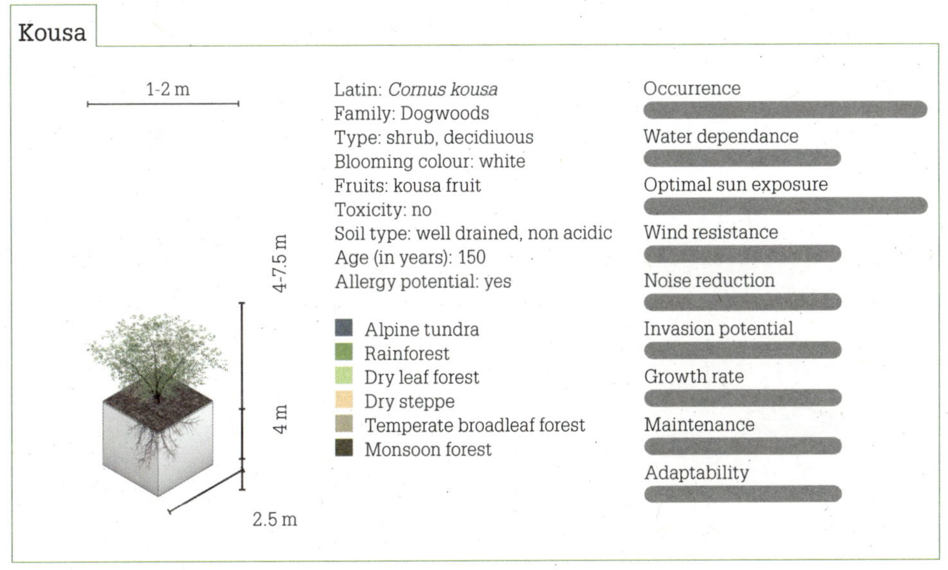

Latin: *Cornus kousa*
Family: Dogwoods
Type: shrub, decidiuous
Blooming colour: white
Fruits: kousa fruit
Toxicity: no
Soil type: well drained, non acidic
Age (in years): 150
Allergy potential: yes

Index of flora

Glauca citrina

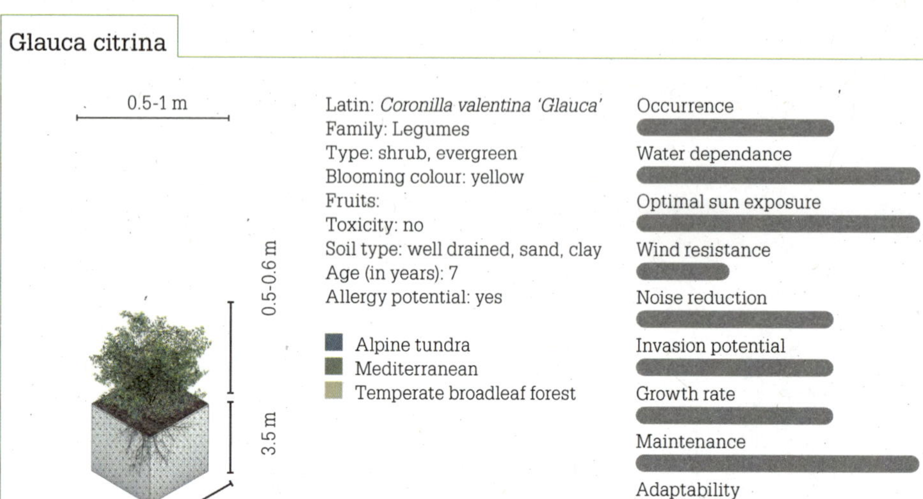

Latin: *Coronilla valentina 'Glauca'*
Family: Legumes
Type: shrub, evergreen
Blooming colour: yellow
Fruits:
Toxicity: no
Soil type: well drained, sand, clay
Age (in years): 7
Allergy potential: yes

- Alpine tundra
- Mediterranean
- Temperate broadleaf forest

Occurrence
Water dependance
Optimal sun exposure
Wind resistance
Noise reduction
Invasion potential
Growth rate
Maintenance
Adaptability

Pampas grass

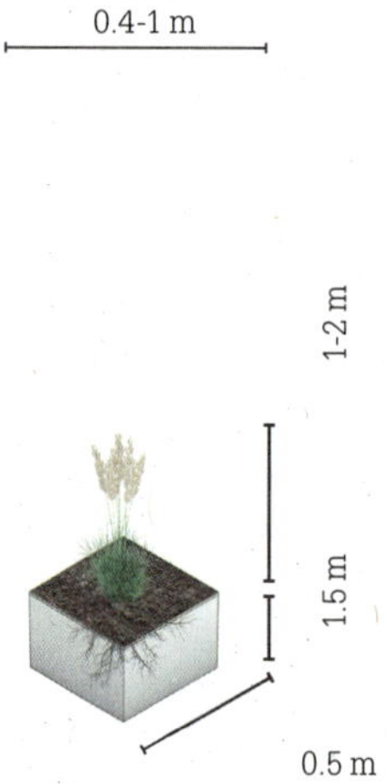

0.4-1 m
1-2 m
1.5 m
0.5 m

Latin: *Cortaderia selloana*
Family: Grasses
Type: shrub, evergreen
Blooming colour: white
Fruits: seeds
Toxicity: no
Soil type: well drained
Age (in years): 15
Allergy potential: yes

- Alpine tundra
- Rainforest
- Semi arid desert
- Arid desert & xeric shrubland
- Dry steppe
- Temperate steppe
- Temperate broadleaf forest
- Monsoon forest

Occurrence
Water dependance
Optimal sun exposure
Wind resistance
Noise reduction
Invasion potential
Growth rate
Maintenance
Adaptability

Index of flora

Common hazel

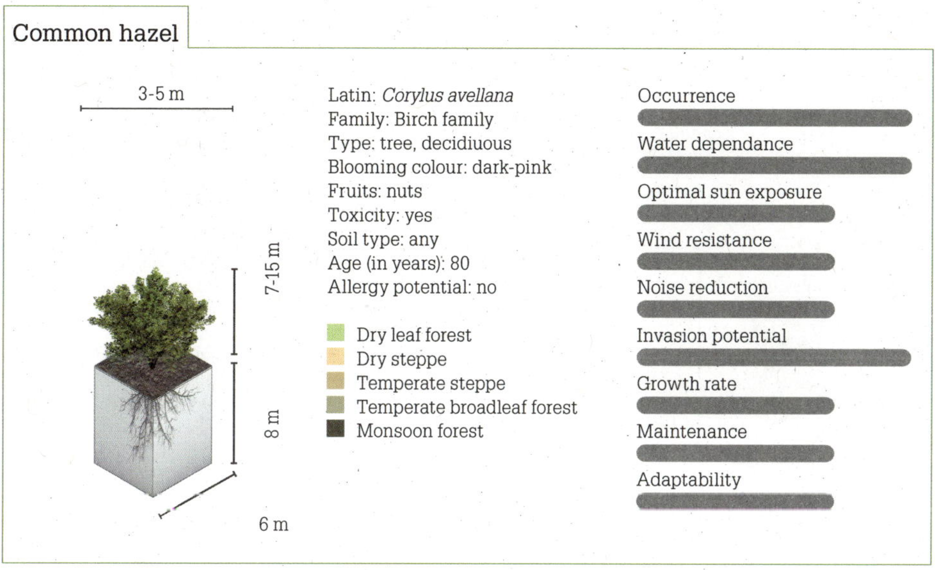

Latin: *Corylus avellana*
Family: Birch family
Type: tree, decidiuous
Blooming colour: dark-pink
Fruits: nuts
Toxicity: yes
Soil type: any
Age (in years): 80
Allergy potential: no

- Dry leaf forest
- Dry steppe
- Temperate steppe
- Temperate broadleaf forest
- Monsoon forest

Purple filbert

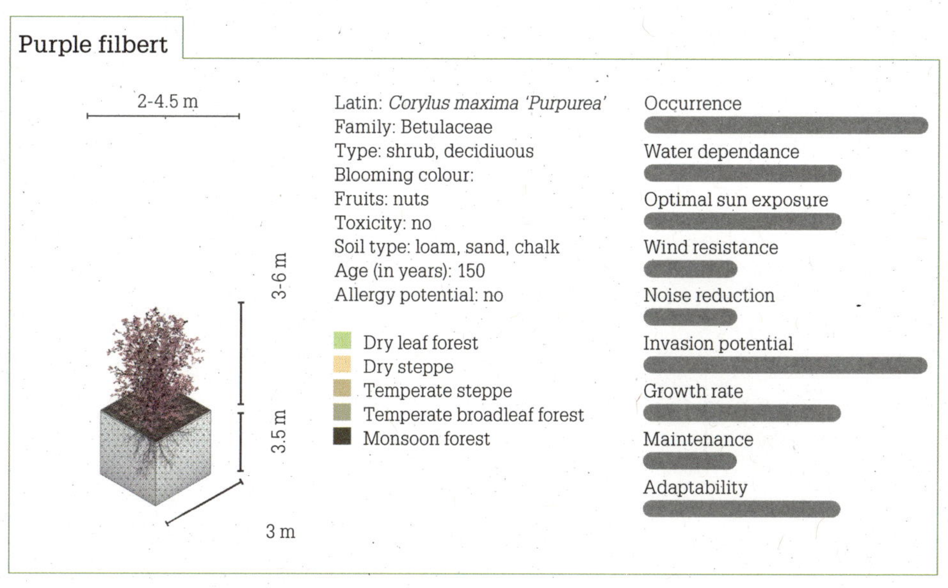

Latin: *Corylus maxima 'Purpurea'*
Family: Betulaceae
Type: shrub, decidiuous
Blooming colour:
Fruits: nuts
Toxicity: no
Soil type: loam, sand, chalk
Age (in years): 150
Allergy potential: no

- Dry leaf forest
- Dry steppe
- Temperate steppe
- Temperate broadleaf forest
- Monsoon forest

Index of flora

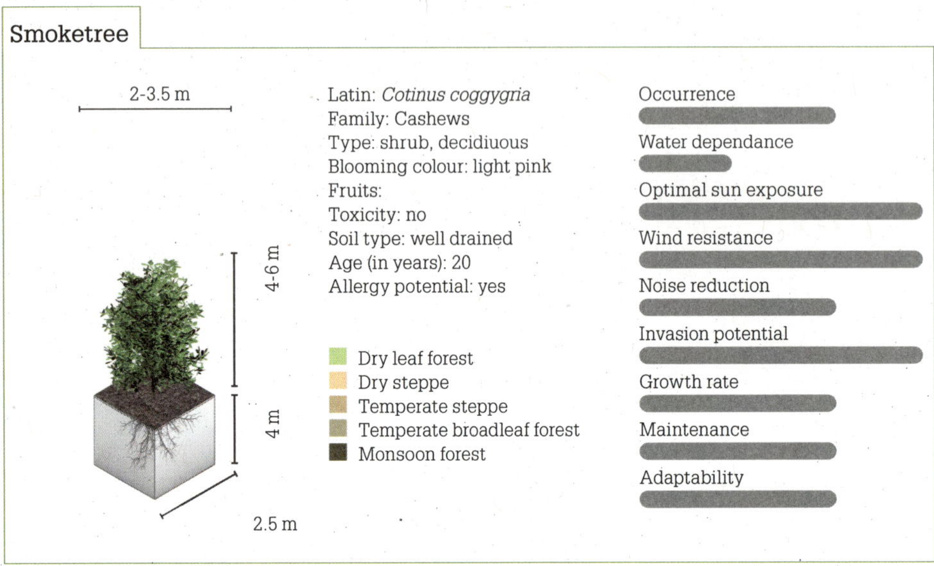

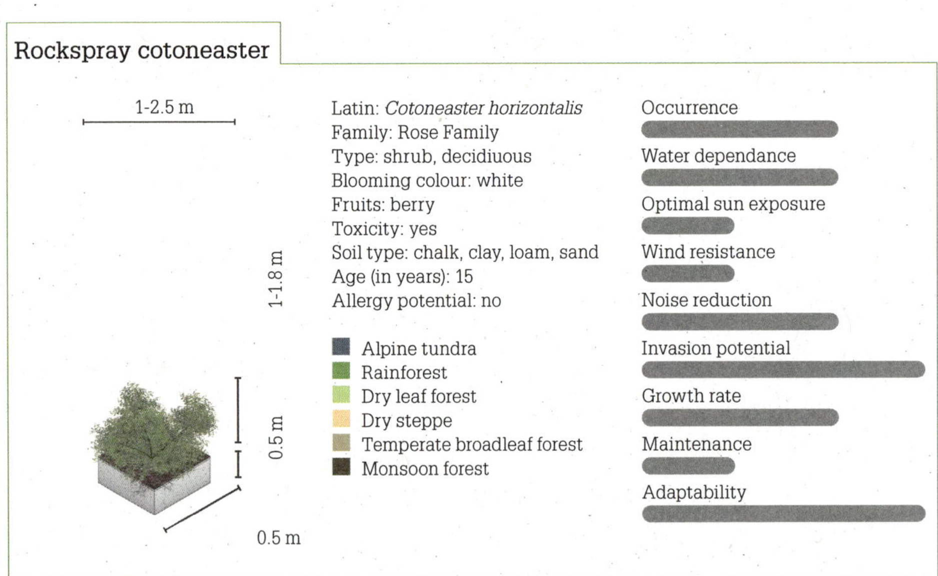

Index of flora

Milkflower cotoneaster

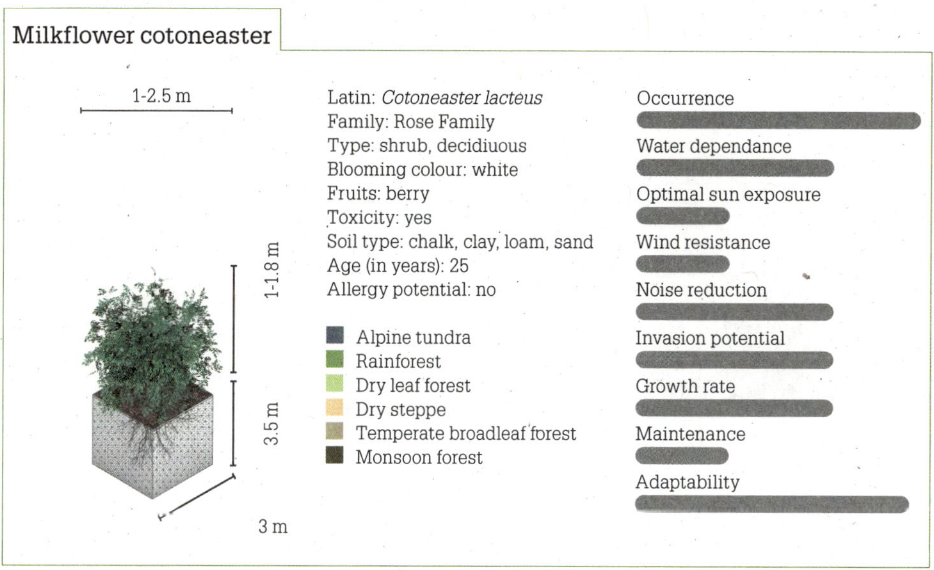

Latin: *Cotoneaster lacteus*
Family: Rose Family
Type: shrub, decidiuous
Blooming colour: white
Fruits: berry
Toxicity: yes
Soil type: chalk, clay, loam, sand
Age (in years): 25
Allergy potential: no

- Alpine tundra
- Rainforest
- Dry leaf forest
- Dry steppe
- Temperate broadleaf forest
- Monsoon forest

Jade

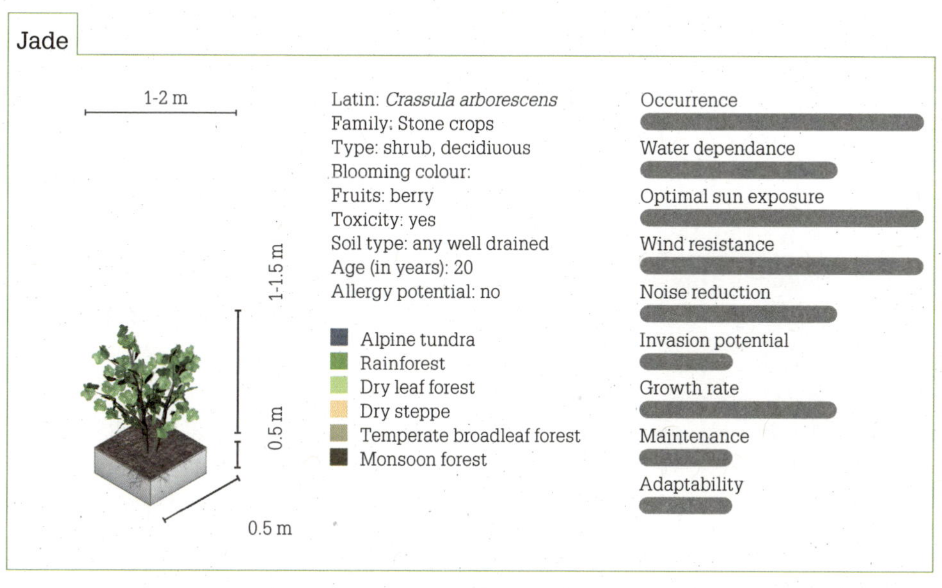

Latin: *Crassula arborescens*
Family: Stone crops
Type: shrub, decidiuous
Blooming colour:
Fruits: berry
Toxicity: yes
Soil type: any well drained
Age (in years): 20
Allergy potential: no

- Alpine tundra
- Rainforest
- Dry leaf forest
- Dry steppe
- Temperate broadleaf forest
- Monsoon forest

Index of flora

Oneseed hawthorn

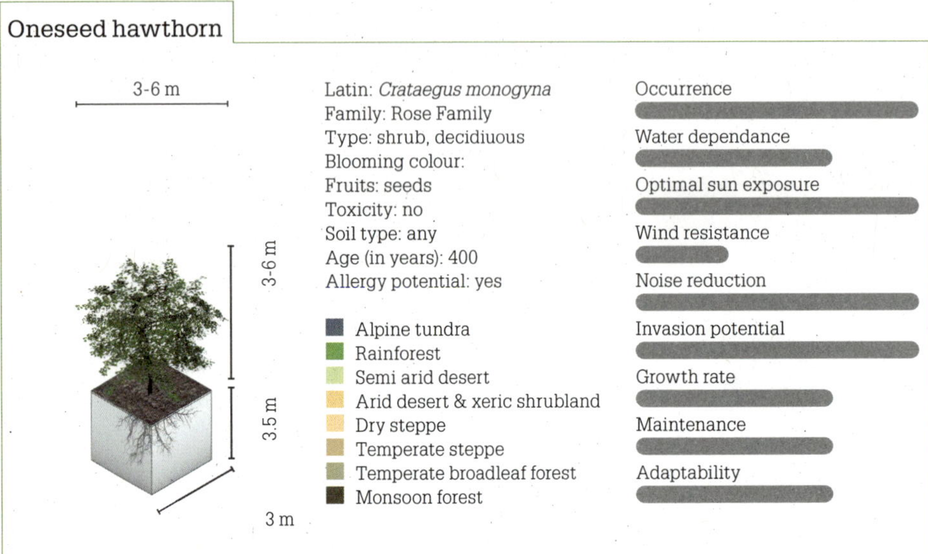

Latin: *Crataegus monogyna*
Family: Rose Family
Type: shrub, decidiuous
Blooming colour:
Fruits: seeds
Toxicity: no
Soil type: any
Age (in years): 400
Allergy potential: yes

- Alpine tundra
- Rainforest
- Semi arid desert
- Arid desert & xeric shrubland
- Dry steppe
- Temperate steppe
- Temperate broadleaf forest
- Monsoon forest

Occurrence
Water dependance
Optimal sun exposure
Wind resistance
Noise reduction
Invasion potential
Growth rate
Maintenance
Adaptability

Japanese cedar

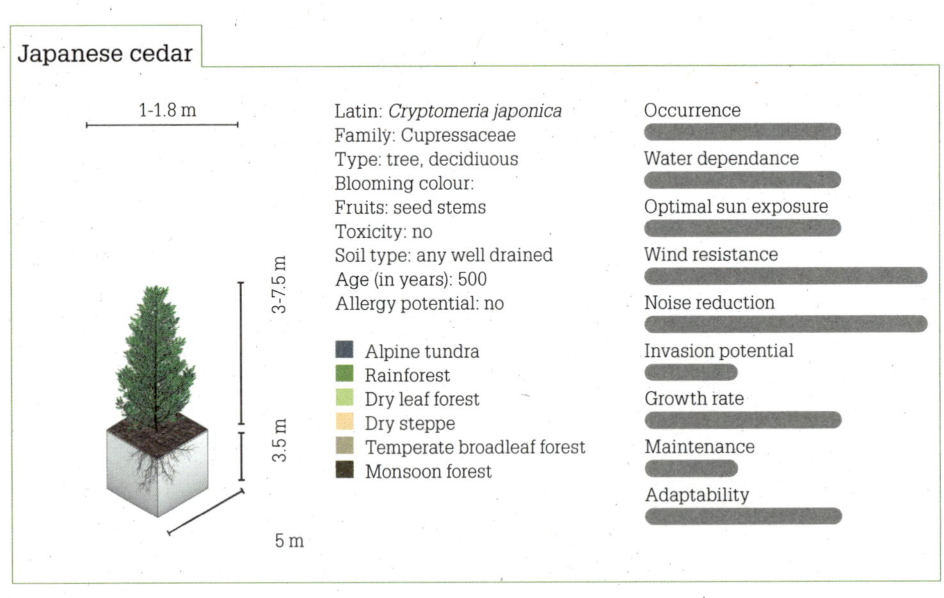

Latin: *Cryptomeria japonica*
Family: Cupressaceae
Type: tree, decidiuous
Blooming colour:
Fruits: seed stems
Toxicity: no
Soil type: any well drained
Age (in years): 500
Allergy potential: no

- Alpine tundra
- Rainforest
- Dry leaf forest
- Dry steppe
- Temperate broadleaf forest
- Monsoon forest

Occurrence
Water dependance
Optimal sun exposure
Wind resistance
Noise reduction
Invasion potential
Growth rate
Maintenance
Adaptability

Index of flora

Leyland cypress

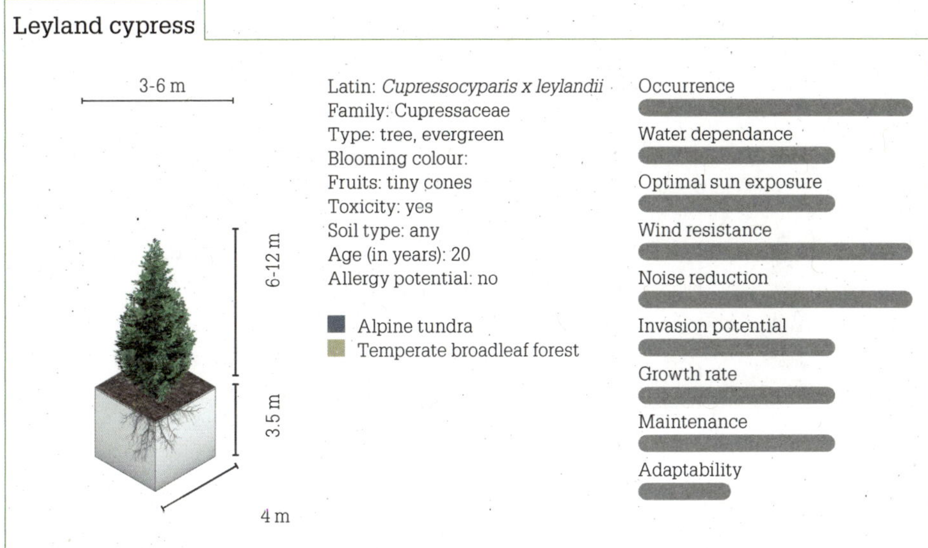

Latin: *Cupressocyparis x leylandii*
Family: Cupressaceae
Type: tree, evergreen
Blooming colour:
Fruits: tiny cones
Toxicity: yes
Soil type: any
Age (in years): 20
Allergy potential: no

- Alpine tundra
- Temperate broadleaf forest

Italian cypress 1

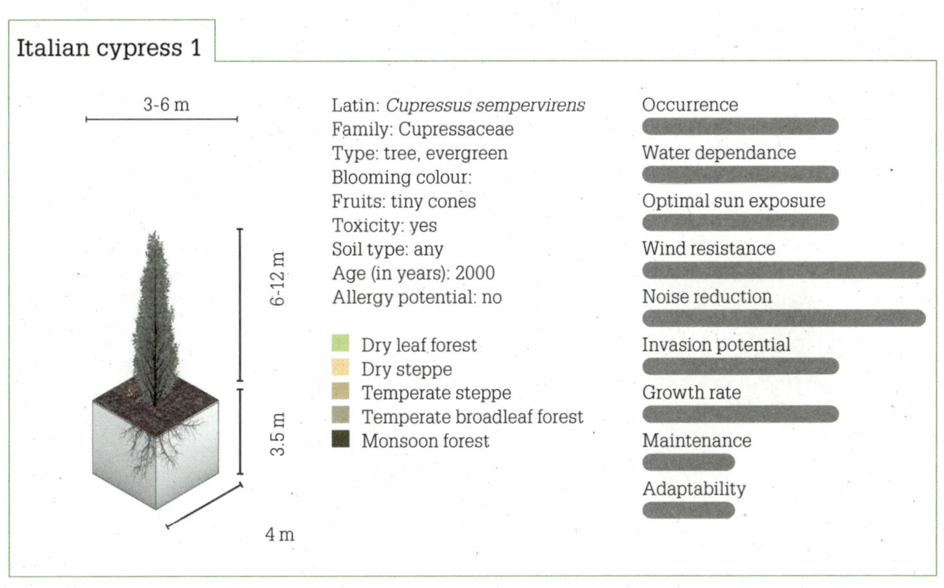

Latin: *Cupressus sempervirens*
Family: Cupressaceae
Type: tree, evergreen
Blooming colour:
Fruits: tiny cones
Toxicity: yes
Soil type: any
Age (in years): 2000
Allergy potential: no

- Dry leaf forest
- Dry steppe
- Temperate steppe
- Temperate broadleaf forest
- Monsoon forest

Index of flora

Italian cypress 2

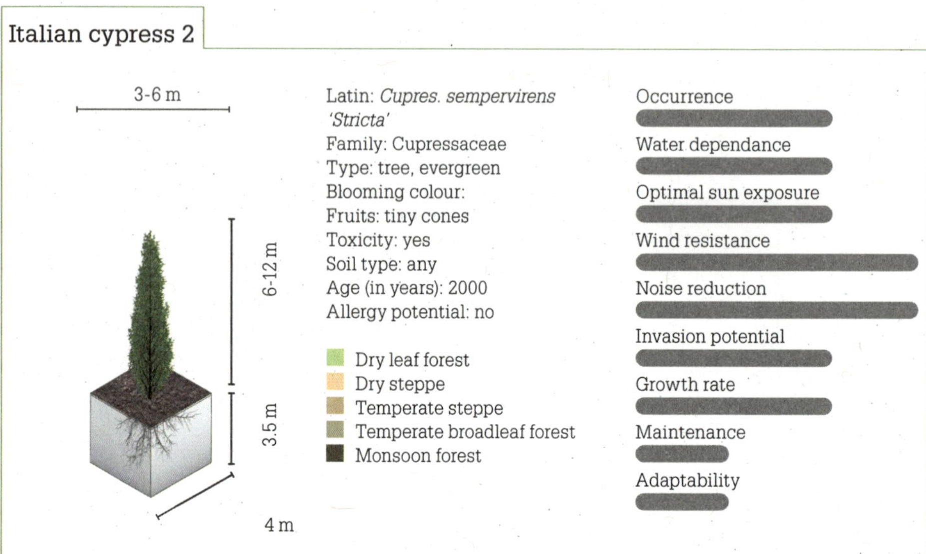

Latin: *Cupres. sempervirens 'Stricta'*
Family: Cupressaceae
Type: tree, evergreen
Blooming colour:
Fruits: tiny cones
Toxicity: yes
Soil type: any
Age (in years): 2000
Allergy potential: no

- Dry leaf forest
- Dry steppe
- Temperate steppe
- Temperate broadleaf forest
- Monsoon forest

Occurrence
Water dependance
Optimal sun exposure
Wind resistance
Noise reduction
Invasion potential
Growth rate
Maintenance
Adaptability

Sago palm

1-3.5 m
1-3.5 m
3.5 m
2 m

Latin: *Cycas revoluta*
Family: Cycad family
Type: tree, evergreen
Blooming colour:
Fruits: huge cone
Toxicity: yes
Soil type: sand, loam, well drained
Age (in years): 100
Allergy potential: no

- Alpine tundra
- Rainforest
- Dry leaf forest
- Dry steppe
- Temperate broadleaf forest
- Monsoon forest

Occurrence
Water dependance
Optimal sun exposure
Wind resistance
Noise reduction
Invasion potential
Growth rate
Maintenance
Adaptability

Index of flora

Umbrella papyrus

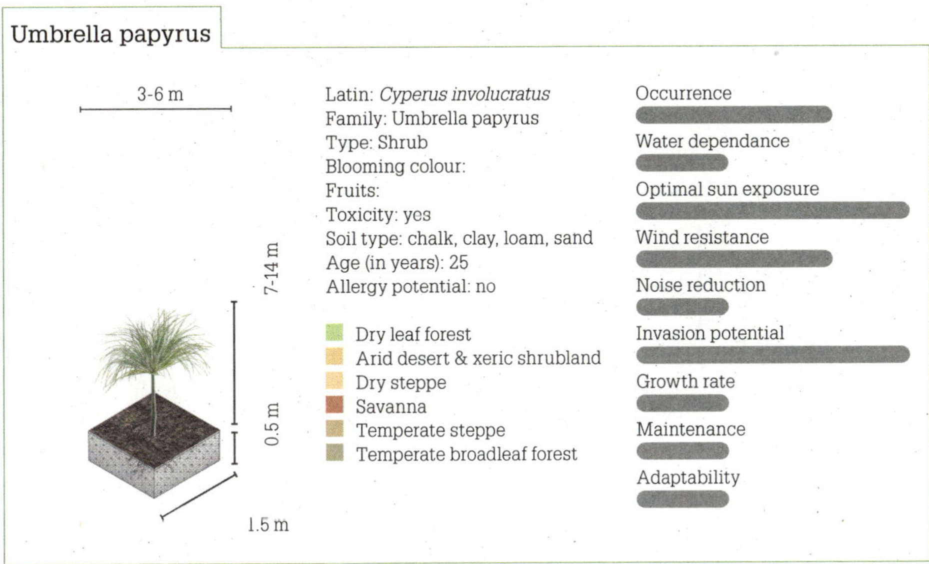

Latin: *Cyperus involucratus*
Family: Umbrella papyrus
Type: Shrub
Blooming colour:
Fruits:
Toxicity: yes
Soil type: chalk, clay, loam, sand
Age (in years): 25
Allergy potential: no

- Dry leaf forest
- Arid desert & xeric shrubland
- Dry steppe
- Savanna
- Temperate steppe
- Temperate broadleaf forest

Hop bush

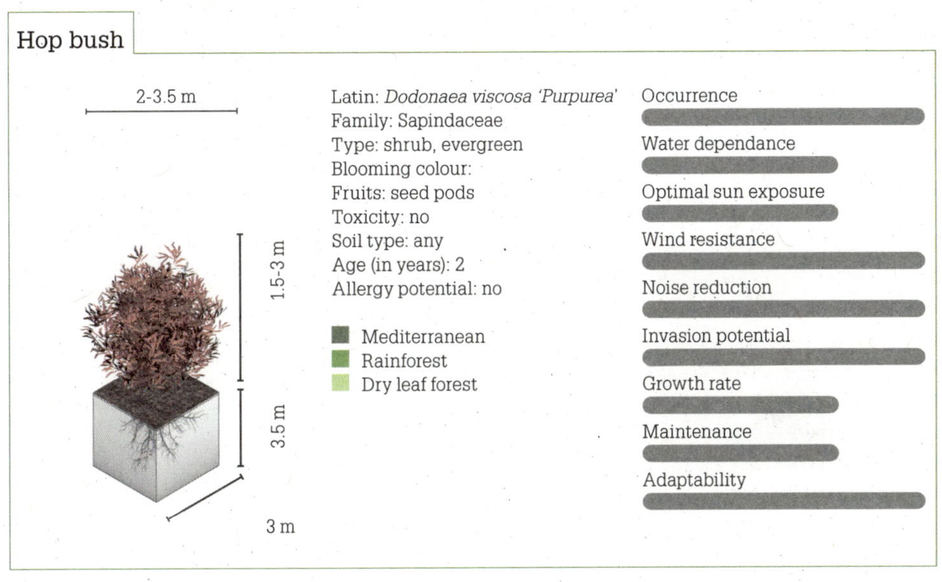

Latin: *Dodonaea viscosa 'Purpurea'*
Family: Sapindaceae
Type: shrub, evergreen
Blooming colour:
Fruits: seed pods
Toxicity: no
Soil type: any
Age (in years): 2
Allergy potential: no

- Mediterranean
- Rainforest
- Dry leaf forest

Index of flora

Skyflower

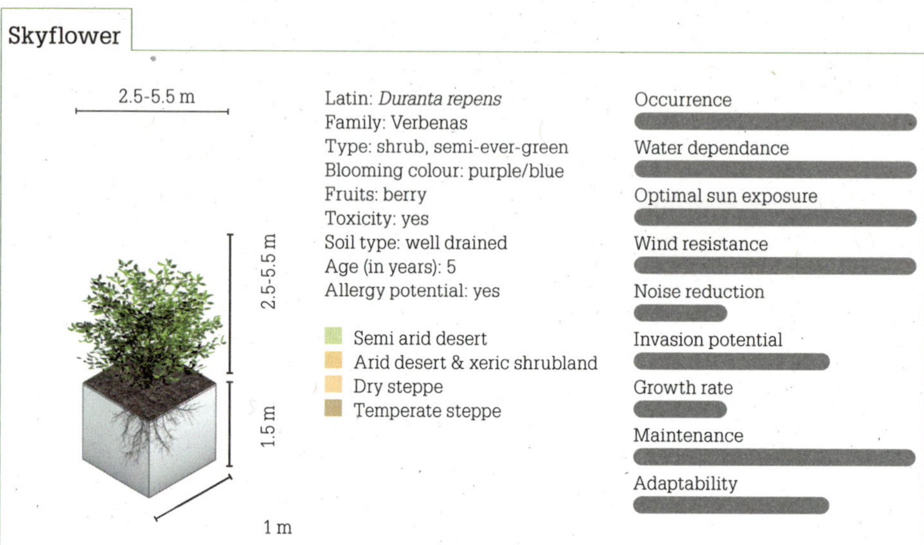

Latin: *Duranta repens*
Family: Verbenas
Type: shrub, semi-ever-green
Blooming colour: purple/blue
Fruits: berry
Toxicity: yes
Soil type: well drained
Age (in years): 5
Allergy potential: yes

- Semi arid desert
- Arid desert & xeric shrubland
- Dry steppe
- Temperate steppe

Golden barrel

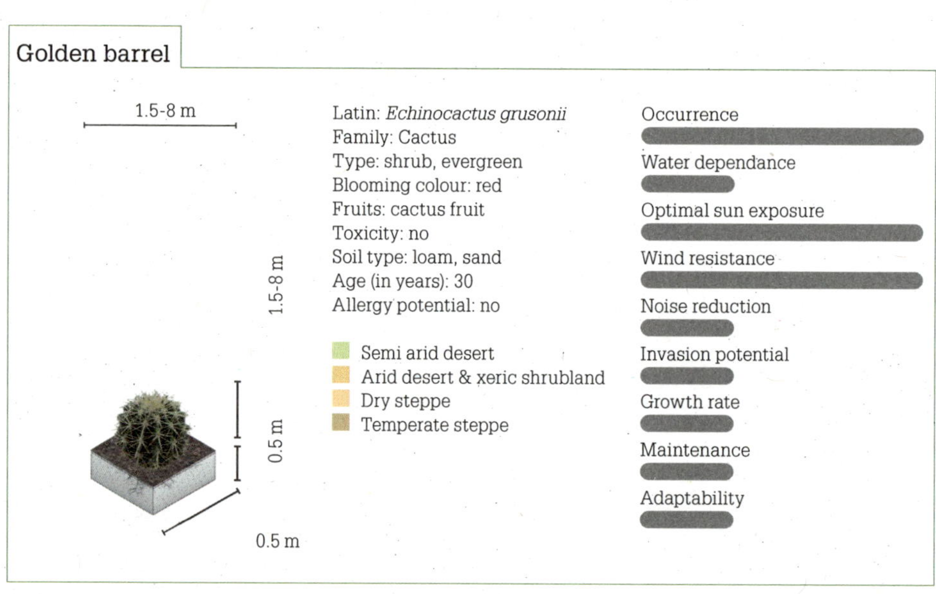

Latin: *Echinocactus grusonii*
Family: Cactus
Type: shrub, evergreen
Blooming colour: red
Fruits: cactus fruit
Toxicity: no
Soil type: loam, sand
Age (in years): 30
Allergy potential: no

- Semi arid desert
- Arid desert & xeric shrubland
- Dry steppe
- Temperate steppe

Index of flora

Trichocereus vollianus

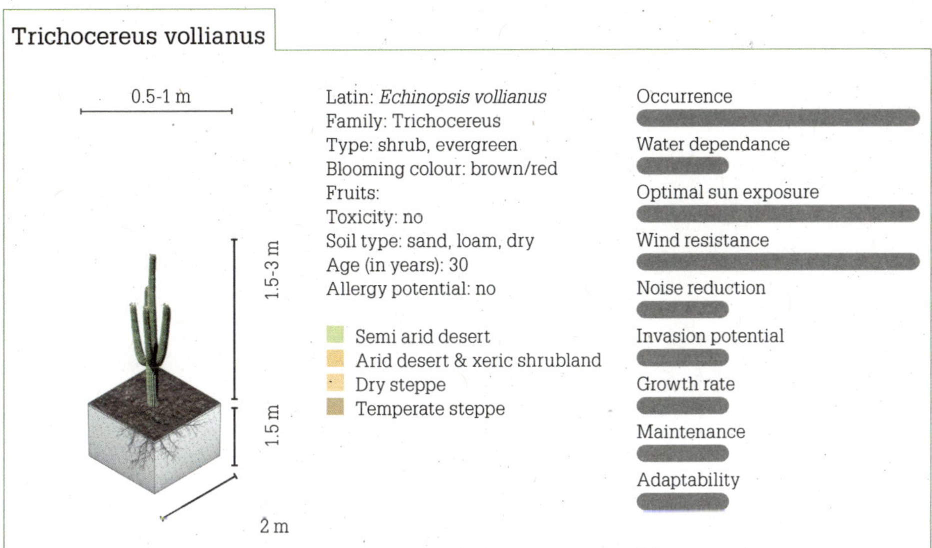

Russian olive

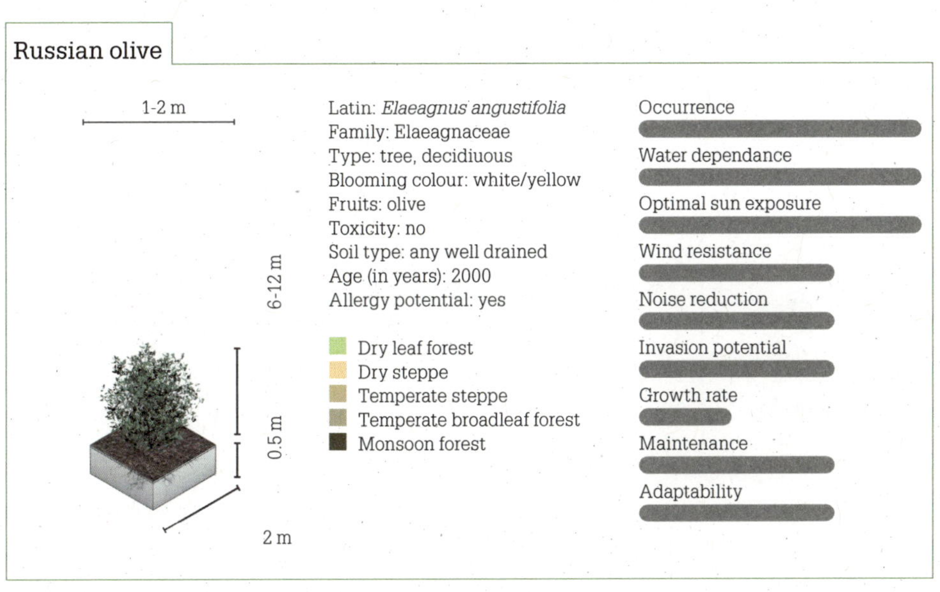

Index of flora

Oleaster

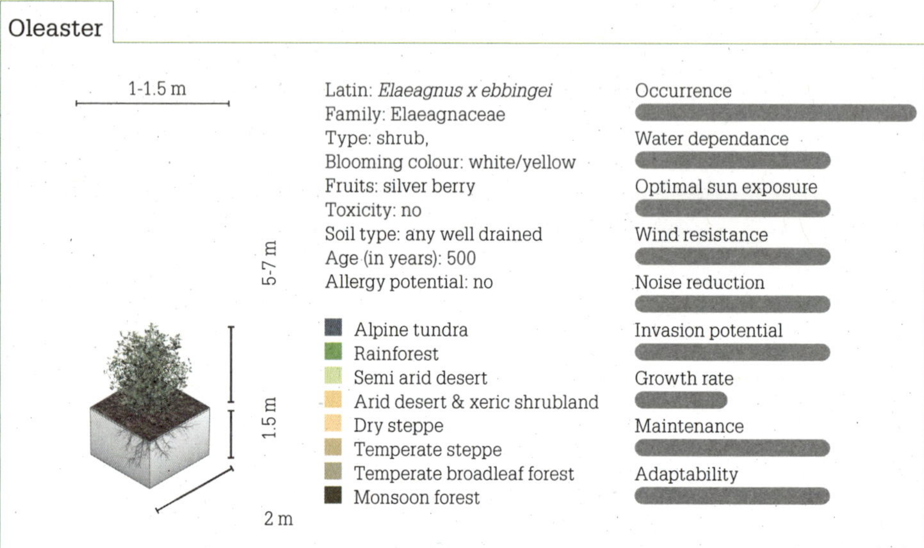

Evergreen Spindle

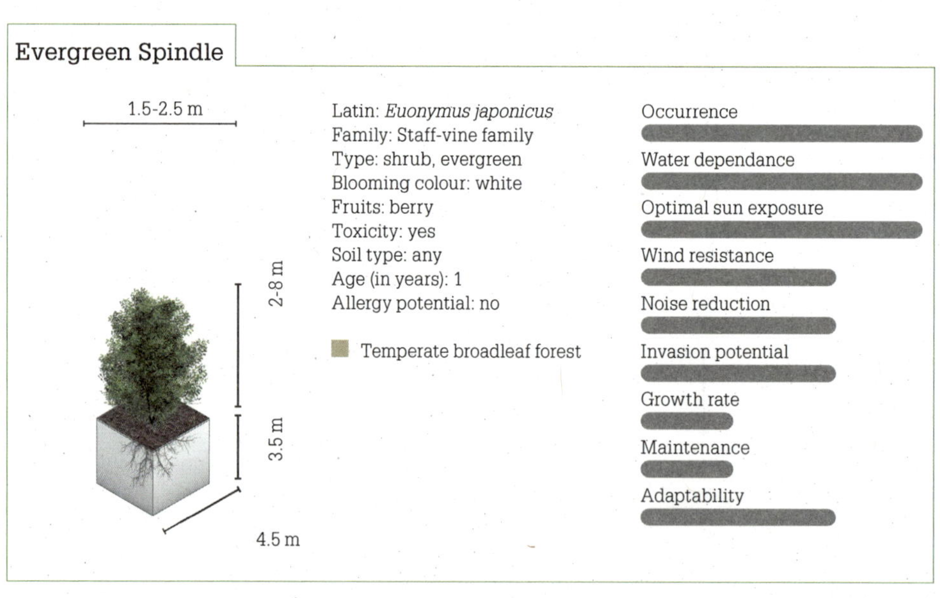

Index of flora

Japanese aralia

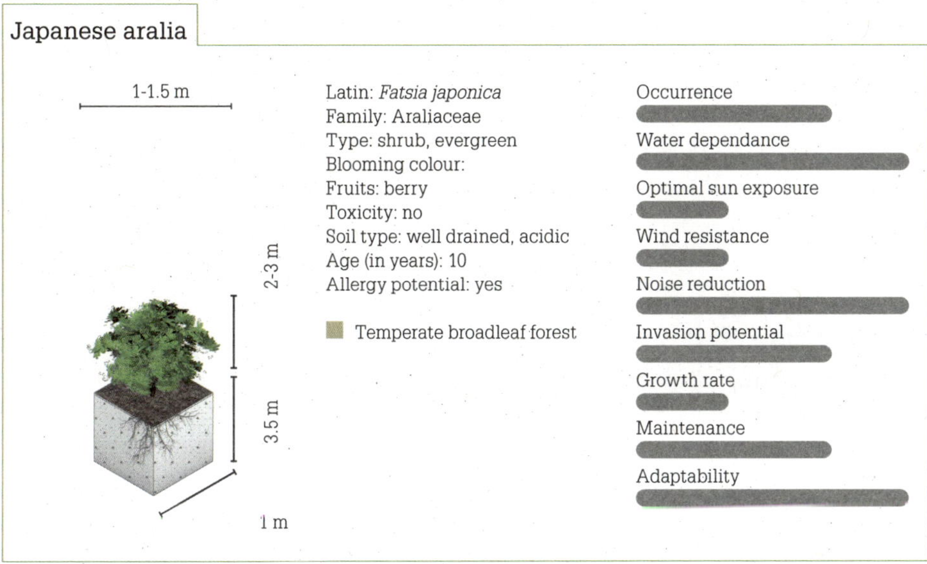

Latin: *Fatsia japonica*
Family: Araliaceae
Type: shrub, evergreen
Blooming colour:
Fruits: berry
Toxicity: no
Soil type: well drained, acidic
Age (in years): 10
Allergy potential: yes

Temperate broadleaf forest

Occurrence
Water dependance
Optimal sun exposure
Wind resistance
Noise reduction
Invasion potential
Growth rate
Maintenance
Adaptability

Pineapple guava

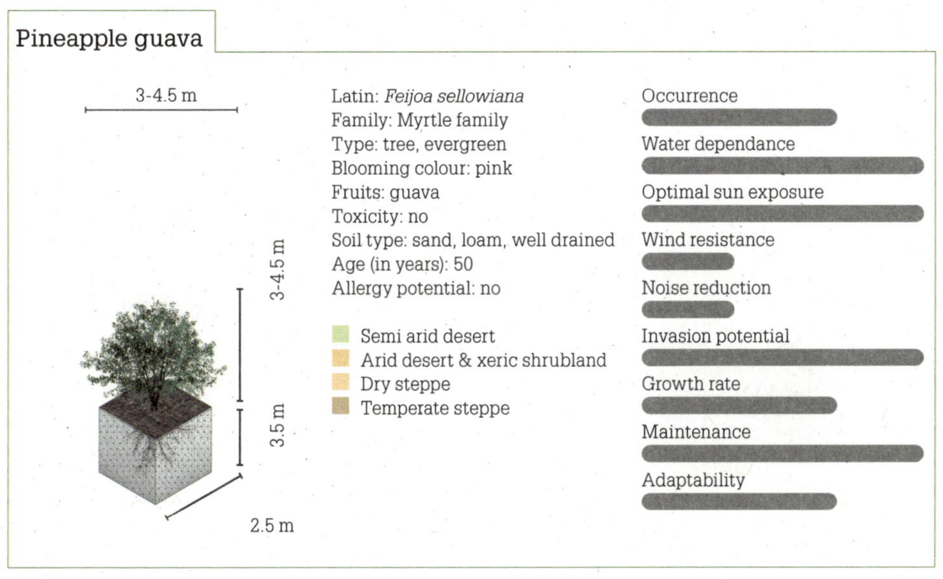

Latin: *Feijoa sellowiana*
Family: Myrtle family
Type: tree, evergreen
Blooming colour: pink
Fruits: guava
Toxicity: no
Soil type: sand, loam, well drained
Age (in years): 50
Allergy potential: no

Semi arid desert
Arid desert & xeric shrubland
Dry steppe
Temperate steppe

Occurrence
Water dependance
Optimal sun exposure
Wind resistance
Noise reduction
Invasion potential
Growth rate
Maintenance
Adaptability

Index of flora

Common fig

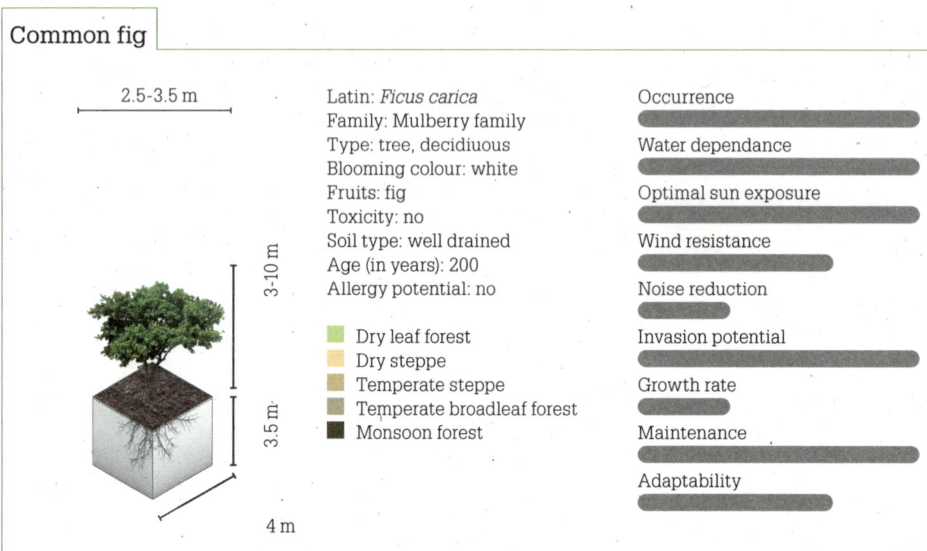

Latin: *Ficus carica*
Family: Mulberry family
Type: tree, decidiuous
Blooming colour: white
Fruits: fig
Toxicity: no
Soil type: well drained
Age (in years): 200
Allergy potential: no

- Dry leaf forest
- Dry steppe
- Temperate steppe
- Temperate broadleaf forest
- Monsoon forest

Occurrence
Water dependance
Optimal sun exposure
Wind resistance
Noise reduction
Invasion potential
Growth rate
Maintenance
Adaptability

Border forsythia

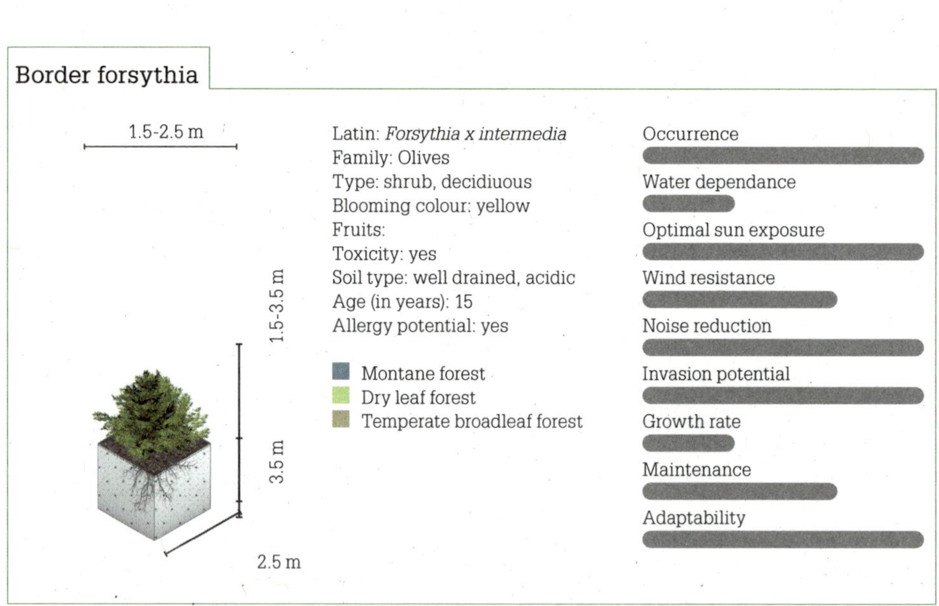

Latin: *Forsythia x intermedia*
Family: Olives
Type: shrub, decidiuous
Blooming colour: yellow
Fruits:
Toxicity: yes
Soil type: well drained, acidic
Age (in years): 15
Allergy potential: yes

- Montane forest
- Dry leaf forest
- Temperate broadleaf forest

Occurrence
Water dependance
Optimal sun exposure
Wind resistance
Noise reduction
Invasion potential
Growth rate
Maintenance
Adaptability

Index of flora

Ash

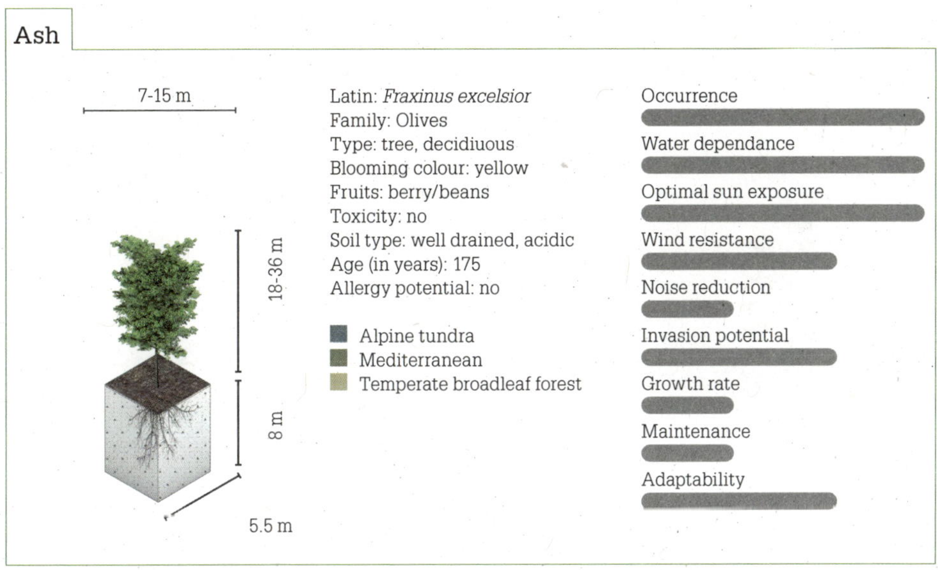

Latin: *Fraxinus excelsior*
Family: Olives
Type: tree, decidiuous
Blooming colour: yellow
Fruits: berry/beans
Toxicity: no
Soil type: well drained, acidic
Age (in years): 175
Allergy potential: no

- Alpine tundra
- Mediterranean
- Temperate broadleaf forest

Occurrence
Water dependance
Optimal sun exposure
Wind resistance
Noise reduction
Invasion potential
Growth rate
Maintenance
Adaptability

Maidenhair tree

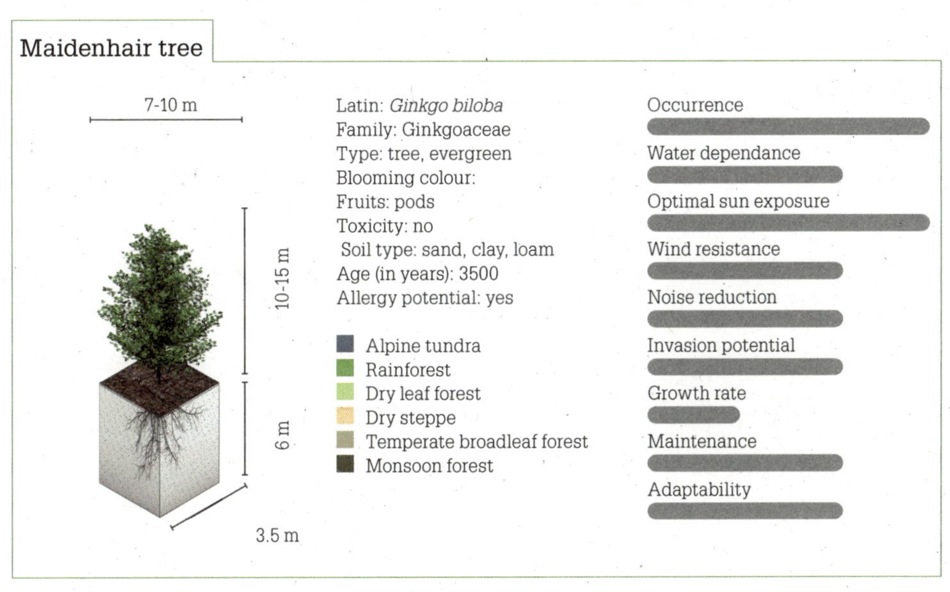

Latin: *Ginkgo biloba*
Family: Ginkgoaceae
Type: tree, evergreen
Blooming colour:
Fruits: pods
Toxicity: no
Soil type: sand, clay, loam
Age (in years): 3500
Allergy potential: yes

- Alpine tundra
- Rainforest
- Dry leaf forest
- Dry steppe
- Temperate broadleaf forest
- Monsoon forest

Occurrence
Water dependance
Optimal sun exposure
Wind resistance
Noise reduction
Invasion potential
Growth rate
Maintenance
Adaptability

Index of flora

Locust

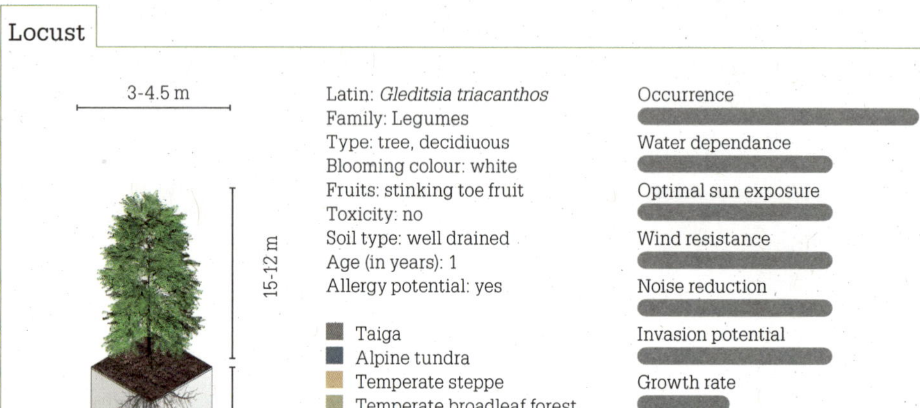

Latin: *Gleditsia triacanthos*
Family: Legumes
Type: tree, decidiuous
Blooming colour: white
Fruits: stinking toe fruit
Toxicity: no
Soil type: well drained
Age (in years): 1
Allergy potential: yes

- Taiga
- Alpine tundra
- Temperate steppe
- Temperate broadleaf forest

Occurrence
Water dependance
Optimal sun exposure
Wind resistance
Noise reduction
Invasion potential
Growth rate
Maintenance
Adaptability

Variegated manna grass

0.3-1.5 m
0.5-1 m
0.5 m
0.5 m

Latin: *Glyceria maxima 'Variegata'*
Family: Grasses
Type: shrub, semi-evergreen
Blooming colour: green/purple
Toxicity: no
Soil type: wett soil
Age (in years): 15
Allergy potential: no

- Dry leaf forest
- Dry steppe
- Temperate steppe
- Temperate broadleaf forest
- Monsoon forest

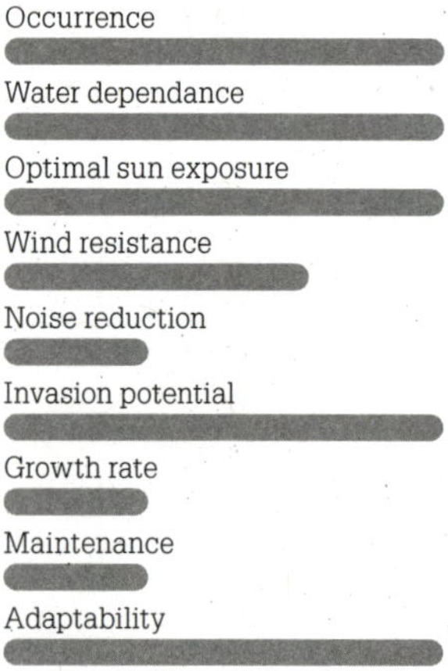

Occurrence
Water dependance
Optimal sun exposure
Wind resistance
Noise reduction
Invasion potential
Growth rate
Maintenance
Adaptability

Index of flora

European ivy

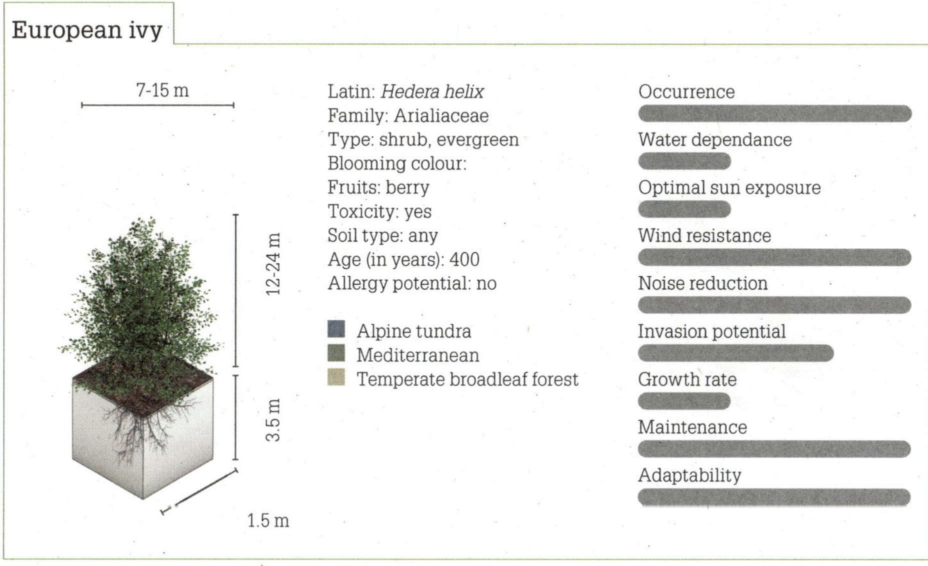

Latin: *Hedera helix*
Family: Arialiaceae
Type: shrub, evergreen
Blooming colour:
Fruits: berry
Toxicity: yes
Soil type: any
Age (in years): 400
Allergy potential: no

- Alpine tundra
- Mediterranean
- Temperate broadleaf forest

Occurrence
Water dependance
Optimal sun exposure
Wind resistance
Noise reduction
Invasion potential
Growth rate
Maintenance
Adaptability

Long yellow daylily

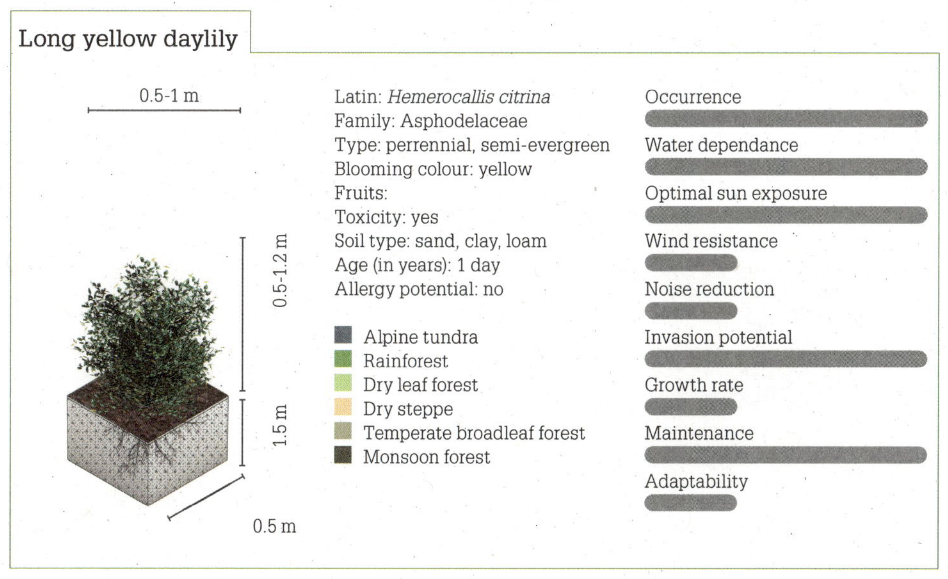

Latin: *Hemerocallis citrina*
Family: Asphodelaceae
Type: perrennial, semi-evergreen
Blooming colour: yellow
Fruits:
Toxicity: yes
Soil type: sand, clay, loam
Age (in years): 1 day
Allergy potential: no

- Alpine tundra
- Rainforest
- Dry leaf forest
- Dry steppe
- Temperate broadleaf forest
- Monsoon forest

Occurrence
Water dependance
Optimal sun exposure
Wind resistance
Noise reduction
Invasion potential
Growth rate
Maintenance
Adaptability

Index of flora

Coral bells

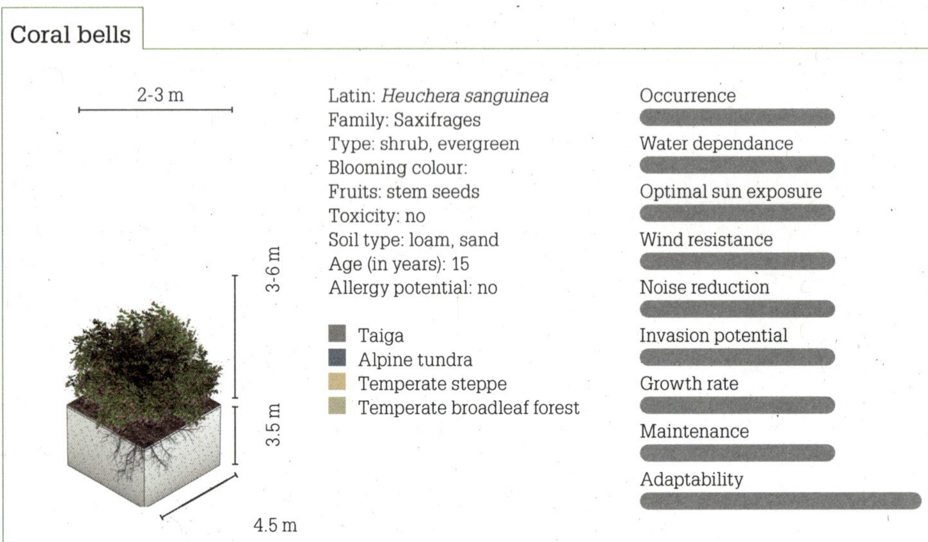

Latin: *Heuchera sanguinea*
Family: Saxifrages
Type: shrub, evergreen
Blooming colour:
Fruits: stem seeds
Toxicity: no
Soil type: loam, sand
Age (in years): 15
Allergy potential: no

- Taiga
- Alpine tundra
- Temperate steppe
- Temperate broadleaf forest

Occurrence
Water dependance
Optimal sun exposure
Wind resistance
Noise reduction
Invasion potential
Growth rate
Maintenance
Adaptability

Hawaiian hibiscus

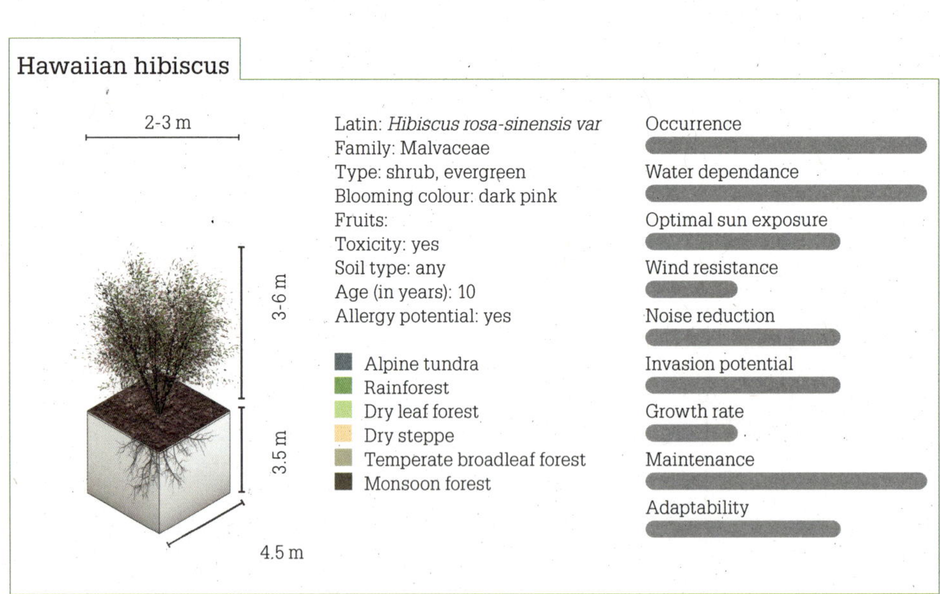

Latin: *Hibiscus rosa-sinensis var*
Family: Malvaceae
Type: shrub, evergreen
Blooming colour: dark pink
Fruits:
Toxicity: yes
Soil type: any
Age (in years): 10
Allergy potential: yes

- Alpine tundra
- Rainforest
- Dry leaf forest
- Dry steppe
- Temperate broadleaf forest
- Monsoon forest

Occurrence
Water dependance
Optimal sun exposure
Wind resistance
Noise reduction
Invasion potential
Growth rate
Maintenance
Adaptability

Index of flora

Bigleaf hydrangea

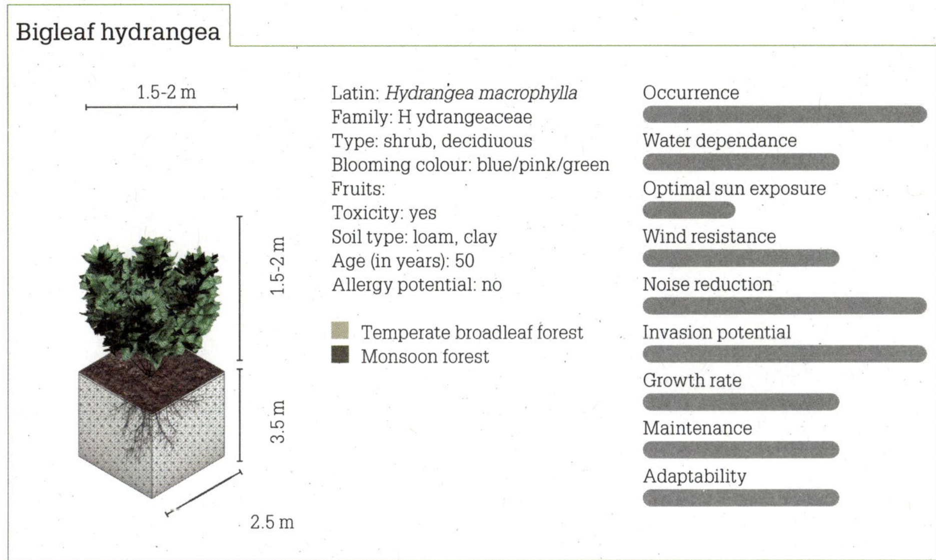

Latin: *Hydrangea macrophylla*
Family: H ydrangeaceae
Type: shrub, decidiuous
Blooming colour: blue/pink/green
Fruits:
Toxicity: yes
Soil type: loam, clay
Age (in years): 50
Allergy potential: no

- Temperate broadleaf forest
- Monsoon forest

Occurrence
Water dependance
Optimal sun exposure
Wind resistance
Noise reduction
Invasion potential
Growth rate
Maintenance
Adaptability

Micro sword

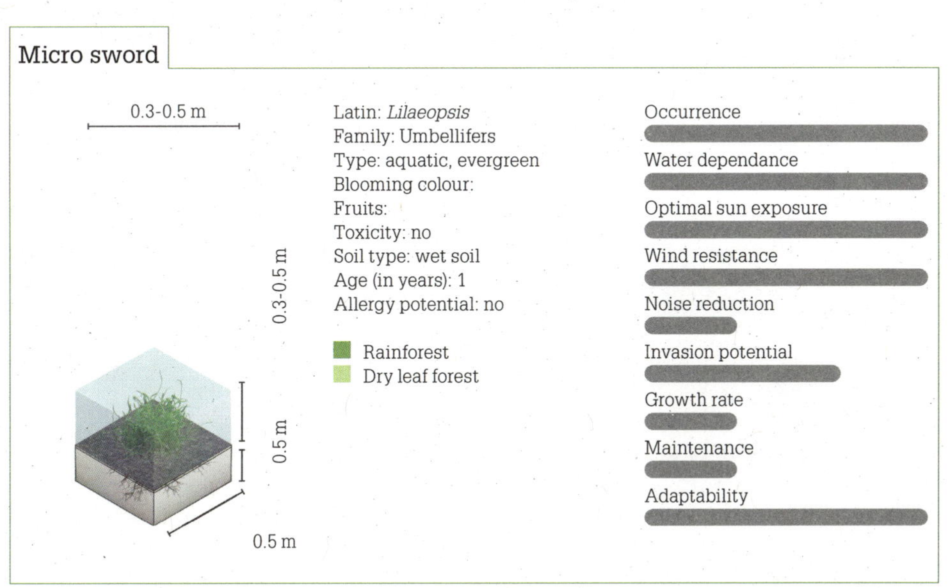

Latin: *Lilaeopsis*
Family: Umbellifers
Type: aquatic, evergreen
Blooming colour:
Fruits:
Toxicity: no
Soil type: wet soil
Age (in years): 1
Allergy potential: no

- Rainforest
- Dry leaf forest

Occurrence
Water dependance
Optimal sun exposure
Wind resistance
Noise reduction
Invasion potential
Growth rate
Maintenance
Adaptability

Index of flora

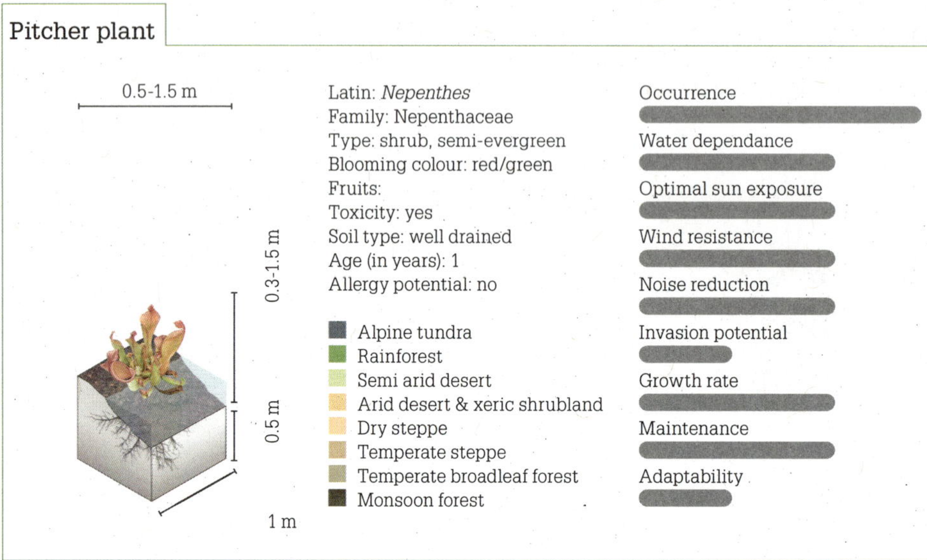

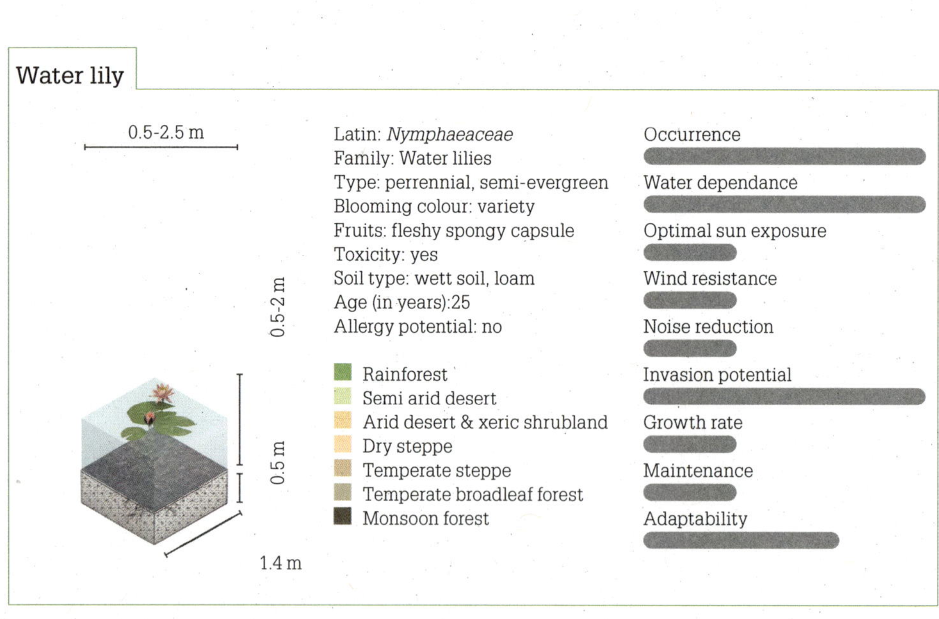

Index of flora

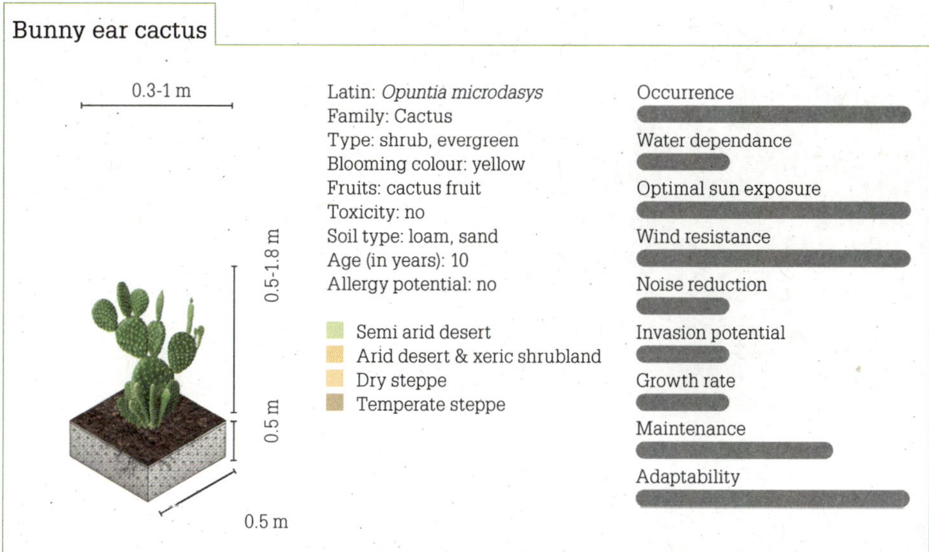

Bunny ear cactus

Latin: *Opuntia microdasys*
Family: Cactus
Type: shrub, evergreen
Blooming colour: yellow
Fruits: cactus fruit
Toxicity: no
Soil type: loam, sand
Age (in years): 10
Allergy potential: no

- Semi arid desert
- Arid desert & xeric shrubland
- Dry steppe
- Temperate steppe

Occurrence
Water dependance
Optimal sun exposure
Wind resistance
Noise reduction
Invasion potential
Growth rate
Maintenance
Adaptability

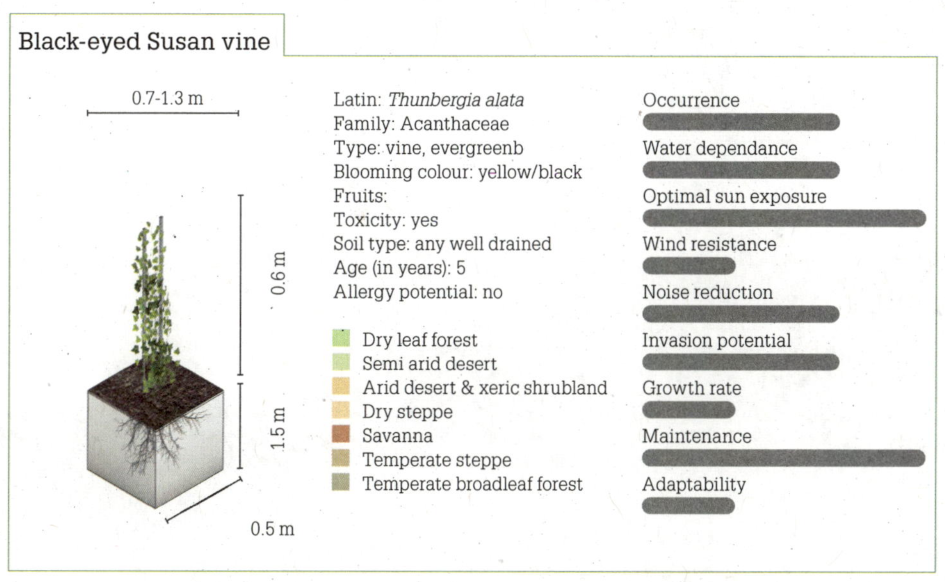

Black-eyed Susan vine

Latin: *Thunbergia alata*
Family: Acanthaceae
Type: vine, evergreenb
Blooming colour: yellow/black
Fruits:
Toxicity: yes
Soil type: any well drained
Age (in years): 5
Allergy potential: no

- Dry leaf forest
- Semi arid desert
- Arid desert & xeric shrubland
- Dry steppe
- Savanna
- Temperate steppe
- Temperate broadleaf forest

Occurrence
Water dependance
Optimal sun exposure
Wind resistance
Noise reduction
Invasion potential
Growth rate
Maintenance
Adaptability

Building with flora

Green components

Building cities that can integrate with flora requires design products. The wide array of products already in the market demonstrates that when botanists, gardeners, and designers collaborate, numerous solutions for integrating vegetation into architecture can be conceived and executed.

This chapter compiles an extensive collection of existing solutions and design proposals that blend vegetation and architecture. From porous brick to clay facades, geotextiles to walls, pavement to rooftops, The Why Factory students have assembled a catalogue of inventions, prototypes, and modules. They compare these based on their functional performance, dimensions, soil capacity, costs, water storage capacity, and biomass.

This is a hypothetical user manual for designing with plants at various scales—from balconies to walls, roofs, streets, neighbourhoods, and entire cities. The catalogue features products that can be applied at different scales and for various elements. These products contribute to and influence multiple environmental phenomena, such as thermal inertia, albedo, shade, evaporation, or wind.

This toolbox should allow architects and residents to choose, customise, and design their environments one day, where each product becomes a new base for nature to flourish.

Architectural components

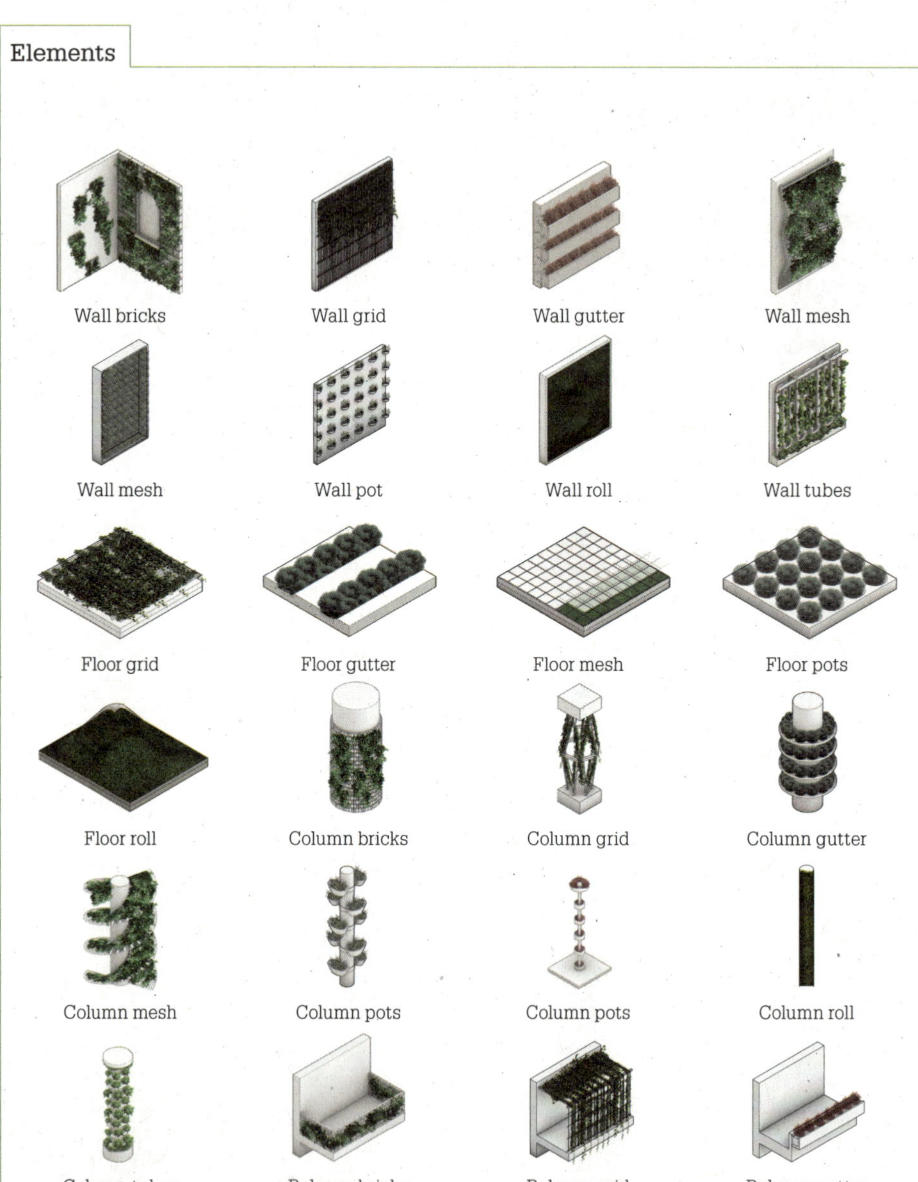

The Green-Maker catalogue is a comprehensive tool for urban greening, allowing users to sort and select components based on architectural elements (such as walls, floors, and roofs), design actions (such as sticking or dripping), plant compatibility, dimensions, soil requirements, water storage capacity, and biome suitability.

Architectural components

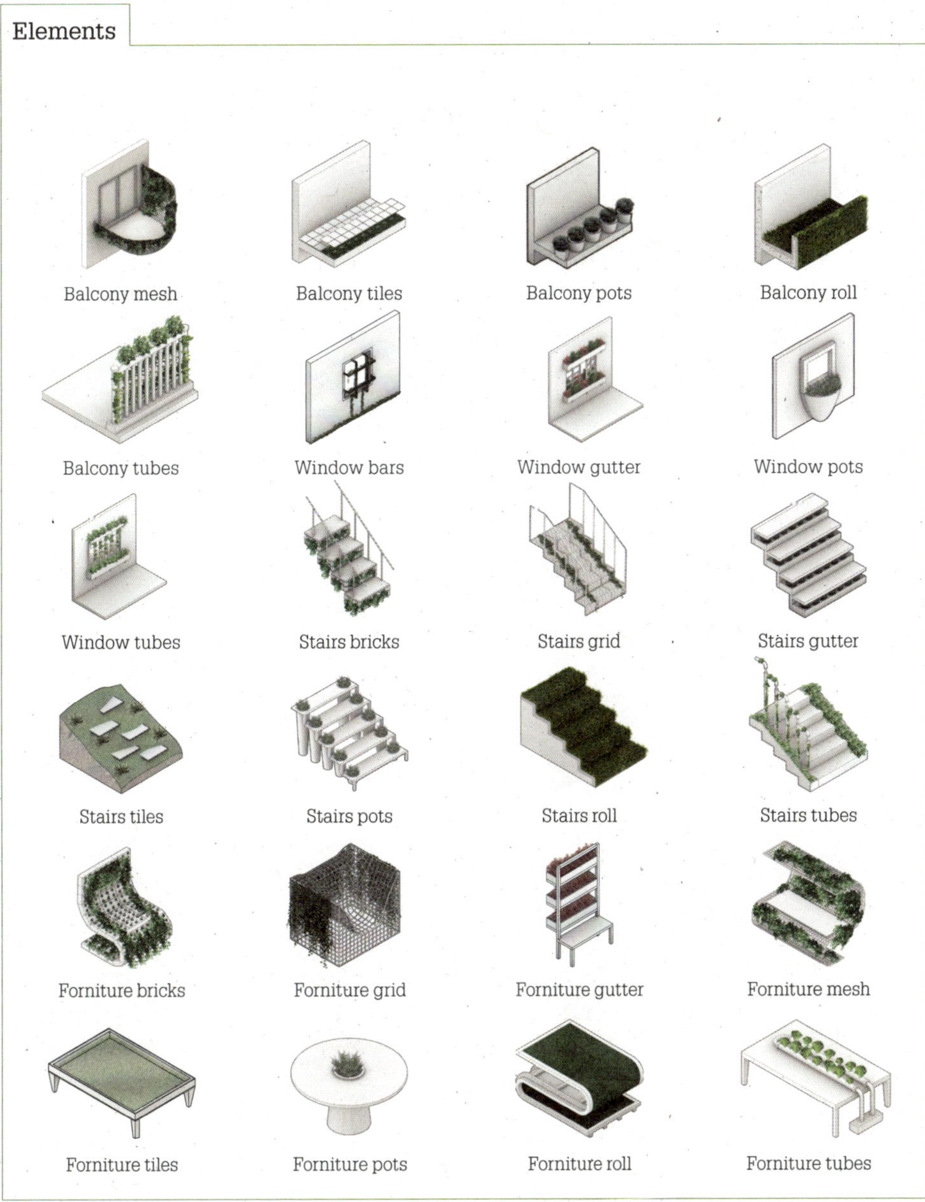

This user-friendly interface lets designers and inhabitants customise their environment using diverse products. Each component has the potential to impact various environmental factors, from thermal inertia to albedo, creating a toolbox for nurturing nature within our urban landscapes.

Architectural components

Elements

Sidewalk bricks

Sidewalk gutter

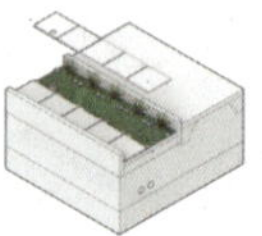
Sidewalk tiles

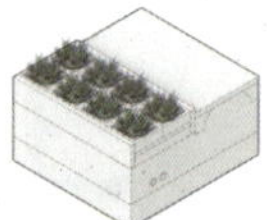
Sidewalk pots

Sidewalk roll

Road gutter

Road roll

Bridge bricks

Bridge gutter

Bridge roll

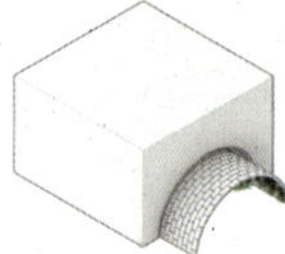
Tunnel bricks

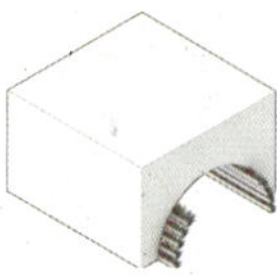
Bridge gutter

Bridge mesh

Bridge roll

Architectural components

Wall

Wall bricks

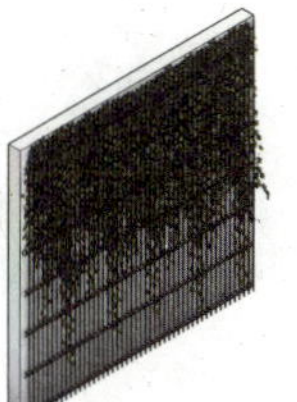

Wall grid

Wall gutter

Wall mesh

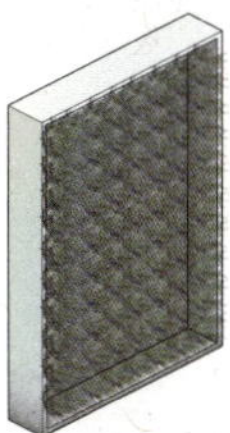

Wall tiles

Wall pots

Wall roll

Wall tubes

Architectural components

Floor

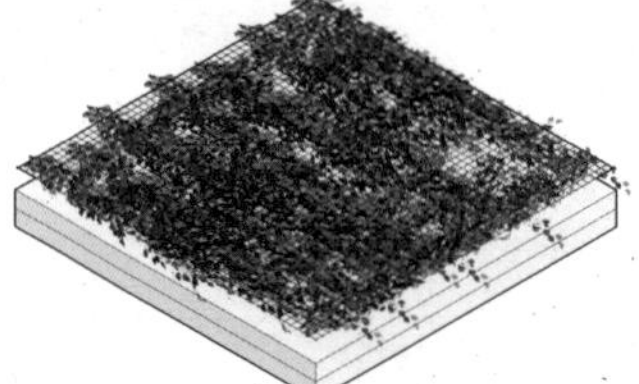

Floor grid

Floor gutter

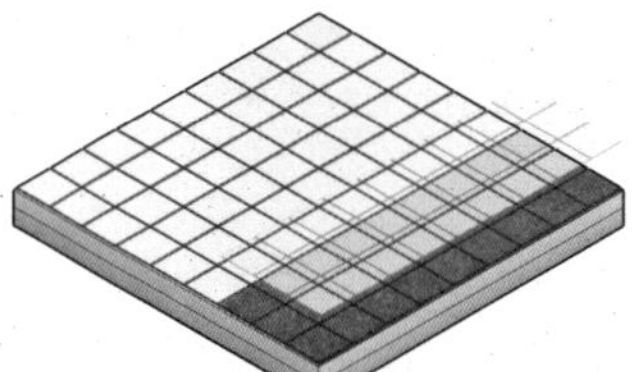

Floor mesh

Floor pots

Floor roll

Architectural components

Ceiling

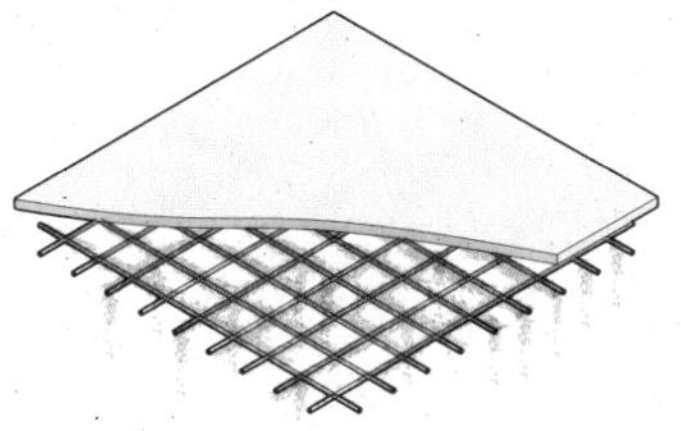

Ceiling grid

Ceiling mesh

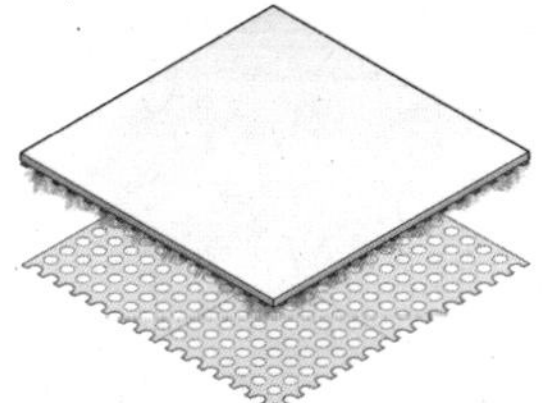

Ceiling tiles

Ceiling pots

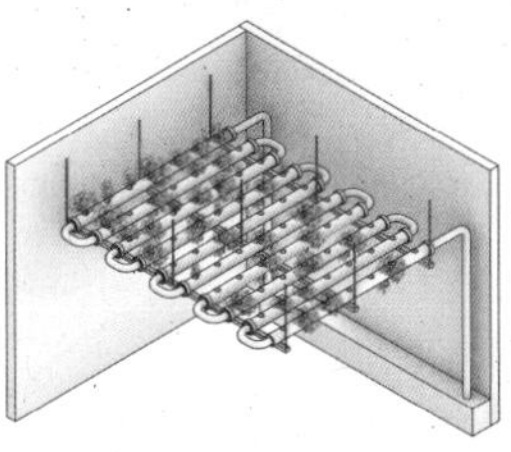

Ceiling tubes

Architectural components

Roof

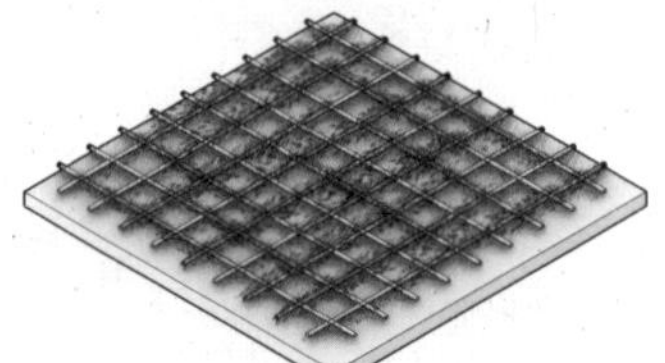

Roof grid

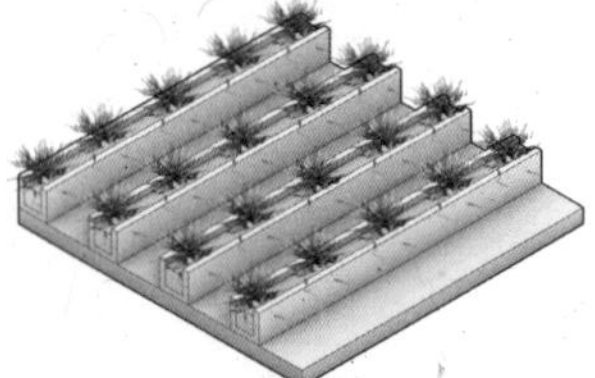

Roof gutter

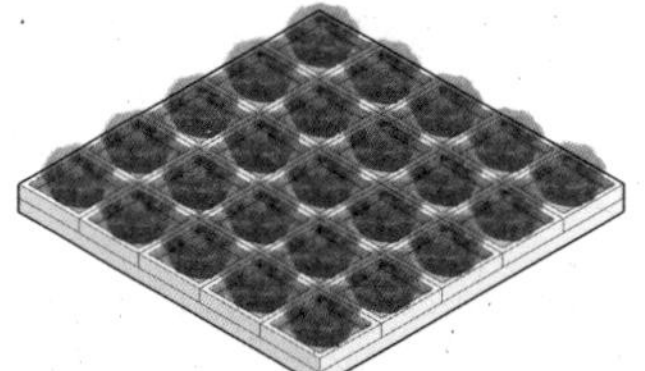

Roof tiles

Roof roll

Architectural components

Column/beam

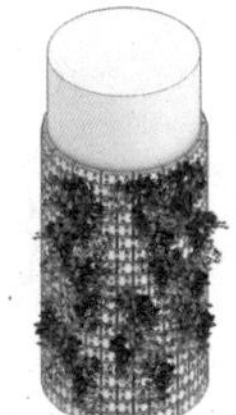
Column bricks

Column grid

Column gutter

Column mesh

Column pots

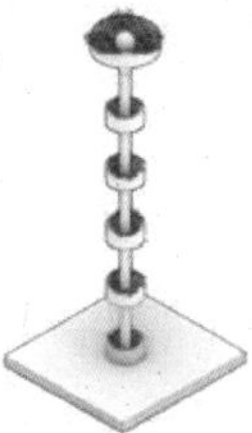
Column pots

Column roll

Column tubes

Architectural components

Balcony

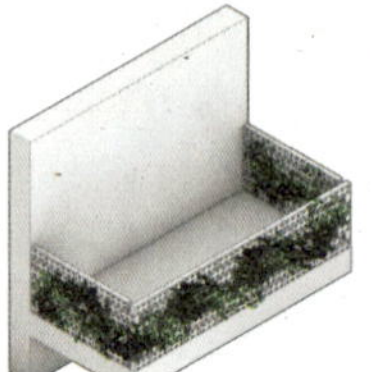

Balcony bricks

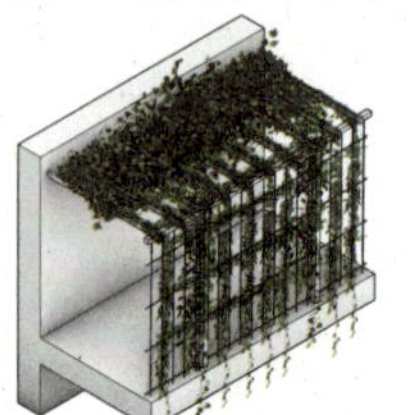

Balcony grid

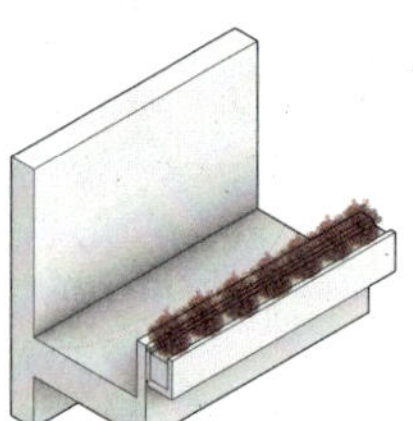

Balcony gutter

Balcony mesh

Balcony tiles

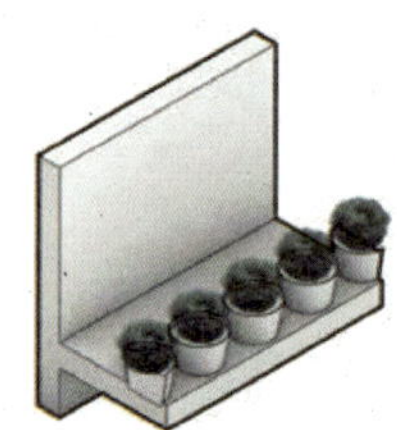

Balcony pots

Balcony roll

Balcony tubes

Architectural components

Window

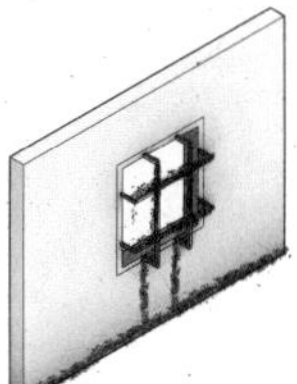

Window bars

Window gutter

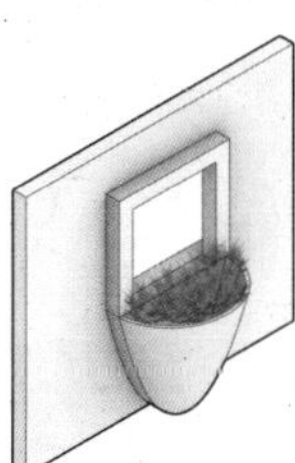

Window pots

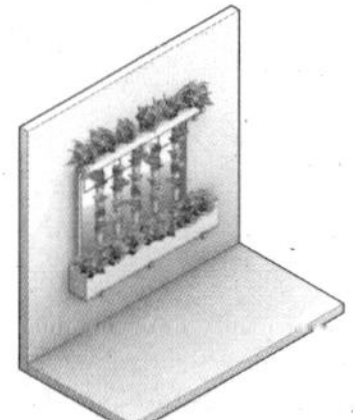

Window tubes

Architectural components

Stairs

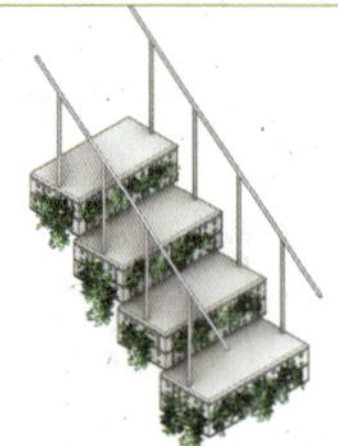

Stairs bricks

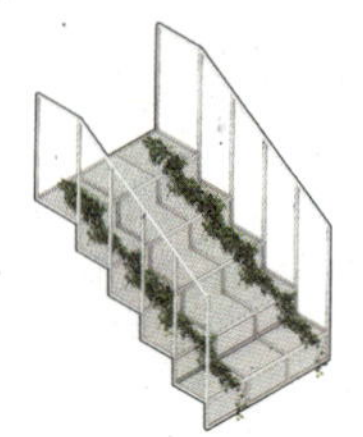

Stairs grid

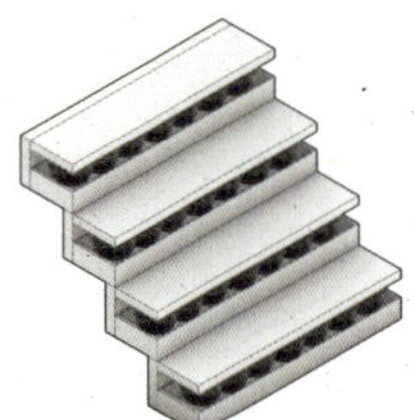

Stairs gutter

Stairs tiles

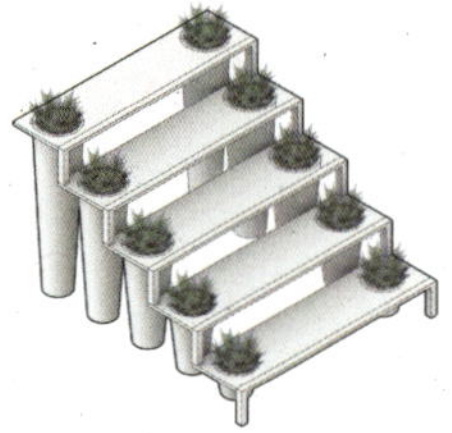

Stairs pots

Stairs roll

Stairs tubes

Architectural components

Furniture

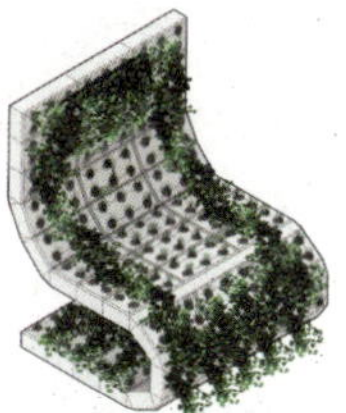

Forniture bricks

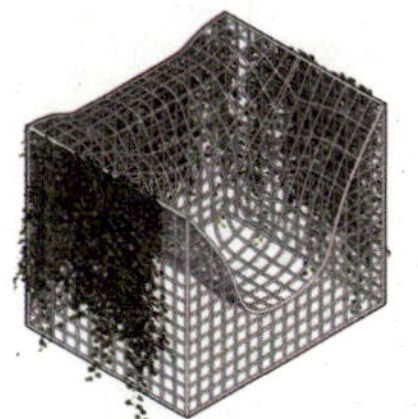

Forniture grid

Forniture gutter

Forniture mesh

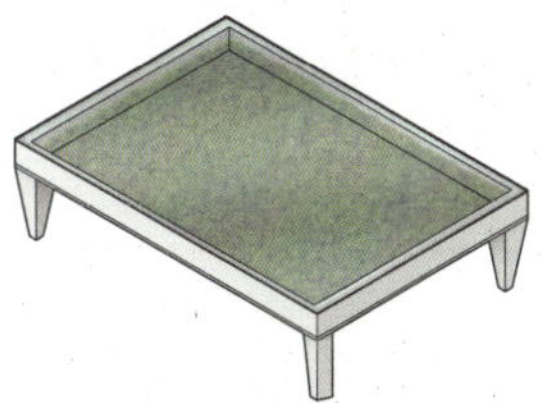

Forniture tiles

Forniture pots

Forniture roll

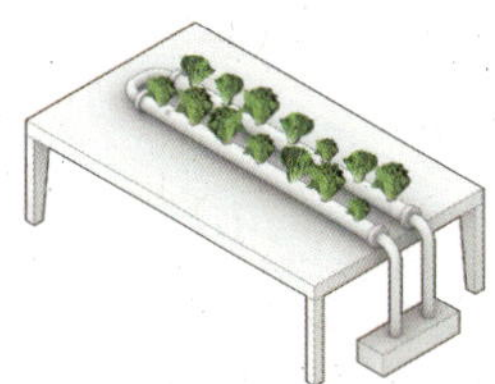

Forniture tubes

Architectural components

Sidewalk

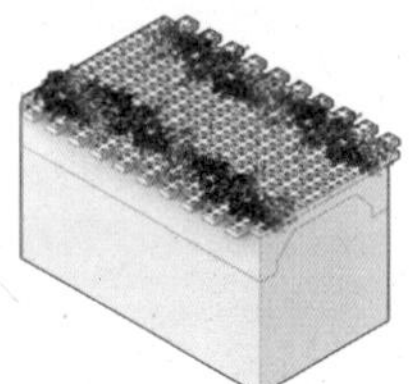

Forniture bricks

Forniture gutter

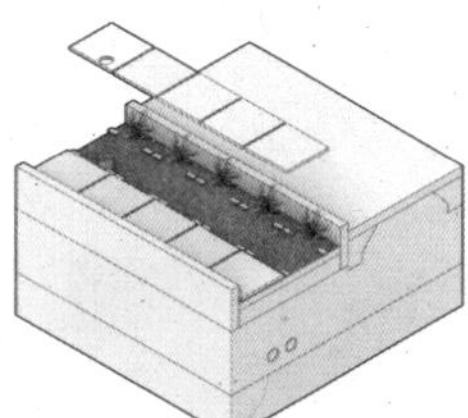

Forniture tiles

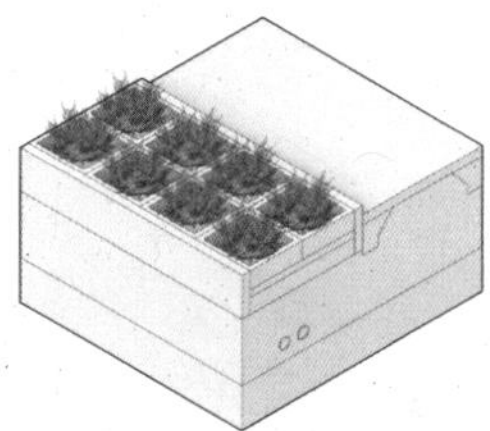

Forniture pots

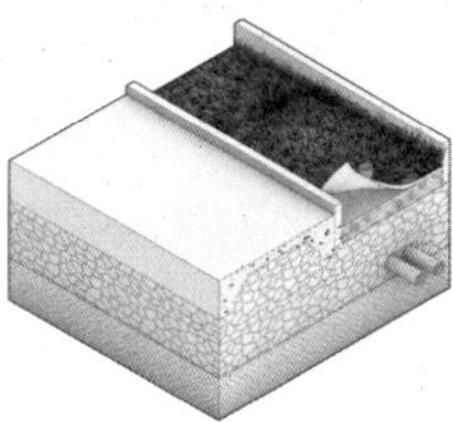

Forniture roll

Architectural components

Road

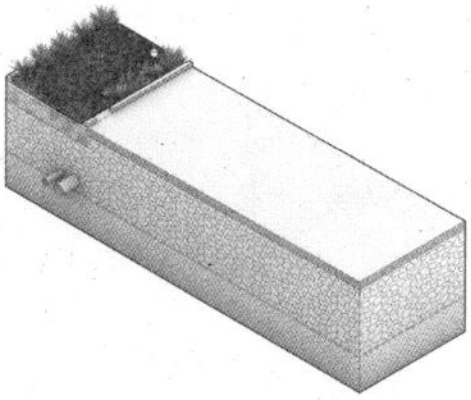

Road gutter

Road roll

Architectural components

Bridge

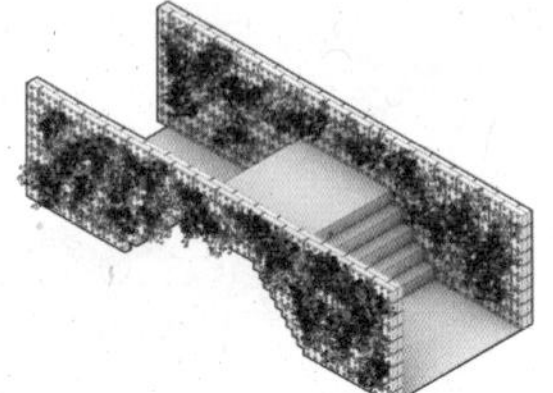

Bridge bricks

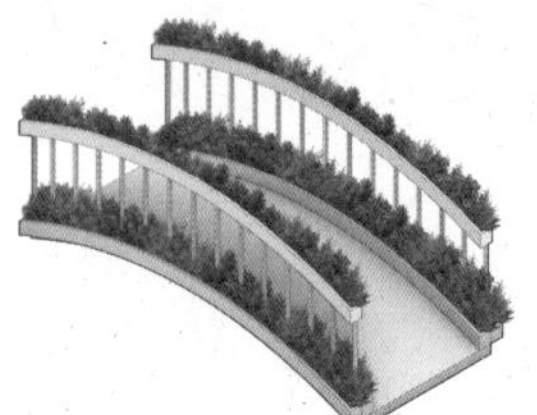

Bridge gutter

Bridge roll

Architectural components

Tunnel

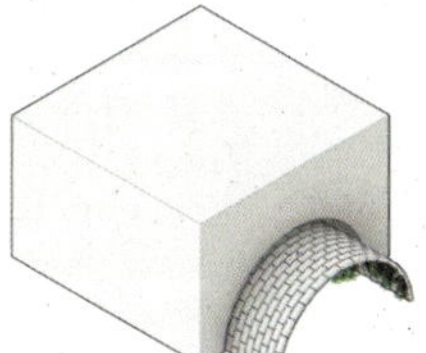

Tunnel bricks

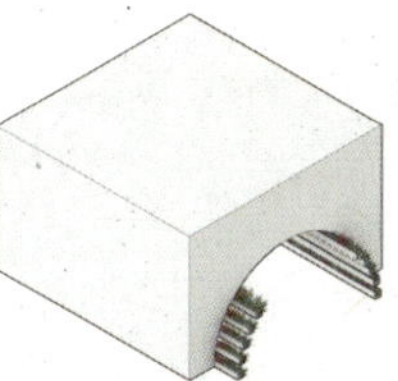

Tunnel gutter

Tunnel mesh

Tunnel roll

Applications

A catalogue of greening strategies

Greening buildings is not new; it has a rich and extensive history of attempts to merge cities and nature. Examples abound: the Hanging Gardens of Babylon; the mighty oak trees atop Tuscany's Torre Guinigi; the productive medieval gardens growing vegetables within the city, the structural elegance of French formal gardens; the romantic charm of English parks; the minimalistic aesthetics of dry Japanese gardens; the organic ornamentation of Art Nouveau; the advent of indoor vegetation facilitated by glass houses, the community-focused garden city movement; and the emergence of landscape architecture as a vital discipline in design. These instances collectively represent a substantial historical record of design solutions that integrate vegetation into buildings and the city—a heritage worth acknowledging.

Over the past decade, many projects have tried to integrate architecture and flora. The success and positive reception of these explorations, combined with their increasing number, have made greening buildings a prominent architectural trend.

This chapter compiles a non-exhaustive series of recipes for integrating greenery into buildings. Students compared the advantages and disadvantages of these diverse design solutions for urban greening and suggested that these strategies, along with their associated urban forms, have the potential to shape the city.

A catalogue of greening strategies

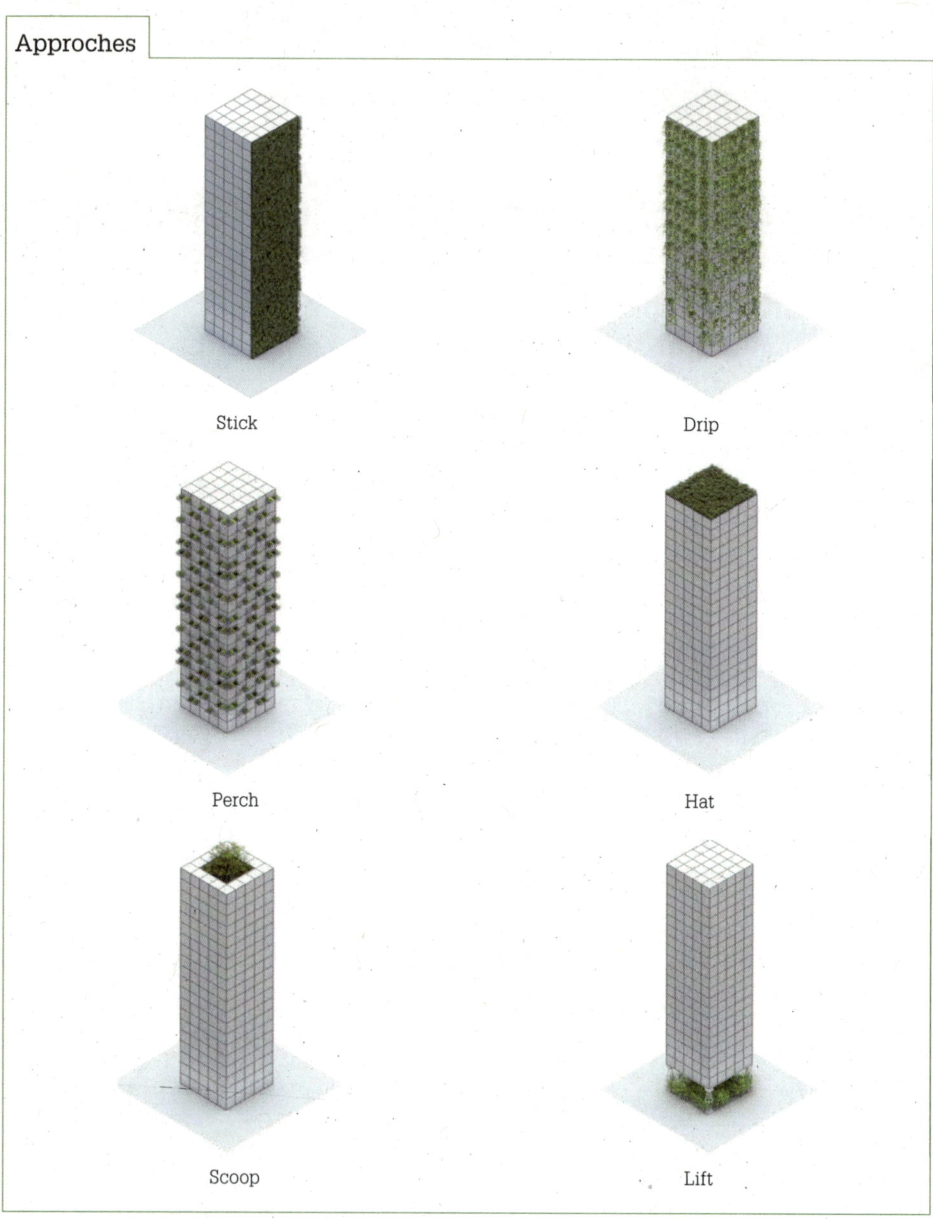

Successful examples of architectural projects that incorporate vegetation in urban environments serve as a source for extracting a non-exhaustive series of strategies for greening buildings.

A catalogue of greening strategies

Various approaches are identified and compared in this study. It highlights that the driving forces behind these design strategies for greening the city, along with their associated urban forms, shape the city.

A catalogue of greening strategies

Green stick

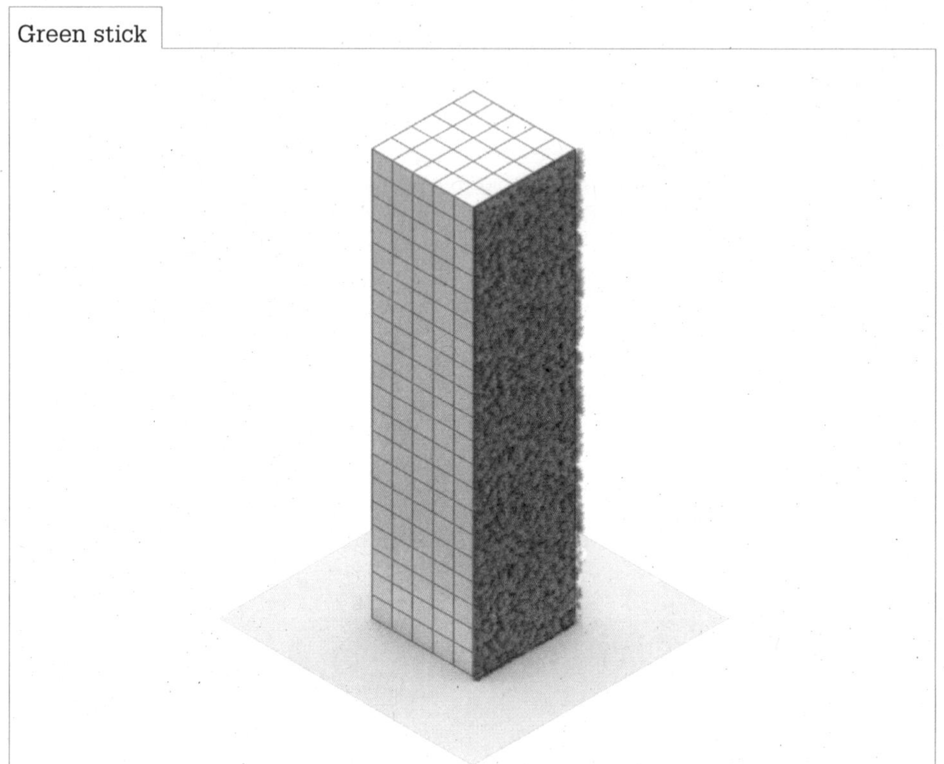

Encompassing green walls and facades, green stick offers a popular approach to integrating greenery into buildings. Numerous products for easily adhering vegetation to building facades have flourished. However, this strategy is often seen as superficial add-ons, expensive and difficult to maintain.

A catalogue of greening strategies

Green drip

Green drip involves hanging plants from buildings, enabling them to grow vertically with minimal maintenance. This cost-effective method requires plant species that thrive with little soil and is a longer-term investment since the plants take time to mature. This method provides privacy to the balconies and could suit densely populated urban areas. Trellises can guide the plants' growth, and the plants' vertical orientation can also provide easy travel routes for certain animals. Moreover, green dripping can improve the energy efficiency of a building by reducing the amount of direct sunlight that reaches the facade, reducing the need for air conditioning.

A catalogue of greening strategies

Green perch

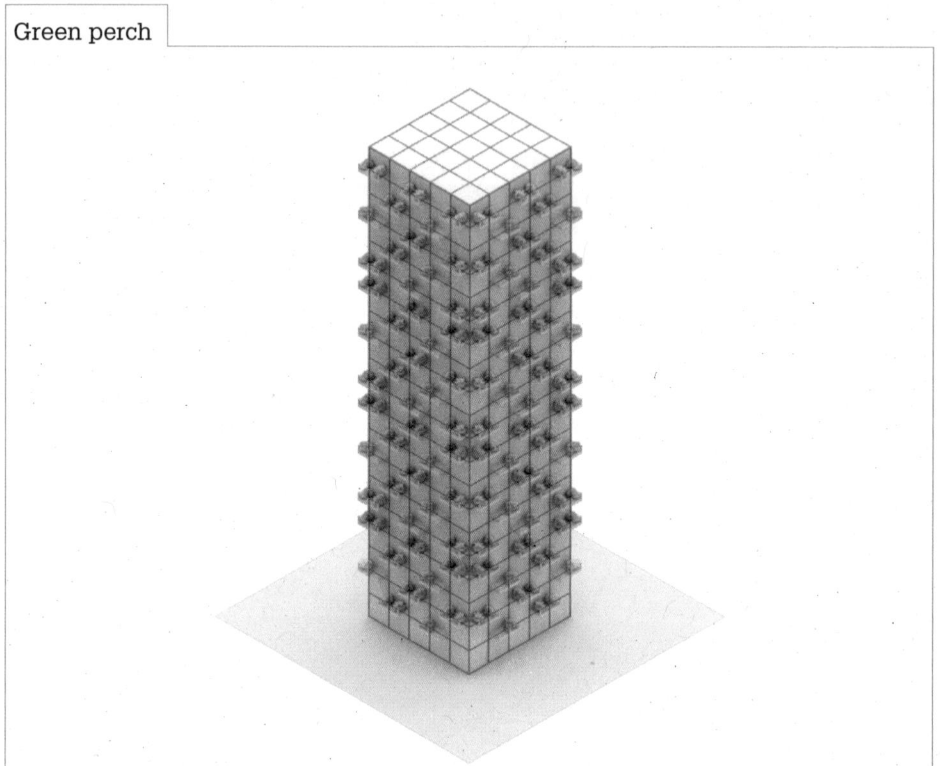

Growing plants on balconies is a common practice that transforms them into small urban gardens. Green balconies provide shade, sound buffering, and potential wildlife habitats. Yet, the weight of soil and plants can be considerable and have an impact on the structure of the building.

A catalogue of greening strategies

Green hat

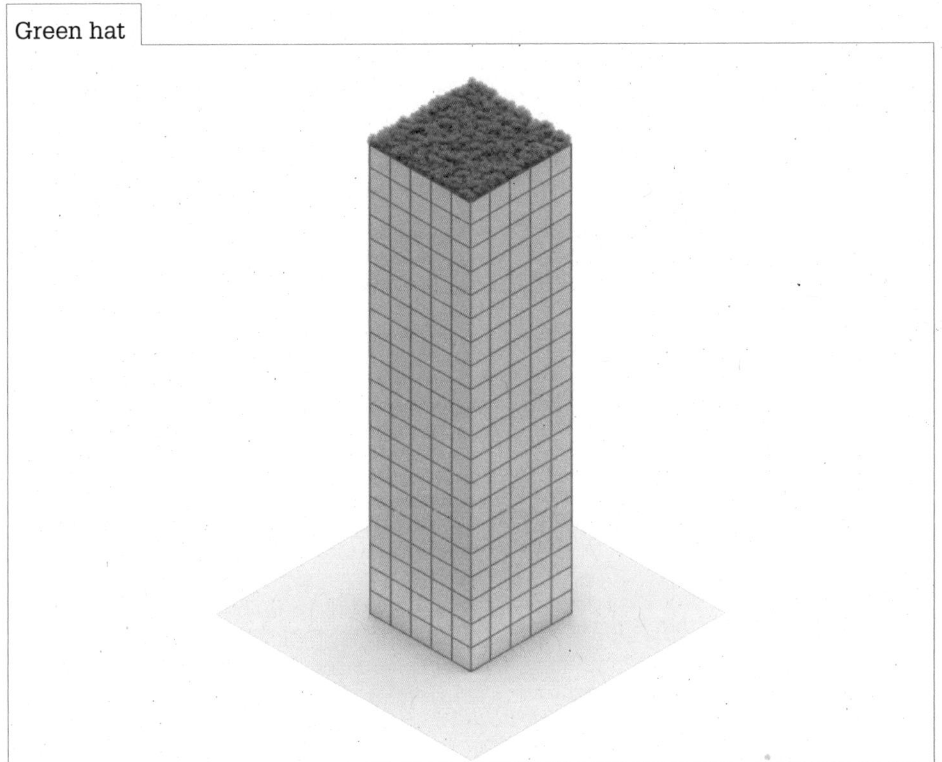

Making green roofs is a well-established architectural strategy that enhances aesthetics, mitigates the heat island effect, and reduces energy consumption. These roofs insulate structures, absorb and filter rainwater, increase biodiversity, and cool and decontaminate the ambient air. Green roofs can also be accessible to the public, encouraging residents to come together and connect with nature in the heart of the city.

A catalogue of greening strategies

Green scoop

Green scoop refers to the use or creation of courtyards within buildings. Courtyards from Beijing's hutongs to Barcelona's Cerdà blocks often foster native plant growth and provide habitats for birds. Courtyards invite natural light, encourage airflow, create spaces to meet, and provide protection from wind and noise. Often enclosed and not visible from the outside, green courtyards give a sense of intimacy. Green scoop is an excellent opportunity for making courtyards accessible to the public and creating more porosity in cities.

A catalogue of greening strategies

Green lift

Green lift elevates buildings to create green spaces, promoting the continuity of public areas and parks in the city. However, the vegetation underneath the building receives less natural light, affecting plant health and growth. Proper maintenance and planning are essential. Green lifts also have the potential to integrate with existing water structures, enhancing overall sustainability and social interaction.

A catalogue of greening strategies

Green camouflage

Sometimes, vegetation is used to make buildings disappear. This approach is defined as camouflaging, which refers to concealing architectural elements with plants and foliage to the extent of completely covering the building. The beauty of green camouflaging lies in its ability to seamlessly blend natural and man-made environments. This technique has practical benefits, such as cooling the building and reducing energy costs.

A catalogue of greening strategies

Green infill

Inviting nature inside buildings has long been a widespread practice. From indoor plants in private apartments or offices, lush gardens in the atriums of shopping malls, to entire post-industrial buildings refurbished as indoor parks, green infill can blur the separation of indoor and outdoor. Indoor vegetation can enhance the mental well-being of the occupants and create serene environments. However, indoor gardens often require indoor climate control and regular watering and upkeep. Indoor gardens may attract unwanted insects and rodents and increase humidity levels.

Cities as canvases

The Green Dip, step by step

The Green-Maker is an imaginary tool that aims to make cities greener, drawing on each city's uniqueness, blending humans and nature. Think of it as a library of plants tailor-made for your city. This pedagogical tool, introduced during The Why Factory's design studio, enabled students to speculate on various methods for incorporating green spaces while simultaneously calculating the environmental impact. As these changes unfold, the cityscape transforms. It's like watching a canvas come to life.

The Green-Maker allows you to navigate around the globe, zoom in, and select any piece of city fabric, one km^2 tile at a time. The software loads and previews a three-dimensional model, revealing the city fabric of each tile along with key parameter—metres of rooftops, facades, sidewalks, roads, public spaces, and squares. The Green-Maker also provides an environmental analysis of each tile, including sunlight, daylight, average temperature, humidity, and wind.

Following a step-by-step approach, you can test a series of design actions for implementing green. First, vegetation is implemented on rooftops, then on facades, squares, sidewalks, roads, balconies, and more. Gradually, each tile is covered with vegetation, and their impact is systematically measured and compared. This systematic approach allows for a comparison of cities and their performance, with an analysis of impacts such as estimated CO_2 absorption, O_2 emission, particle absorption, average temperature, average noise reduction, wood production, water needs, soil volume, soil weight, maximum water storage, and maximum added weight.

New York

Urbanised areas of the world and their corresponding biomes

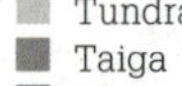

- Tundra
- Taiga
- Alpine tundra
- Montane forest
- Mediterranean
- Rainforest
- Dry leaf forest
- Semi arid desert
- Arid desert & xeric shrubland
- Dry steppe
- Savanna
- Temperate steppe
- Temperate broadleaf forest
- Monsoon forest

Moscow
Dubai
Mumbai

Green Dip – Mumbai (India)

Dry leaf forest

Trees	271
Shrubs	2276
Other	33
Total	2579

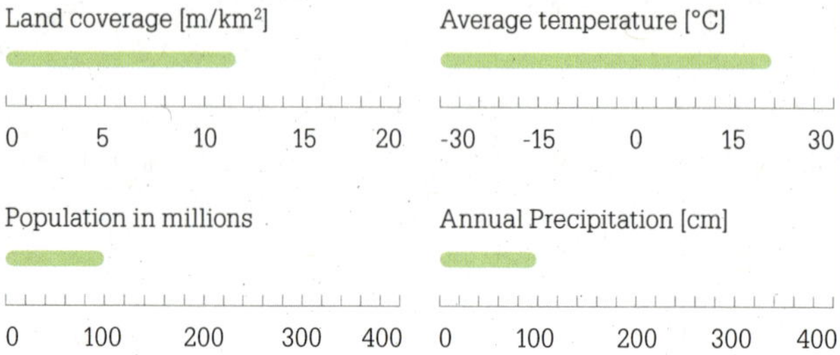

Land coverage [m/km²]
0 5 10 15 20
Average temperature [°C]
-30 -15 0 15 30
Population in millions
0 100 200 300 400
Annual Precipitation [cm]
0 100 200 300 400

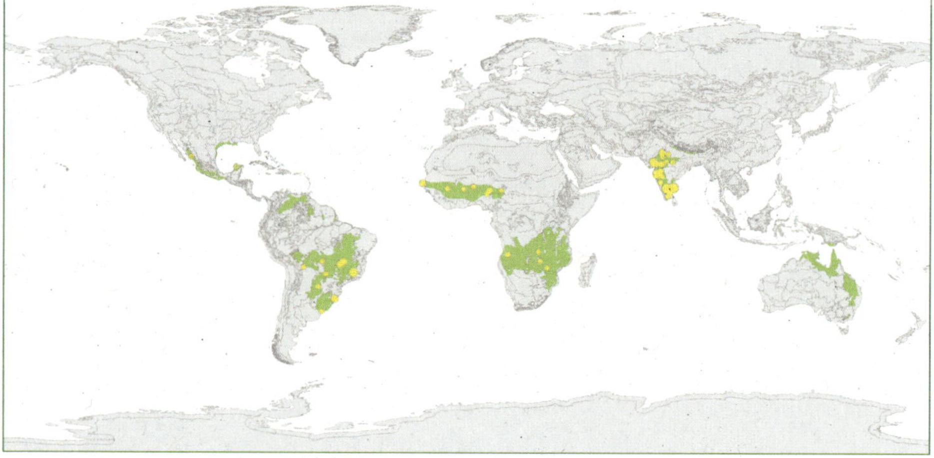

Step 1: Choose a city in its corresponding biome

Location

3D Model

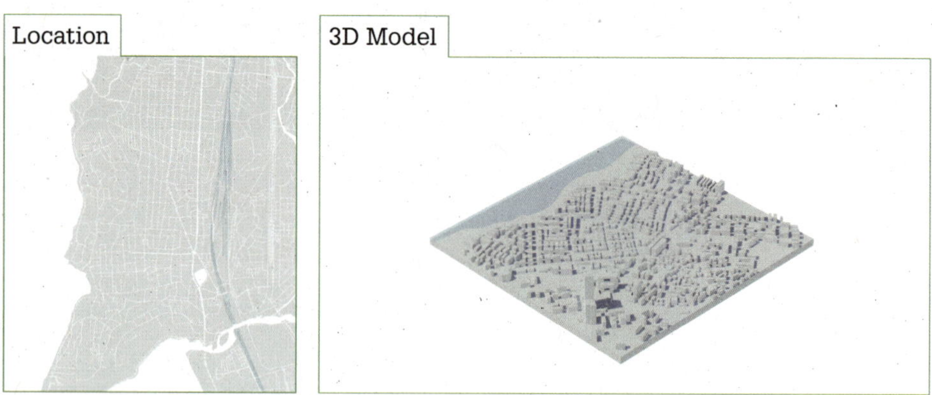

Step 2: Select an area and display the 3D model

Green Dip – Mumbai (India)

Step 3: Load the catalogue of plants associated with its biome

Step 4: Explore design strategies

Green Dip – Mumbai (India)

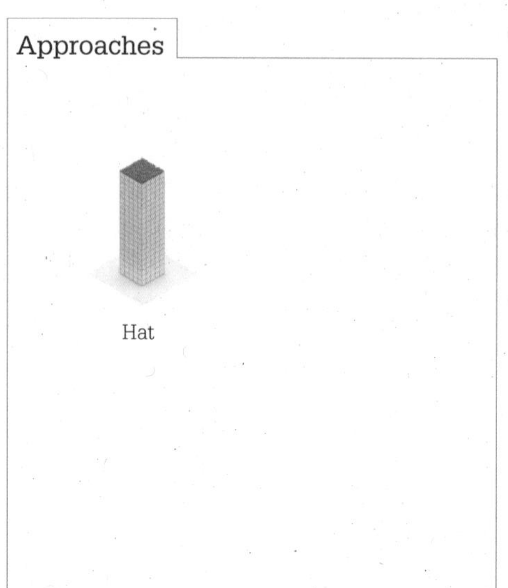

Step 5: Select rooftops (*Hat* button)

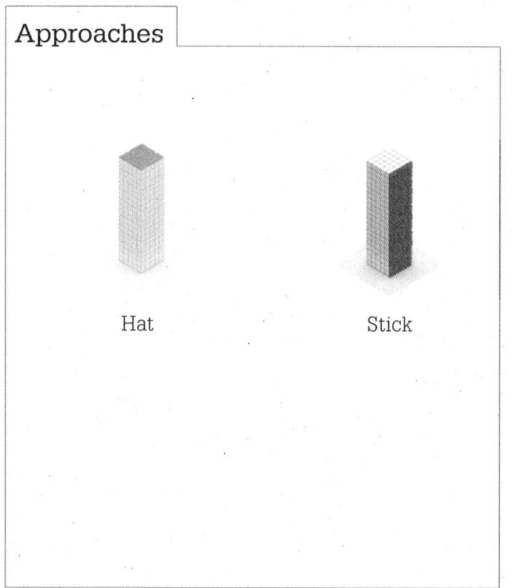

Step 6: Select facades (*Stick* button)

Green Dip – Mumbai (India)

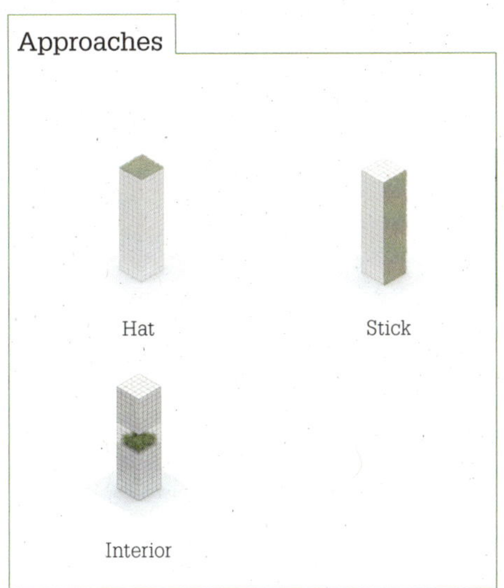

Step 7: Select interiors (*Interior* button)

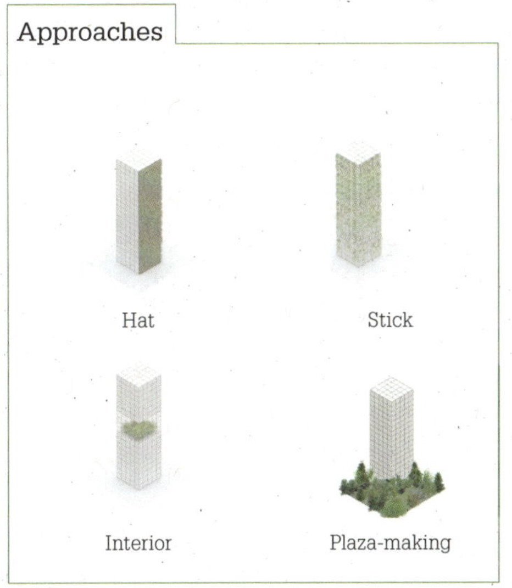

Step 8: Select public space (*Plaza-making* button)

Green Dip – Mumbai (India)

Analysis

Step 9: Display performance analysis

Green Dip – Mumbai (India)

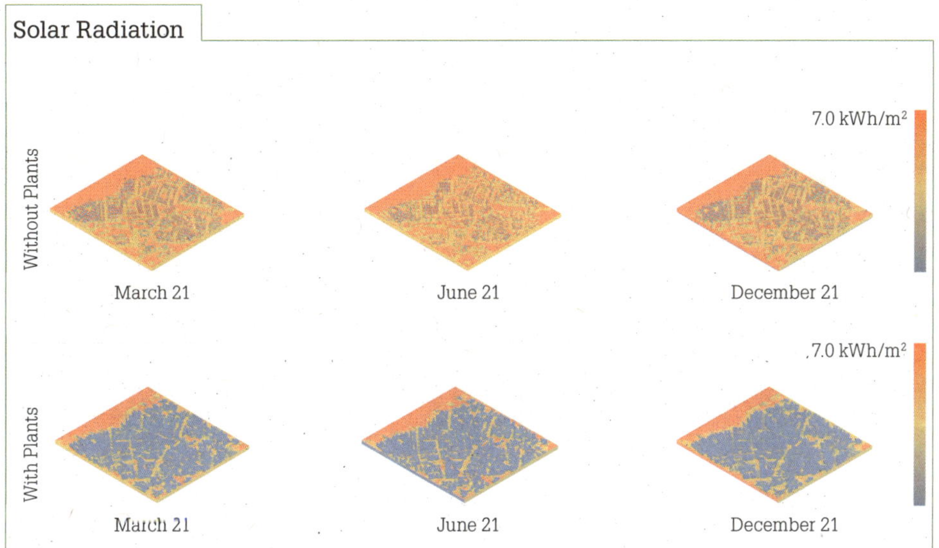

Step 10: Display solar radiation

Step 11: Display impacts after Green Dip

Green Dip – Mumbai (India)

Step 12: Display *The Green Dip*

Green Dip – Mumbai (India)

Green Dip – Dubai (UAE)

Arid Desert & Xeric Shrubland

Trees	108
Shrubs	662
Other	21
Total	681

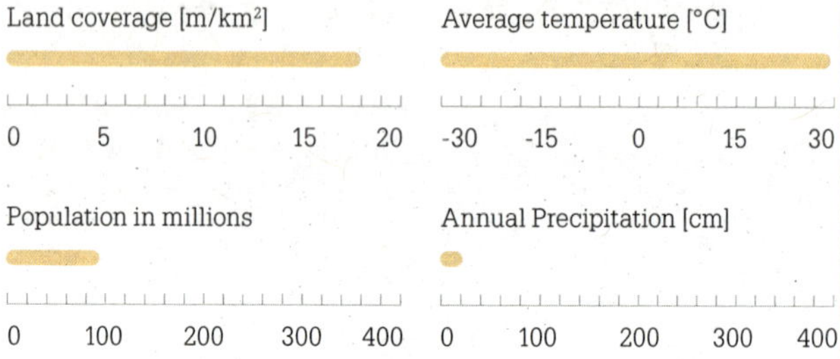

Land coverage [m/km²]
0 5 10 15 20
Average temperature [°C]
-30 -15 0 15 30
Population in millions
0 100 200 300 400
Annual Precipitation [cm]
0 100 200 300 400

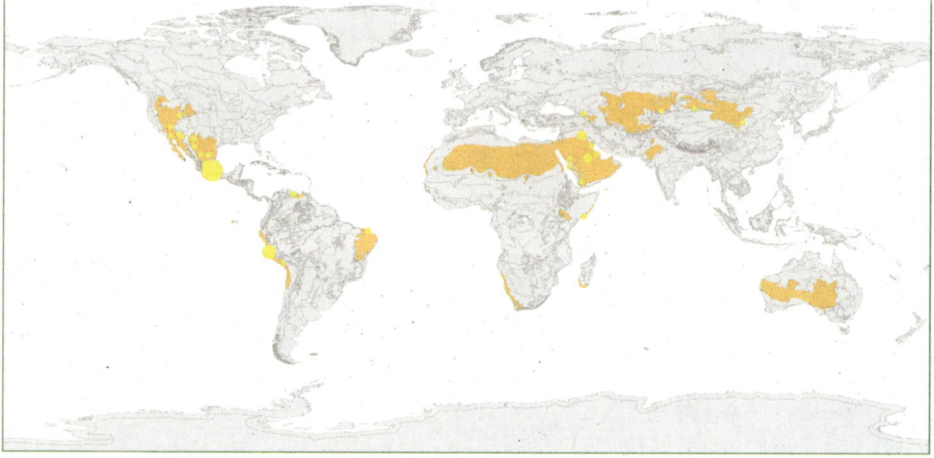

Step 1: Choose a city in its corresponding biome

Location

3D Model

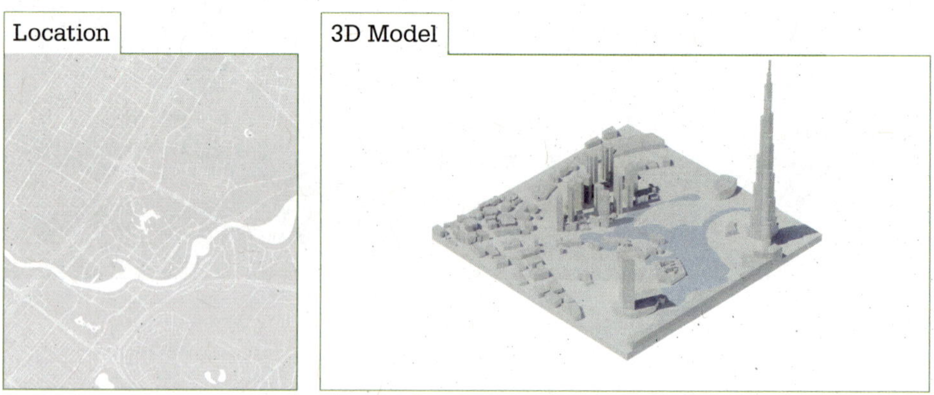

Step 2: Select an area and display the 3D model

Green Dip – Dubai (UAE)

Step 3: Load the catalogue of plants associated to its biome

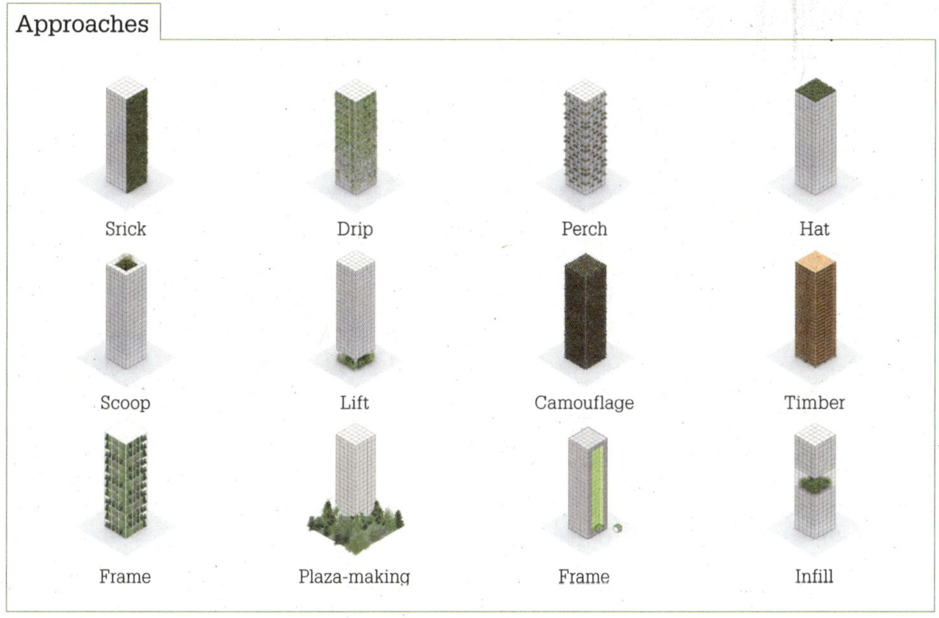

Step 4: Explore design strategies

Green Dip – Dubai (UAE)

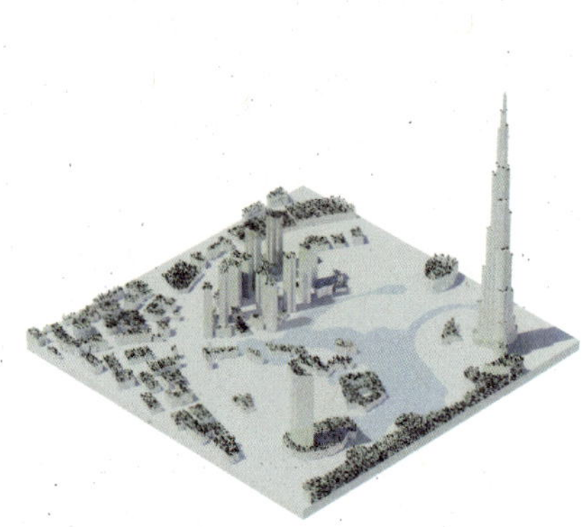

Step 5: Select rooftops (*Hat* button)

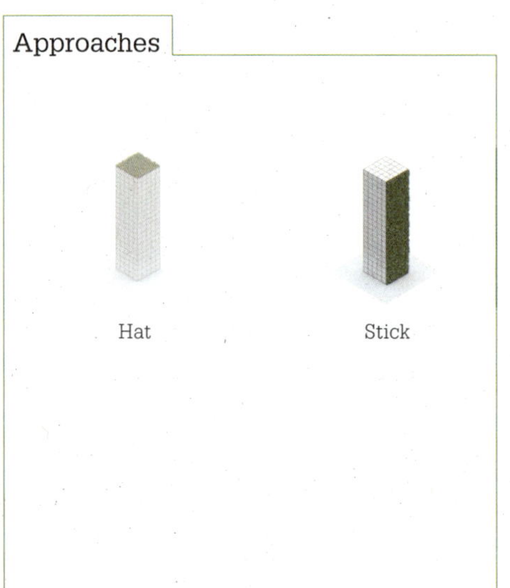

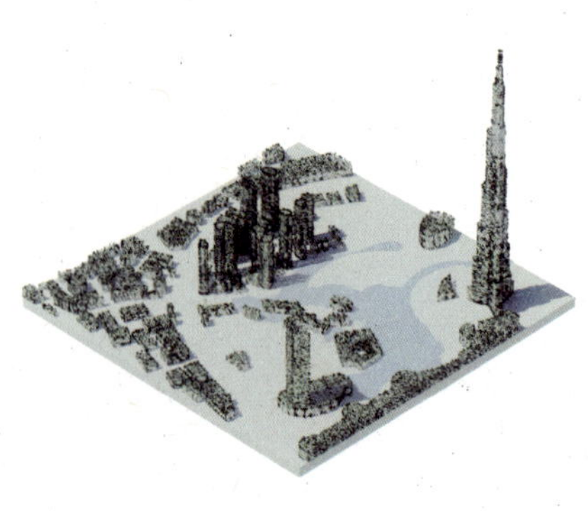

Step 6: Select facades (*Stick* button)

Green Dip – Dubai (UAE)

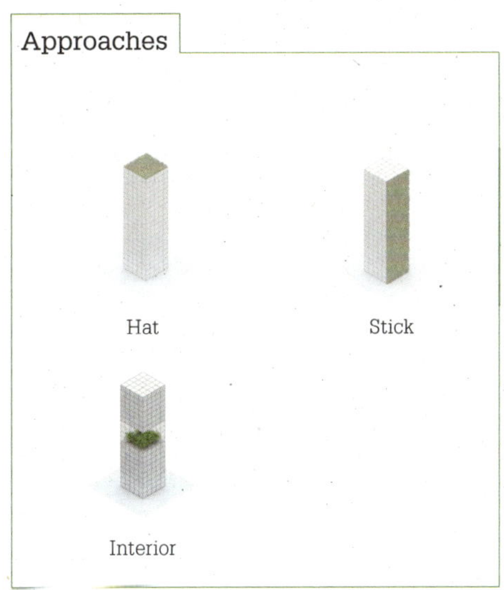

Step 7: Select interiors (*Interior* button)

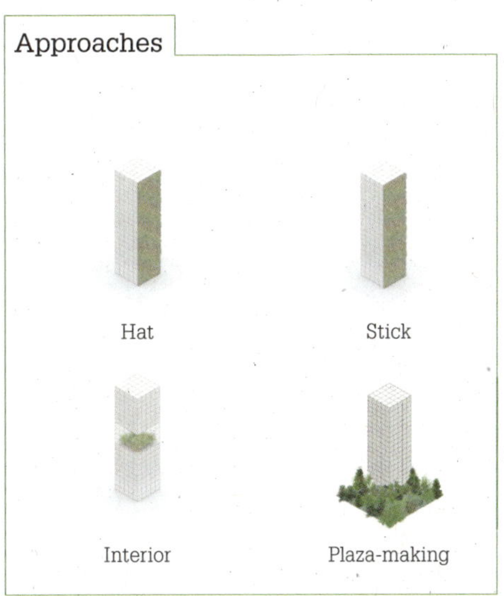

Step 8: Select public space (*Plaza-making* button)

Green Dip – Dubai (UAE)

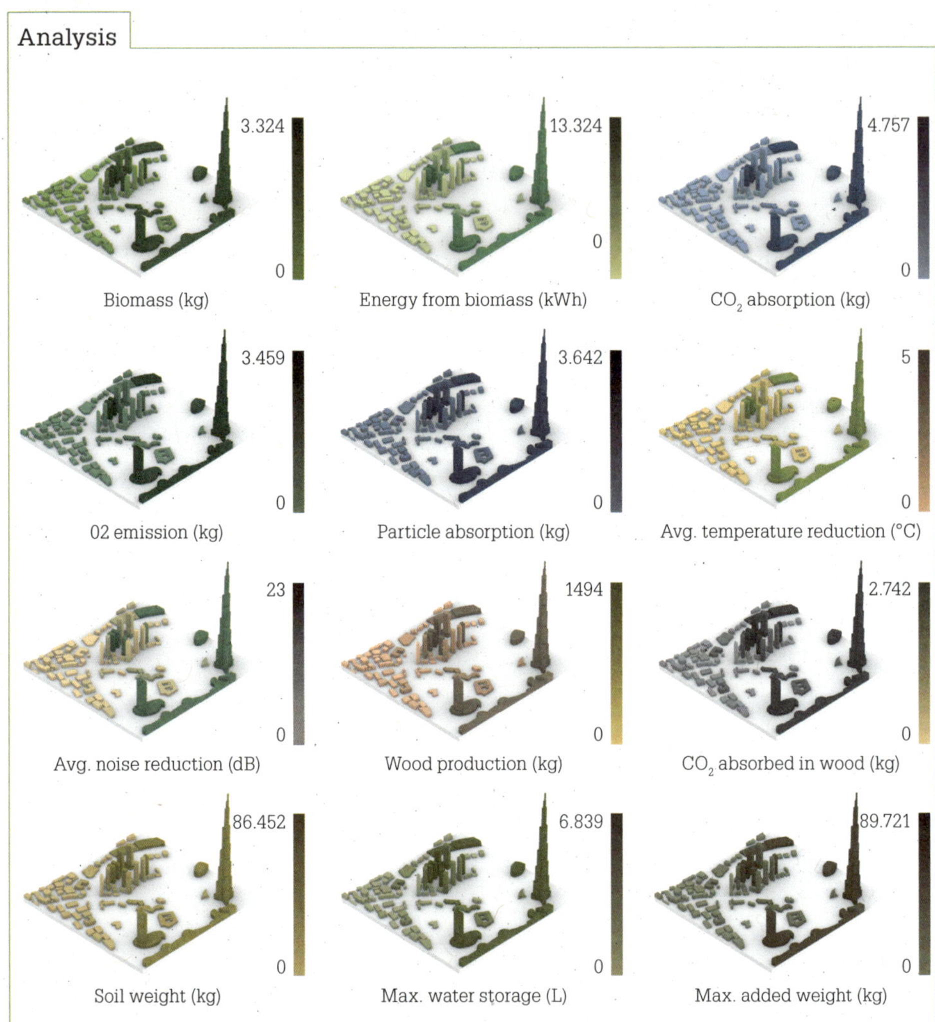

Step 9: Display performances analysis

Green Dip – Dubai (UAE)

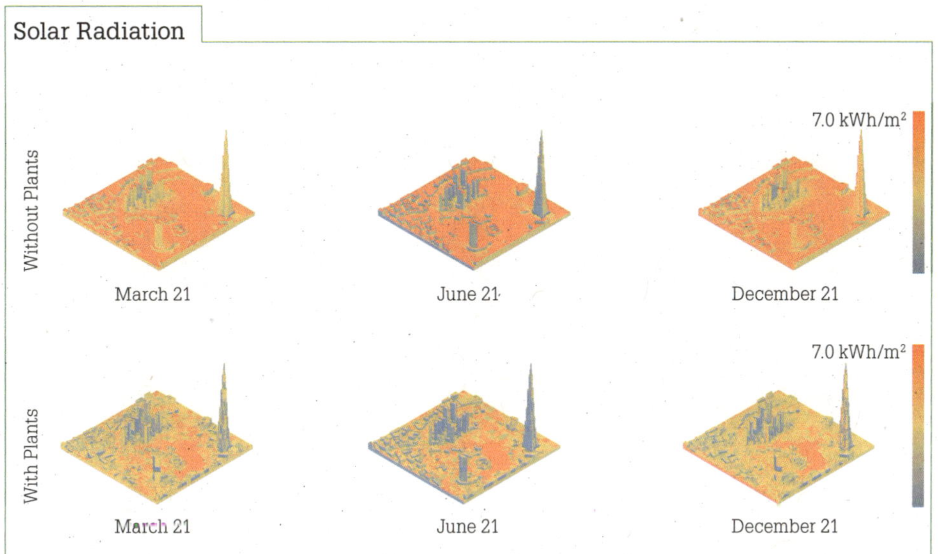

Step 10: Display solar radiation

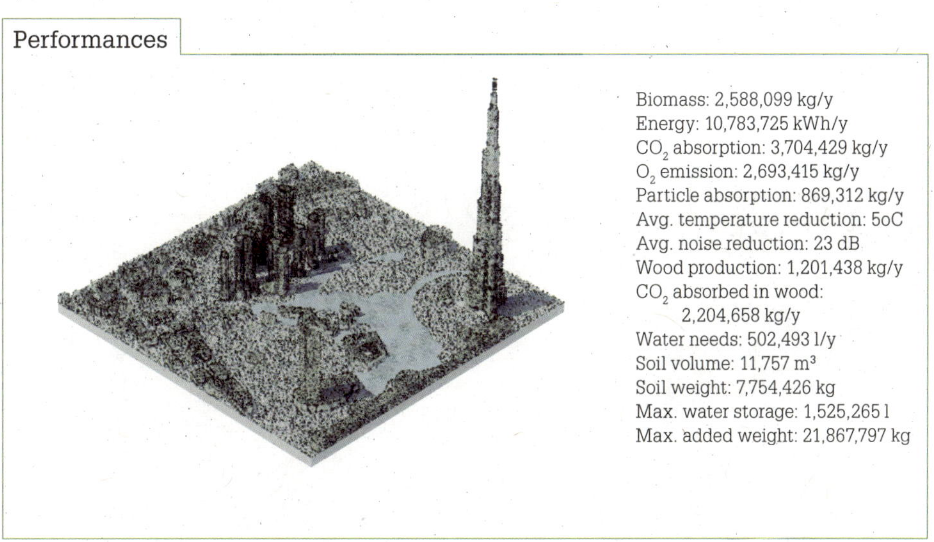

Step 11: Display impacts after Green Dip

Green Dip – Dubai (UAE)

Step 12: Display *The Green Dip*

Green Dip – Dubai (UAE)

Green Dip – Moscow (Russia)

Taiga

Trees	90
Shrubs	467
Other	16
Total	563

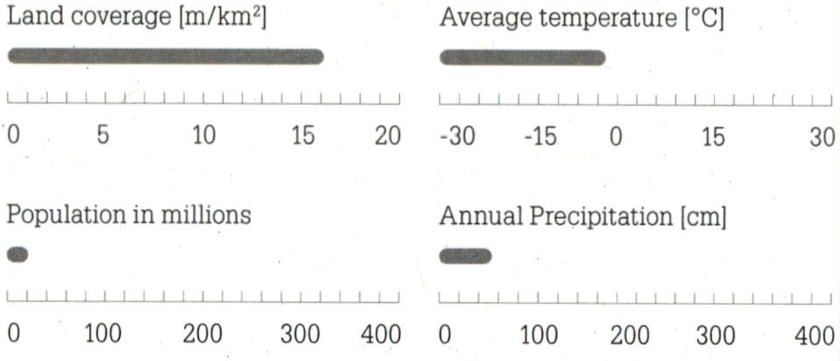

Land coverage [m/km²]
0 5 10 15 20
Average temperature [°C]
-30 -15 0 15 30
Population in millions
0 100 200 300 400
Annual Precipitation [cm]
0 100 200 300 400

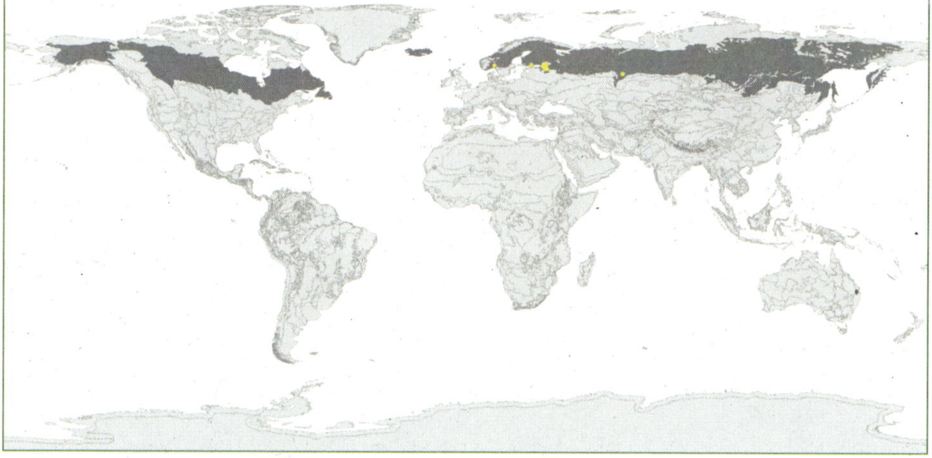

Step 1: Choose a city in its corresponding biome

Location

3D Model

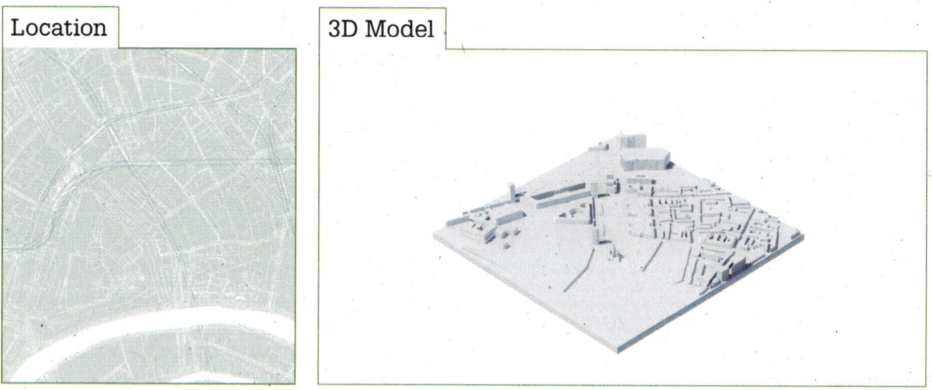

Step 2: Select an area and display the 3D model

Green Dip – Moscow (Russia)

Step 3: Load the catalogue of plants associated to its biome

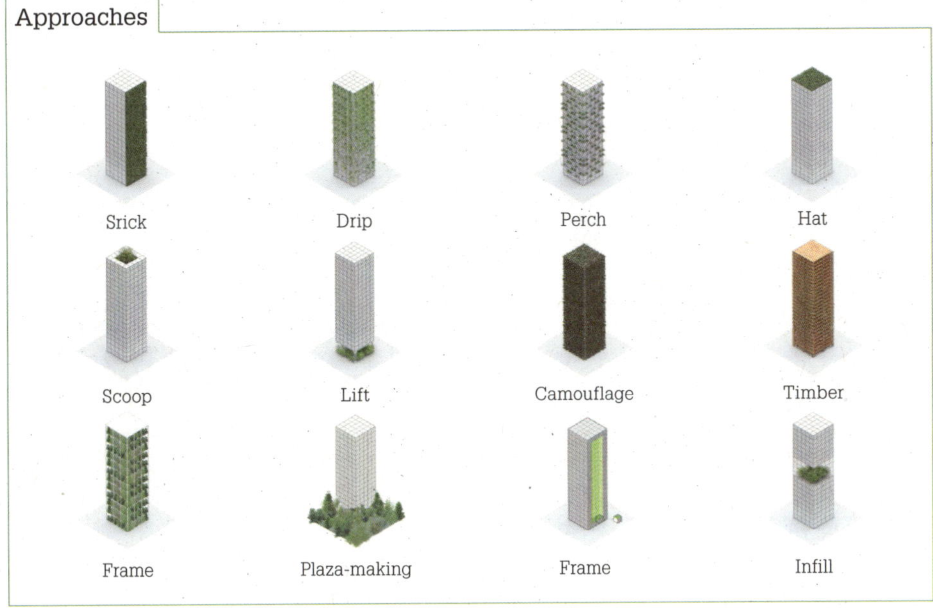

Step 4: Explore design strategies

Green Dip – Moscow (Russia)

Step 5: Select rooftops (*Hat* button)

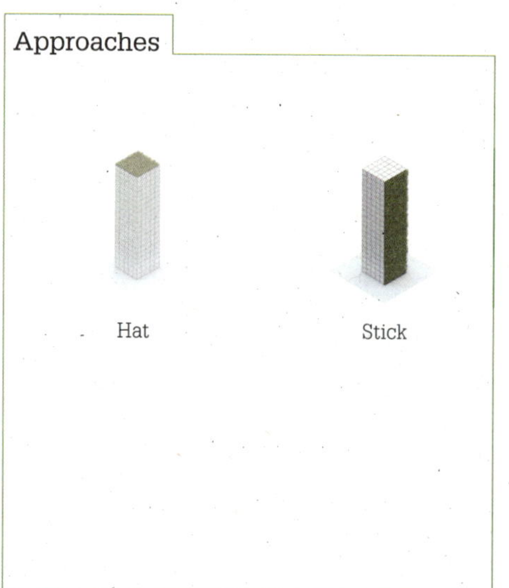

Step 6: Select facades (*Stick* button)

Green Dip – Moscow (Russia)

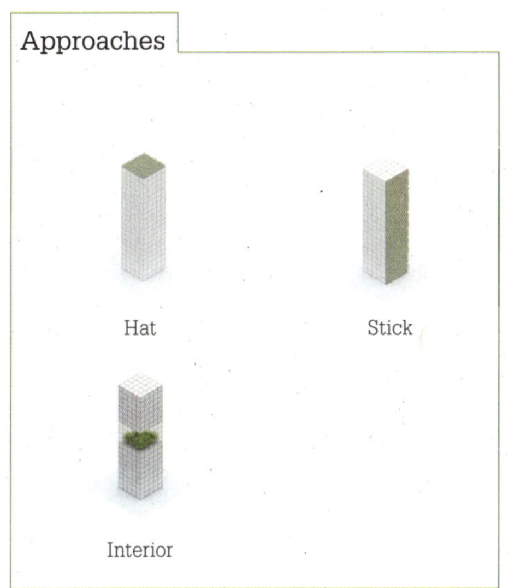

Step 7: Select interiors (*Interior* button)

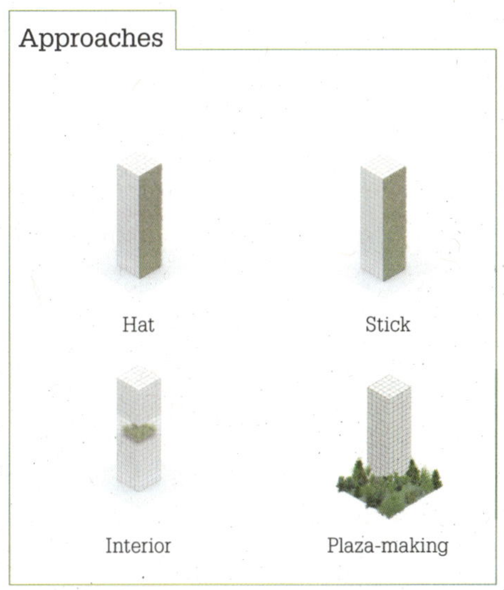

Step 8: Select public space (*Plaza-making* button)

Green Dip – Moscow (Russia)

Analysis

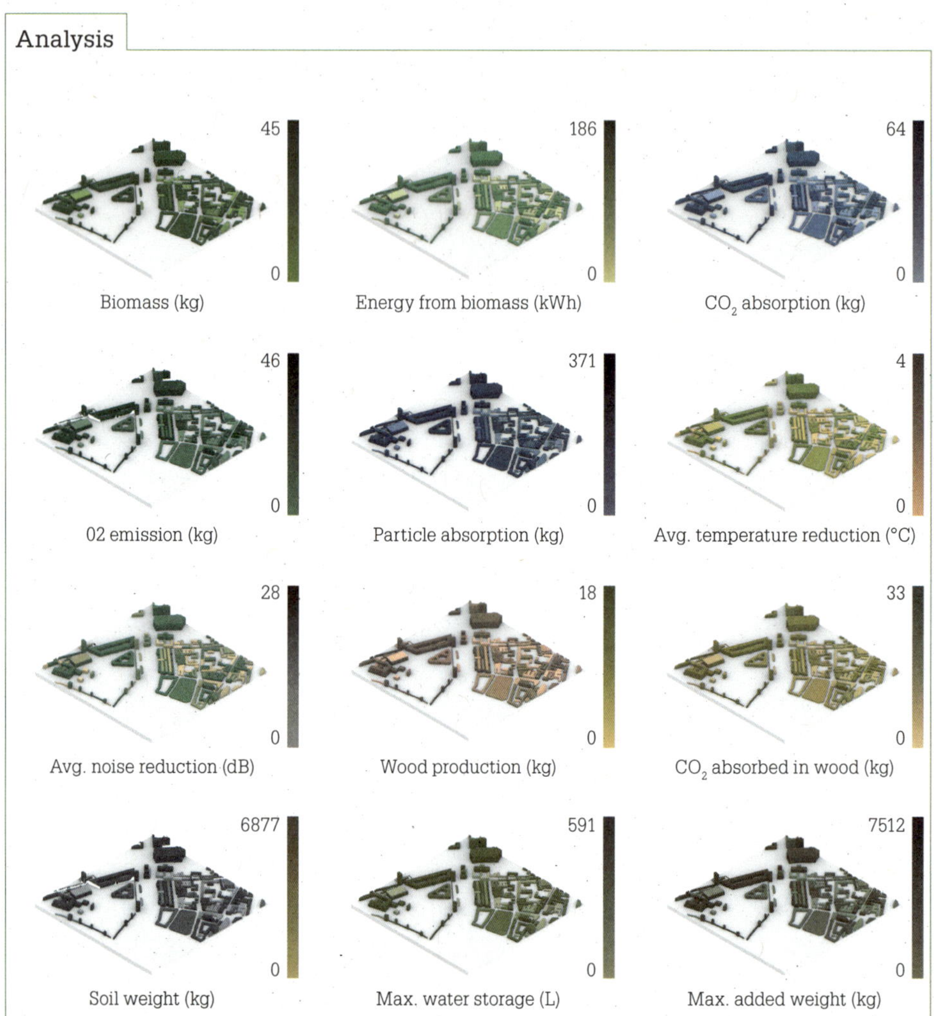

Step 9: Display performances analysis

Green Dip – Moscow (Russia)

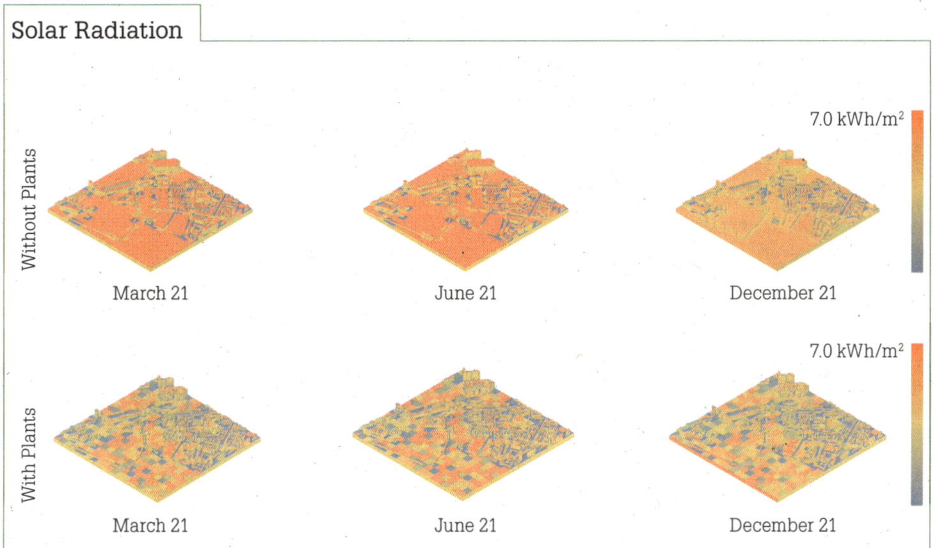

Step 10: Display solar radiation

Step 11: Display impacts after Green Dip

Green Dip – Moscow (Russia)

Step 12: Display *The Green Dip*

Green Dip – Moscow (Russia)

Green Dip – New York (USA)

Temperate Broadleaf Forest

Trees	388
Shrubs	2430
Other	51
Total	2869

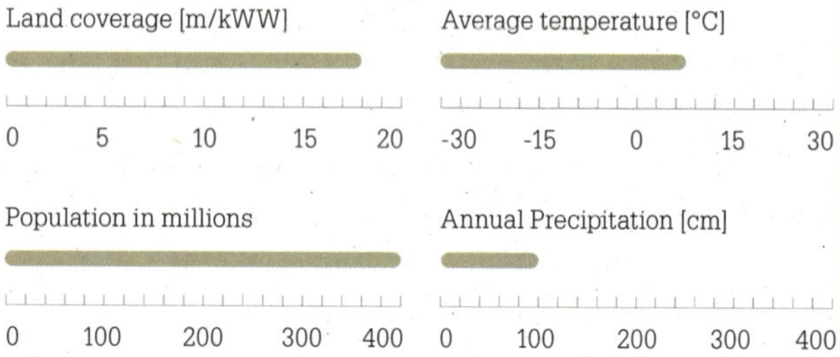

Land coverage [m/kWW]
0 5 10 15 20
Average temperature [°C]
-30 -15 0 15 30
Population in millions
0 100 200 300 400
Annual Precipitation [cm]
0 100 200 300 400

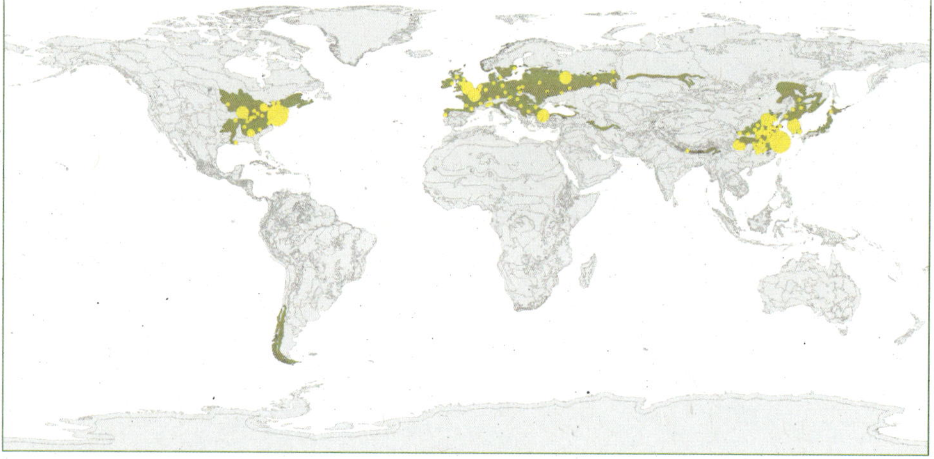

Step 1: Choose a city in its corresponding biome

Location

3D Model

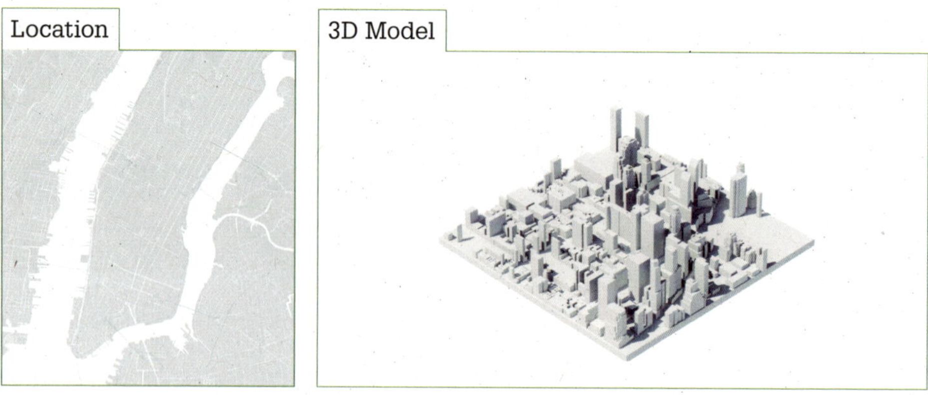

Step 2: Select an area and display the 3D model

Green Dip – New York (USA)

Step 3: Load the catalogue of plants associated to its biome

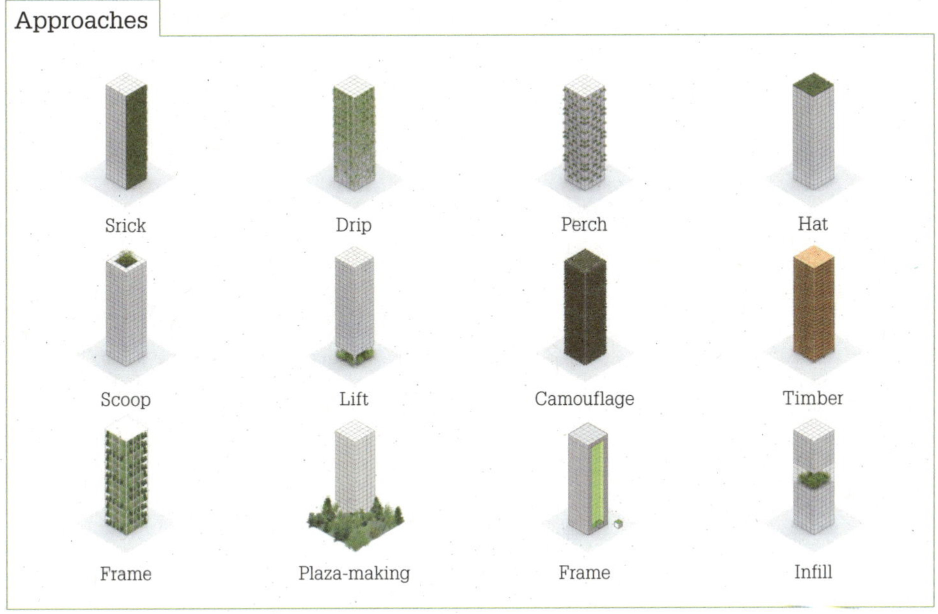

Step 4: Explore design strategies

Green Dip – New York (USA)

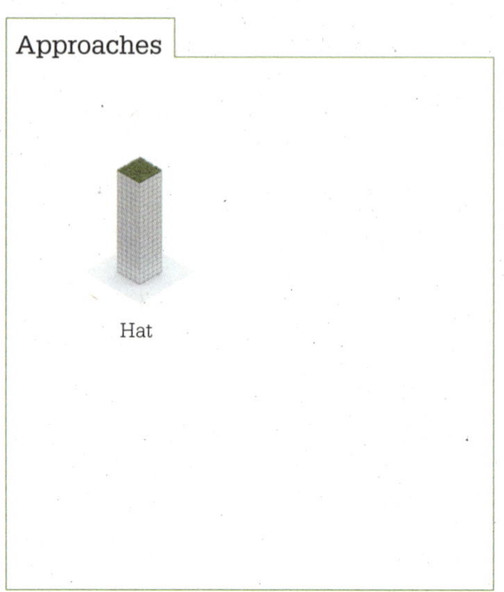

Step 5: Select rooftops (*Hat* button)

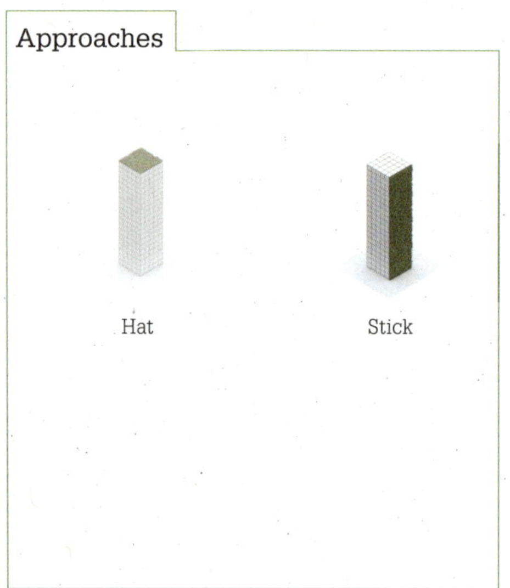

Step 6: Select facades (*Stick* button)

Green Dip – New York (USA)

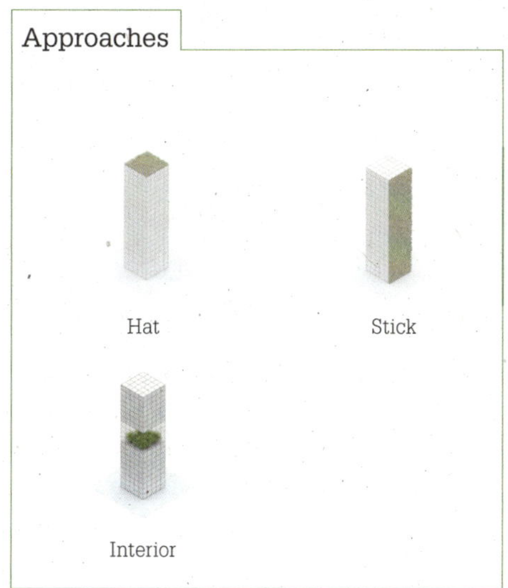

Step 7: Select interiors (*Interior* button)

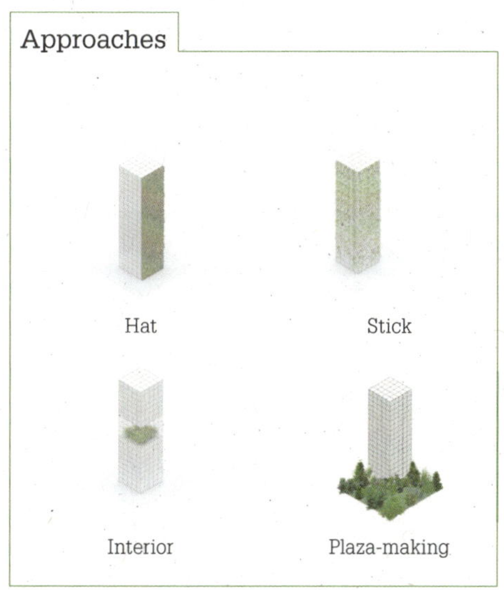

Step 8: Select public space (*Plaza-making* button)

Green Dip – New York (USA)

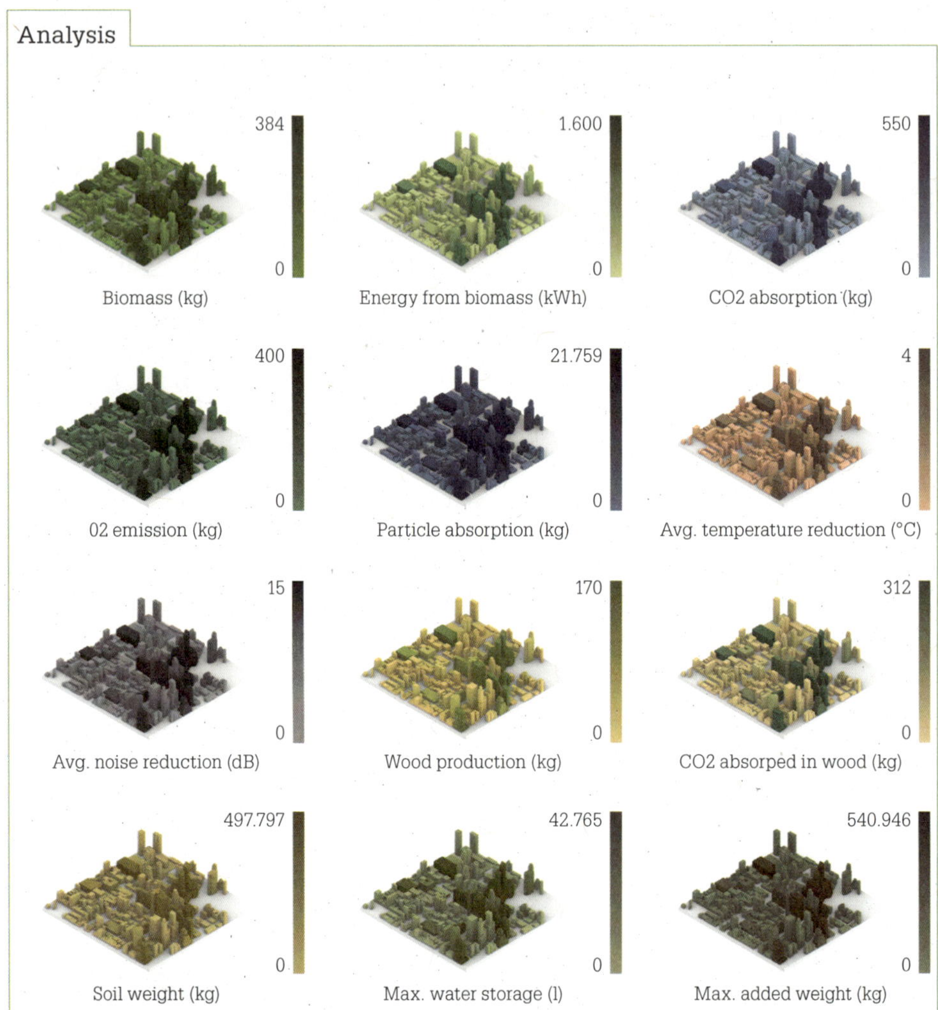

Step 9: Display performances analysis

Green Dip – New York (USA)

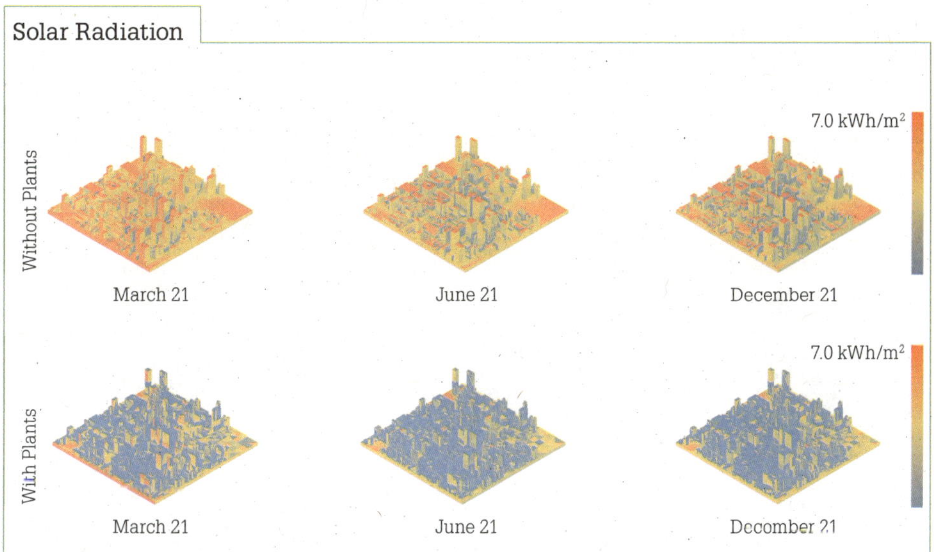

Step 10: Display solar radiation

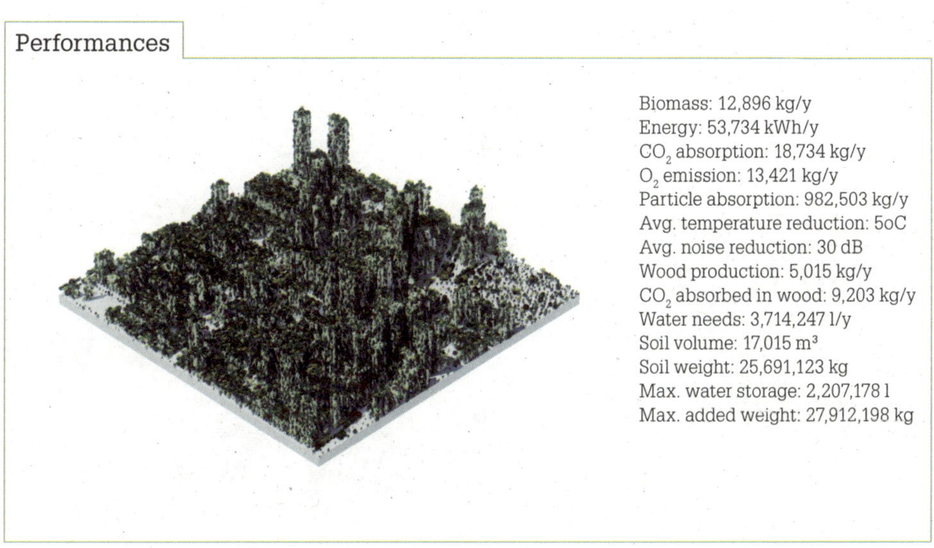

Step 11: Display impacts after Green Dip

Green Dip – New York (USA)

Step 12: Display *The Green Dip*

Green Dip – New York (USA)

Part 3

Welcome to *The Green Dip*

The exhibition

Experience *The Green Dip*
Hangzhou, China (2023)

The O2 Museum in Hangzhou welcomed visitors for the first time in September 2023 with 'The Green Dip' exhibition. In this show, visitors were immersed in a 360-degree audio-visual experience that invited them to imagine a future in which Hangzhou, Singapore, Dubai, Paris, and New York are covered in vegetation.

'The Green Dip' exhibition, occupying the central area of a former industrial building, began by illustrating the impact of human activity on the planet with a giant section of the Earth's crust. This powerful display underscored the environmental challenges of our world, acting as a backdrop for reimagining cities. After traversing this section of the Earth's crust, visitors gained insights into The Green-Maker methodology.

Upon entering the installation's centrepiece, a space measuring 35 by 15 m, visitors experienced skyscrapers transforming into vertical forests, urban facades becoming extensions of the natural world, and green balconies replacing conventional climate control systems. Riverbanks and waterfronts transform into lush public parks, and the urban forest extends to hilltops, casting a verdant canopy over the city.

The exhibition at the O2 Museum was an immersive journey into a future of green havens. Hangzhou, Singapore, Dubai, Paris, and New York are just the beginning—inviting all to reimagine a world where cities and nature coexist.

The show displays how cities can become living ecosystems, teeming with vibrant plant life and providing new habitats for diverse species.

The Green Dip exhibition aims to raise awareness not only among architects, urban planners, citizens, politicians, and policymakers, but also among the wider public. It serves as an invitation to all individuals to acquire and share knowledge about plants, biodiversity, and their integration in the built environment.

The centrepiece of the exhibition is the 360-degrees immersive film. The film allows the imagination to soar, transforming the streets of five cities worldwide into lush green boulevards that help alleviate the scorching summer temperatures. These avenues also evolve into urban biodiversity corridors.

The film additionally presents lush interiors suitable for living and working within each of the highlighted cities. Visitors are invited to picture themselves wandering through a city that transitions from a savanna to a rainforest or from a swamp to the tundra. They can experience these interiors, where the climate is regulated by the presence of vegetation.

Visitors have the opportunity to imagine and draw inspiration from the film, showcasing that the benefits of greening cities surpass ecosystem services, aesthetic beauty, and environmental, social, and economic value.

The film demonstrates that, if thoughtfully executed, *The Green Dip* has the potential to enhance our thinking, design practices, lifestyle, and interactions with the built environment.

The references to the planet in the film encourage us to extrapolate and imagine a future where urbanisation could evolve and blend with nature, envisioning a continuous planetary forest. This transformation could redefine cities as hubs for biodiversity to thrive.

The Green Dip film provides the opportunity for visitors to virtually walk or fly through city fragments entirely covered with greenery.

The imagery is reflected in the mirrored floors, offering an even more immersive experience to visitors.

Cities selected

- Tundra
- Taiga
- Alpine tundra
- Montane forest
- Mediterranean
- Rainforest
- Dry leaf forest
- Semi arid desert
- Arid desert & xeric shrubland
- Dry steppe
- Savanna
- Temperate steppe
- Temperate broadleaf forest
- Monsoon forest

Paris
Hangzhou
Dubai
Singapore

Hangzhou (China)

Take a look at Hangzhou from the air after the Green Dip is executed. What would it be like to inhabit this 'next Hangzhou'?

Imagine waking up surrounded by an urban forest, going for a walk outside, and gazing upon the transformation of your city streets into a lush woodland. Step out onto your roof garden or onto the street below to collect fruits for breakfast...

...now made possible as all plazas and parks have been converted into vegetable gardens.

Singapore (Singapore)

Welcome to ‘next Singapore’...

Picture yourself residing in a cooler, fresher city, all thanks to the greenery covering its buildings and streets.

How would it feel to stay at the iconic Marina Bay Sands hotel?

Fly through a newly green-covered Singapore and witness the aquatic vegetation gradually filling up the harbour too.

Dubai (UAE)

Now, let's shift our focus to Dubai, where a dense layer of desert vegetation covers the glass facades of the city's towers, significantly reducing energy consumption for cooling during the scorching summer months.

Picture Dubai transforming into a walkable city. Envision yourself leisurely strolling in the shade of palm trees and cacti.

Did you imagine Dubai could one day look like this?

A true oasis in the Persian Gulf, untouched by the desert's sandstorms.

Paris (France)

Let's now imagine Paris blending seamlessly into the temperate broadleaf forest. Do you recognise the Île de la Cité?

Vegetation covers the entire city and its monuments, including Notre Dame cathedral, now converted into a public garden after restoration.

As plants flourish on buildings and streets, the city turns into a peaceful forest.

The scent of plants replaces pollution, and birds chirp at your doorstep.

New York (USA)

The beauty of the East Coast Forest now envelops Manhattan in its autumn splendour.

Imagine working in a Midtown office surrounded by flourishing vegetation, fostering a more relaxed atmosphere.

Envision strolling through the Fifth Avenue Forest, where pedestrians, bikes, and birds replace cars and pollution.

Enjoy lunch in one of the numerous public plazas covered with greenery atop the skyscrapers.

Summer in New York is no longer sweltering but refreshing and revitalizing.

Green impacts

Towards a planetary forest

The Green Dip initiative holds the promise of radical transformation. As we contemplate its implementation across all cities globally, a cascade of transformative effects becomes apparent, each with far-reaching implications for our environment, economy, and quality of life.

The Why Factory students conducted a series of calculations to estimate the global impacts of implementing *The Green Dip*. While these results may lack scientific precision, they provide a promising glimpse into the potential for radical change.

+30%

CARBON STORED

Storage (Mg ha^{-1}) = C Sequestration (Mg ha^{-1} yr^{-1}) × No. of years(y)
C Sequestration = Carbon Sequestration [1]

The Green Dip is estimated to boost carbon storage in flora by 30 per cent. This calculation, performed for each biome, accounts for the biome's population and specific metrics.

+25%

BIOMASS

Biomass net(Mg) = AGB(Mg ha^{-1}) × Area(ha)
AGB = Aboveground Biomass [2]

The global biomass, estimated at 550 billion tonnes of carbon, is projected to increase after *The Green Dip*. The biomass productivity of forests within these urban areas is calculated for each biome.

-0.26°C

URBAN HEAT ISLAND EFFECT

UHI = Urban Temperature difference (°C)
UHI = Urban Heat Island [3]

The Green Dip is projected to decrease the urban heat island effect, with an average temperature drop of 0.26°C.

+2.6%

HUMIDITY

$RH = (ele_w) \times 100$
RH = Relative Humidity, e= Actual Vapour Density, e_w = Saturation Vapour Densit [4]

Relative Humidity (RH), measuring air's water vapour concentration, is estimated to rise by 2.6 per cent.

+8%

O_2 PRODUCTION

net O^2 Release(kg yr^{-1}) = net C Sequestration (kg yr^{-1}) × 32/12
C Sequestration = Carbon Sequestration [5]

Global O_2 production is estimated to increase by 8 per cent thanks to *The Green Dip*. The increase is estimated through research on the trees native to each biome

-10%

NO_2 CONCENTRATION

$AQI = (AQI_{high} \quad AQI_{low}) / (C_{high} - C) \times (C - C_{low}) + AQI_{low}$
AQI = Air Quality Index, C = The concentration of breakpoint [6]

After implementing *The Green Dip*, the absorption of NO_2 by plants is estimated to increase by 10 per cent.

-0.65°C

TEMPERATURE

Temperature = 5.35 In (C/CO) × A
C = Carbon concentration in ppm, A = Climate sensitivity [7]

The Green Dip strategy could lead to a temperature drop of 0.65°C. This decrease is expected due to the reduction in carbon concentration from 400ppm to 360ppm, which should have a cooling effect..

+19%

EVAPOTRANSPIRATION

$E\ (mm/day) = K.f(u)(e_w - e_a)$

E = Evaporation, e = Vapour Pressure, f(u) = wind speed correction function, K = coefficient [8]

The Green Dip is anticipated to boost evapotranspiration by 19 per cent. Evapotranspiration (E) is influenced by several factors, including temperature, sunshine, wind, and air humidity, with temperature and sunshine being the most significant..

+6.4%

WATER STORAGE CAPACITY

SWS (mm) = RD(m) x AWSC ($mm\ m^{-1}$)
SWS = Soil Water Storage, RD = Crop Rooting Depth, AWSC = Available water storage capacity of soil [9]

The Green Dip is projected to increase soil water storage capacity (SWS) by 6.4 per cent. The strategy is estimated to capture an amount of water equivalent to the Caspian Sea every year, approximately 258.57 km^3 of water. Additionally, tropical and subtropical moist broadleaf forests are expected to capture an additional 0.3 mm, equivalent to three times the volume of Lake Baikal.

Soil Water Storage Capacity (SWS) is defined as the total amount of water that is stored in the soil. The total soil water storage capacity refers to when all the apiol pores or voids are filled with water.

+10%

PRECIPITATION

$Pann = E\,P_{day}$, $Pann$ = annual rainfall, P_{day} = daily rainfall [10]

The Green Dip is projected to increase precipitation by 10%. Precipitation refers to the combination of rainfall and snowfall reaching the land surface.

-0.7%

ALBEDO

$a = F^{+}/F^{-}$

a = Albedo, F^{+} =flux of reflected solar radiation, F^{-}= flux of incident solar radiation [11]

The albedo of urban areas is lower than that of areas with vegetation. Hence, adding vegetation in urban areas, the albedo increases by 0.76, which causes the global temperature to drop by 1.5°C.

[1] UN Environment Program
[2] ORNL DAAC for Biochemical Dynamics
[3] charteredforests.org, sustainability and governance of urban forests
[4] NA
[5] the Nature Project, Brittanica.com
[6] Worlds Air Population AQI Index
[7] www.scepticalscience.com
[8] www.waterandclimatechange.eu
[9] www.fao.org
[10] www.waterandclimatechange.eu
[11] climatedata.info

What's next?

Towards *Biotopia*

Winy Maas

The Green Dip is not enough. The current state of immediate apocalypse requires a decisive paradigm change at the very epicentre of urbanisation. We must understand the planet as a single city of eight or more billion human bodies and a myriad other living creatures.

We can only survive on this planet if we turn Earth into a place where humans can sustainably cohabit with nature: respecting the limits, without waste, in a fully biodegradable, adaptable, recyclable, clean, and energy-neutral environment.

It's time to design *with*, *for*, and *as* nature (no matter what preposition we want to use). It's time to use our imagination to invent and change; it's time to direct ourselves, our environments, and our behaviour into a world where we not only make nature but live like nature. In short: it is a world determined by biology.

From *The Green Dip*, I will move into an exploration of *BiodiverCity*—the second publication of this trilogy—to ultimately reach the state of *Biotopia*.

In 1973, psychoanalyst Erich Fromm coined the term *biophilia* in his book *The Anatomy of Human Destructiveness*, pointing out that humans have an innate tendency to seek connections with nature and other forms of life. Biologist Edward O. Wilson later explored the *biophilia hypothesis* in his work Biophilia (1984), which proposed that the tendency of humans to focus on and affiliate with nature and other life forms has, in part, a genetic basis.

Was this the beginning of an *age of biology*? Unfortunately, no. We grow. We consume more. We waste more. Until when? Until resources are fully depleted? Until fresh water, soil, or energy come to an end? It is appalling how humanity disconnected itself from all forms of biological balance to the extent that we are running out of not only resources but also time.

As moving off the planet is a solution limited to just a privileged few, we must face the challenges instead of ignoring them—and act before it's too late.

Let's finally enter the age of biology. Let's construct *Biotopia*.

What can we innovate, technically and spatially? How can natural sciences, automation, nanomaterials, robotics, biotechnology, or biomimicry contribute to establishing new relationships among humans and all other living organisms?

Let's invent and dream. Let's imagine *Biotopia*.

Fortunately, there are more and more inventions: from energy-generating glass to bioengineered products. But more inventions are still needed to achieve *Biotopia*. Can we imagine these inventions merging into a new material or ecological complex? Can we imagine a material that gives light, creates energy, and filters, contains and produces fresh water? Can we create a material that grows and shrinks instantly—that recycles, makes soils, feeds, and moves, or loosens itself and can fly and transport us? Can we invent a material, or a *bio-matter*, that can even form clouds for shading, produce food and manage water?

Today, more than ever, everything is biology. Everything is nature.

Welcome to *Biotopia*.

Credits

Authors

Winy Maas

Winy Maas is the Director of The Why Factory–an internationally engaged think tank established in 2008–and Founding Partner and Principal Architect of MVRDV. He has received international acclaim for his broad range of urban planning and building projects, across all typologies and scales. At TU Delft's The Why Factory Maas challenges the boundaries of established standards in order to produce solutions that reimagine how we live, work, and play. In addition to his dedicated leadership role at MVRDV and professorship at TU Delft and elsewhere, Maas is widely published, actively engaged in the advancement of the design profession, and sits on numerous boards and juries.

> *'I advocate denser, greener, more attractive and liveable cities, with an approach to design that centres around user-defined, innovative and sustainable ideas for the built environment, regardless of typology or scale.'*
> *- Maas*

Javier Arpa Fernández

Javier Arpa Fernández is an architecture and urbanism teacher, researcher, author, and curator. Having completed a Master of Science in Architecture at the Delft University of Technology, Javier specialises in the dissemination of architectural and urbanism practice. Javier is the Research and Education Coordinator of The Why Factory and the Curator of Public Programs at the Faculty of Architecture of TU Delft. Javier gives public lectures and participates in colloquia worldwide. Javier has been lecturer at the University of Pennsylvania, Design Critic at Harvard GSD, Adjunct Professor at Columbia GSAPP, Visiting Professor at ENSA-Belleville and ENSA-Versailles. He was Deputy Editor of Domus Magazine and Senior Editor for *a+t* research group. He is the co-author of *a+t*'s *Density*, *Hybrids*, *Civilities*, *In Common* and the *Strategy* series, and *The Public Chance* volume. He was the curator of the exhibition *Paris Habitat*, about a century of social housing in Paris, held in 2015 at the Pavillon de l'Arsenal in Paris, and the author of the monograph *Paris Habitat: One Hundred Years of City, One Hundred Years of Life*.

Adrien Ravon

Adrien Ravon is an architect and academic. In September 2011, he joined The Why Factory at the Faculty of Architecture and the Built Environment, TU Delft. He has participated in research and education projects, been responsible for the production of digital design tools and actively collaborated in the public dissemination of ideas about the city of the future. He co-authored The Why Factory's Future Cities Series publications *Barba, Life in a Fully Adaptable Environment* (2015), *Copy Paste, the Badass Copy Guide* (2017), *PoroCity, Opening up Solidity* (2018), *Le Grand Puzzle*, Manifesta 13 Marseille (2020), (w) Ego, *Dream Homes in Density* (2022). He has collaborated with numerous international institutions, including ETH (Zurich), KTH (Stockholm), GSAPP (New York), IAAC (Barcelona), Centre Pompidou (Paris), Dutch Design Week (Eindhoven), Manifesta 13 (Marseille) and Mori Art Museum (Tokyo). Adrien has worked as an architect and consultant for firms in Argentina, France, and the Netherlands.

Content Credits

The Green Dip by The Why Factory (TU Delft)

Authors: Winy Maas, Javier Arpa Fernández, Adrien Ravon
Research assistants: Lex te Loo and Anna Sujkowska

Graphic Designer: Selina Landis

Text Editor: Becky Quintal

Copy editor: Leo Reijnen

Contributors: Anna Yudina, Marco Roos, Wim Beining, Sander de Kler, Nicholas Pevzner

Urgent Earth
Javier Arpa Fernández and Adrien Ravon
Developed and illustrated by The Why Factory, and by the students of The Why Factory's Msc2 Design Studio at the Faculty of Architecture and the Built Environment (TU Delft) during the Spring semester, 2022.
Tutors: Winy Maas, Javier Arpa Fernández, Adrien Ravon, Lex te Loo
Students: Dali Baran, David Bernatek, Ainhoa Church, Nicole Filippoli, Aleksandra Jodlowska, Anna-Lena Kleiner, Sander van der Kooij, Fruzsi Kovacs, Feline van Lierop, Emilie Lodewijks, Javier Marcos, Reem Al-Muraikhi, Matteo Saba, Fabio Sala, Regina Salazar Gayo, Alexandra Sapounaki, Tijmer Smith, Melanie Waidler, Aphitchaya Wongnitchakul, Jiaying Wu, Mirko Zucchini

Green? Yes, green!
Winy Maas

Part 1
What can green do?

Green fashions
Javier Arpa Fernández and Adrien Ravon
Developed and illustrated by The Why Factory and by the students of Columbia University GSAPP Summer Workshop at The Why Factory (TU Delft), 2019
Tutors: Winy Maas, Javier Arpa Fernández, Adrien Ravon, Lex te Loo, Abraham Murrell
Students: Gauri Bahuguna, Héctor García, Wenya Liu, Ran Ma, Lucy Navarro, Matthew Ninivaggi, Adam Susaneck, Qingying Wang

Green assets
Javier Arpa Fernández and Adrien Ravon
Developed and illustrated by the students of Columbia University GSAPP Summer Workshop at The Why Factory (TU Delft), 2019.
Tutors: Winy Maas, Javier Arpa Fernández, Adrien Ravon, Lex te Loo, Abraham Murrell
Students: Gauri Bahuguna, Héctor García, Wenya Liu, Ran Ma, Lucy Navarro, Matthew Ninivaggi, Adam Susaneck, Qingying Wang
And by the students of The Why Factory's Msc1 Design Studio at The Why Factory (TU Delft) during the Fall semester, 2019.
Tutors: Winy Maas, Javier Arpa Fernández, Adrien Ravon, Leo Stuckardt, Lex te Loo
Students: Ugo Azoulay, Alex Da Costa Gomez, Anne de Schepper, Clara Beckers, Antonia Bohn, Dries Brøns, Fraser Carroll, Daryna Chernyshova, Emma Chris Avramiea, Júlia Dubois Auleda, David Fritz, Ton van Giessen, Gongbu Han, Jesslyn Humardani, Siddharth Jain, Eszter Katona, Natalie Keynton, Stanisław Klajs, Michelle Li, Yuchen Li, Maja Lindborg, Koen Meijman, Maciej Moszant, Hannah Namuth, Sophie van Riel, Yi Shan, Daniel Sobieraj, Katharina Stommel, Mikołaj Strzelczuk, Loen Sung, Ludvig Sundberg, Rogier Tamminga,

Mihaela Tomova, Sophie Vrisekoop, Jacqueline Yueh

If cities were covered with forests
Javier Arpa Fernández and Adrien Ravon
Developed and illustrated by the students of The Why Factory's MaCT Workshop at the Institute of Advanced Architecture of Catalonia (IAAC) during the Spring semester, 2019.
Tutors: Winy Maas, Javier Arpa Fernández, Adrien Ravon, Lex te Loo
Students: Natalie Adhiambo Ouma, Natali Barada, Sarine Bekarian, David Casanovas Tatxé, Raeshma Janardhanan Nair, Jarosław Kowalski, Luna Nagatomo, Mahsa Nikoufar, Polina Skorina, Maria Uporova, Wei Wei, Luyang Zhang, Xinyu Zhang, Haining Zhou

Green voices
Interviews conducted by Javier Arpa Fernández and Adrien Ravon
Contributors: Anna Yudina, Marco Roos, Wim Beining, Sander de Kler, Nicholas Pevzner

Part 2
How to green?

The Green-Maker
Javier Arpa Fernández and Adrien Ravon
Developed and illustrated by the students of The Why Factory's Msc1 Design Studio at The Why Factory (TU Delft) during the Fall semester, 2019.
Tutors: Winy Maas, Javier Arpa Fernández, Adrien Ravon, Leo Stuckardt, Lex te Loo
Students: Ugo Azoulay, Alex Da Costa Gomez, Anne de Schepper, Clara Beckers, Antonia Bohn, Dries Brøns, Fraser Carroll, Daryna Chernyshova, Emma Chris Avramiea, Júlia Dubois Auleda, David Fritz, Ton van Giessen, Gongbu Han, Jesslyn Humardani,

Siddharth Jain, Eszter Katona, Natalie Keynton, Stanisław Klajs, Michelle Li, Yuchen Li, Maja Lindborg, Koen Meijman, Maciej Moszant, Hannah Namuth, Sophie van Riel, Yi Shan, Daniel Sobieraj, Katharina Stommel, Mikołaj Strzelczuk, Loen Sung, Ludvig Sundberg, Rogier Tamminga, Mihaela Tomova, Sophie Vrisekoop, Jacqueline Yueh

Mapping flora

Javier Arpa Fernández and Adrien Ravon
Developed and illustrated by the students of The Why Factory's Msc1 Design Studio at The Why Factory (TU Delft) during the Fall semester, 2019.
Tutors: Winy Maas, Javier Arpa Fernández, Adrien Ravon, Leo Stuckardt, Lex te Loo
Students: Ugo Azoulay, Alex Da Costa Gomez, Anne de Schepper, Clara Beckers, Antonia Bohn, Dries Brøns, Fraser Carroll, Daryna Chernyshova, Emma Chris Avramiea, Júlia Dubois Auleda, David Fritz, Ton van Giessen, Gongbu Han, Jesslyn Humardani, Siddharth Jain, Eszter Katona, Natalie Keynton, Stanisław Klajs, Michelle Li, Yuchen Li, Maja Lindborg, Koen Meijman, Maciej Moszant, Hannah Namuth, Sophie van Riel, Yi Shan, Daniel Sobieraj, Katharina Stommel, Mikołaj Strzelczuk, Loen Sung, Ludvig Sundberg, Rogier Tamminga, Mihaela Tomova, Sophie Vrisekoop, Jacqueline Yueh

Library of plants

Javier Arpa Fernández and Adrien Ravon
Developed and illustrated by the students of The Why Factory's Msc1 Design Studio at The Why Factory (TU Delft) during the Fall semester, 2019.
Tutors: Winy Maas, Javier Arpa Fernández, Adrien Ravon, Leo Stuckardt, Lex te Loo
Students: Ugo Azoulay, Alex Da Costa Gomez, Anne de Schepper, Clara Beckers, Antonia Bohn, Dries Brøns, Fraser Carroll, Daryna Chernyshova, Emma Chris Avramiea, Júlia Dubois Auleda, David Fritz, Ton van Giessen, Gongbu Han, Jesslyn Humardani, Siddharth Jain, Eszter Katona, Natalie Keynton, Stanisław Klajs, Michelle Li, Yuchen Li, Maja Lindborg, Koen Meijman, Maciej Moszant, Hannah Namuth, Sophie van Riel, Yi Shan, Daniel Sobieraj, Katharina Stommel, Mikołaj Strzelczuk, Loen Sung, Ludvig Sundberg, Rogier Tamminga, Mihaela Tomova, Sophie Vrisekoop, Jacqueline Yueh

Building with flora

Javier Arpa Fernández and Adrien Ravon
Developed and illustrated by the students of The Why Factory's Msc1 Design Studio at The Why Factory (TU Delft) during the Fall semester, 2019.
Tutors: Winy Maas, Javier Arpa Fernández, Adrien Ravon, Leo Stuckardt, Lex te Loo
Students: Ugo Azoulay, Alex Da Costa Gomez, Anne de Schepper, Clara Beckers, Antonia Bohn, Dries Brøns, Fraser Carroll, Daryna Chernyshova, Emma Chris Avramiea, Júlia Dubois Auleda, David Fritz, Ton van Giessen, Gongbu Han, Jesslyn Humardani, Siddharth Jain, Eszter Katona, Natalie Keynton, Stanisław Klajs, Michelle Li, Yuchen Li, Maja Lindborg, Koen Meijman, Maciej Moszant, Hannah Namuth, Sophie van Riel, Yi Shan, Daniel Sobieraj, Katharina Stommel, Mikołaj Strzelczuk, Loen Sung, Ludvig Sundberg, Rogier Tamminga, Mihaela Tomova, Sophie Vrisekoop, Jacqueline Yueh

Applications

Javier Arpa Fernández and Adrien Ravon
Developed and illustrated by the students of The Why Factory's Msc1 Design Studio at The Why Factory (TU Delft) during the Fall semester, 2019.
Tutors: Winy Maas, Javier Arpa Fernández, Adrien Ravon, Leo Stuckardt, Lex te Loo
Students: Ugo Azoulay, Alex Da Costa Gomez, Anne de Schepper, Clara Beckers, Antonia Bohn, Dries Brøns, Fraser Carroll, Daryna Chernyshova, Emma Chris Avramiea, Júlia Dubois Auleda, David Fritz, Ton van Giessen, Gongbu Han, Jesslyn Humardani, Siddharth Jain, Eszter Katona, Natalie Keynton, Stanisław Klajs, Michelle Li, Yuchen Li, Maja Lindborg, Koen Meijman, Maciej Moszant, Hannah Namuth, Sophie van Riel, Yi Shan, Daniel Sobieraj, Katharina Stommel, Mikołaj Strzelczuk, Loen Sung, Ludvig Sundberg, Rogier Tamminga, Mihaela Tomova, Sophie Vrisekoop, Jacqueline Yueh

Cities as canvases

Javier Arpa Fernández and Adrien Ravon
Developed and illustrated by the students of The Why Factory's Msc1 Design Studio at The Why Factory (TU Delft) during the Fall semester, 2019.
Tutors: Winy Maas, Javier Arpa Fernández, Adrien Ravon, Leo Stuckardt, Lex te Loo
Students: Ugo Azoulay, Alex Da Costa Gomez, Anne de Schepper, Clara Beckers, Antonia Bohn, Dries Brøns, Fraser Carroll, Daryna Chernyshova, Emma Chris Avramiea, Júlia Dubois Auleda, David Fritz, Ton van Giessen, Gongbu Han, Jesslyn Humardani, Siddharth Jain, Eszter Katona, Natalie Keynton, Stanisław Klajs, Michelle Li, Yuchen Li, Maja Lindborg, Koen Meijman, Maciej Moszant, Hannah Namuth, Sophie van Riel, Yi Shan, Daniel Sobieraj, Katharina Stommel, Mikołaj Strzelczuk, Loen Sung, Ludvig Sundberg, Rogier Tamminga, Mihaela Tomova, Sophie Vrisekoop, Jacqueline Yueh

Part 3
Welcome to The Green Dip

The exhibition
The Why Factory (TU Delft) with MVRDV
Developed and illustrated by Winy Maas, Javier Arpa Fernández, Adrien Ravon, Anna Sujkowska, with Feng Yu Zhu, Daniel van Loenen.

Green impacts
Developed and illustrated by the students of The Why Factory's MaCT Workshop at the Institute of Advanced Architecture of Catalunya (IAAC) during the Spring semester, 2020.
Tutors: Winy Maas, Javier Arpa Fernández , Adrien Ravon, Lex te Loo
Students: Pawitra Bureerak, Byron Esteban Cadena Campos, Aryo Dhaneswara, Rashid Gilfanov, Jianne Libunao, Akshay Marsute, Jochen Morandell, Elijah Munn, Alejandro Quinto Ferrández, Michelle Carolina Rodríguez Ruiz, Linara Salikhova, Andrew Saltzman, Rovianne Santiago, Kushal Saraiya

What's next?
The Why Factory (TU Delft)
Winy Maas

Image credits

All images in this publication were produced by The Why Factory, which holds their copyright, except for the following images:

p.32 El Oasis, Fernando Higueras, Madrid, Spain, 1972
p.32 Planeta building, Josep Maria Fargas and Enric Tous, Barcelona, Spain, 1978
p.32 Bosco Verticale, Stefano Boeri Architetti, Milan, Italy, 2014
p.32 One Central Park, Ateliers Jean Nouvel, Sydney, Australia, 2014
p.32 – Chicland Hotel, VTN Architects, Da Nang, Vietnam, 2020
p.32 Urban Farming Office, VTN Architects, Ho Chi Minh, Vietnam, 2022
p.33 Les Etoiles, Jean Renaudy, Ivry-sur-Seine, France, 1975
p.33 Alterlaa, Harry Glück, Vienna, Austria, 1986
p.33 La piece pointue, Atelier Iwona Buczkowska, Blanc-Mesnil, France, 1992
p.33 Tower Flower, Édouard François, Paris, France, 2004
p.33 M6B2 Tour de la Biodiversité, Édouard François, Paris, France, 2016
p.33 Trudeau Vertical Forest, Stefano Boeri Architetti, Eindhoven, The Netherlands, 2021
p. 34 Musée du Quai Branly, Ateliers Jean Nouvel, Patrick Blanc, Paris, France, 2006
p. 34 Caixa Forum, Herzog & de Meuron, Patrick Blanc, Madrid, Spain, 2008
p. 34 The Palace Hotel, Gary Grant, London, United Kingdom, 2013
p. 34 L'Oasis d'Aboukir, Patrick Blanc, Paris, France, 2013
p. 34 Sportplaza Mercator, VenhoevenCS, , Amsterdam, The Netherlands, 2013
p. 34 Edifício Santalaia, Exacta proyecto total, Groncol, Bogota, Colombia, 2015
p.35 ACROS Fukuoka, Emilio Ambasz, Fukuoka City, Japan, 1995
p.35 Green Roof, Chicago City Hall, William McDonough + Partners, Chicago, United States of America, 2001
p.35 Kampung Admiralty, WOHA, Singapore, 2017
p.35 Hilldegarden Bunker, Hamburg, Germany, 2018
p.35 Kö-Bogen II, Ingenhouven, Dusseldorf, Germany, 2020
p.35 View of Montecarlo with green rooftops, Monaco

p.36 Chichu Art Museum, Tadao Ando, Japan, 2004
p.36 Pool Pavilion Gluck+, , United States of America, 2009
p.36 Earth House, BCHO Architects, South Korea, 2009
p.36 Shilda Winery, X-architecture, Kakheti, Georgia, 2016
p.36 Taoyunju Community Center, Vector Architects, Chongqing, China, 2016
p.36 Skamlingsbanken, CEBRA architecture, Danemark, 2021
p.37 Barbican Conservatory, Chamberlin, Powell and Bon, London, United Kingdom, 1976
p.37 Biosphere 2, John P. Allen, Arizona, United States of America, 1991
p.37 National Botanic Garden of Wales, Foster + Partners, Llanarthney, United Kingdom, 2000
p.37 Gardens by the Bay WilkinsonEyre, , Singapore, 2012
p.37 Jewel Changi Airport, Moshe Safdie, Singapore, 2019
p.37 Tropicalia, Coldefy, France, 2023
p.38 Ford Foundation Center for Social Justice, New York City, United States of America, 1967
p.38 Naturescape, Kengo Kuma, Milan, Italy, 2013

p.38 Ecole Polytechnique Learning Centre, Sou Foujimoto, Saclay, France, 2015
p.38 Naman Retreat Pure Spa, MIA Design Studio, Da Nang, Vietnam, 2019
p.38 James Ramsey, Jonggak Station Solar Garden, Seoul, South Korea, 2019
p.38 Lowline Lab, James Ramsey, New York City, United States of America, 2019
p.38 1Hotel Paris, Kengo Kuma, Paris, France, 2017
p.38 Amata, Triptyque, Sao Paulo, Brazil, 2017
p.38 Toronto Tree Tower, Studio Precht, Toronto, Canada, 2017
p.38 The Farmhouse Studio Precht, 2019. Unbuilt
p.38 WoHO, Mad Arkitekter, Berlin, Germany, 2021
p.38 C6, Fraser and Partners, Perth, Australia, 2023
p.40 Cheonggyecheon Restorsation, Seoul Development Institute urban design team, Dongmyung Eng, Daelim E&C, Seoul, South Korea, 2005
p.40 Camden Highline, Oliver O'Brien, London, United Kingdom, 2015
p.40 Madrid Rio, West 8, Fernando Porras-Isla, Burgos-Garrido, Madrid, 2015
p.40 BAM Park, Inside Outside and Petra Blaisse, with Simona and Franco Giorgetta, Milan, Italy, 2022
p.40 Highline, Diller Scofidio + Renfro, Field Operations, New York City, United States of America, 2023
p.40 Beltline, Atlanta, United States of America, 2023
p.41 Emirates Golf Club, BSBG, Dubai, 1988
p.41 Reunion Resort, BMA, Florida, USA, 2007
p.41 Godrej Golf Links, BDP, Greater Noida, Delhi, India, 2016

p.41 Caitriona, Ambience, Gurgaon, India, 2016
p.41 The Camellias Development, Hafeez Contractor, Gurgaon, India, 2021
p.41 Serenity Alcaidesa, One Eden, San Roque, Spain, 2021
p.42 New Town, Cytonn, Kenya 2016
p.42 Green River, Dar Al Handasah Landscape Architects, Cairo, Egypt, 2019
p.42 Makadi Heights, EDSA, Makadi, Egypt, 2021
p.42 The Line, Neom, Saudi Arabia, 2021
p.42 Desert Rose city, Khatib & Alami, Dubai, 2022
p.42 XZERO City, URB, United Arab Emirates, 2022
p.43 Tianjin Ecocity, SSTEC, Binhai, China, 2007
p.43 Paris smart city 2050, Vincent Callebaut Architectures, Paris, France, 2015
p.43 Paris smart city 2050, Vincent Callebaut Architectures, Paris, France, 2015
p.43 Flemington Sustainable City, Tony Owen Partners, Sydney, Australia, 2018
p.43 AI generated
p.43 AI generated
p.97 L'île Derborence, Gilles Clément, Lille, France, 1995
p.97 Le Jardin des Fonderies, Doazan + Hirschberger, Nantes, France, 2009
p.100-101 Breatheaustria, Austrian Pavilion at Expo Milano, Klaus K. Loenhart, Milan, Italy, 2015
p.109 Philadelphia, USA
p.114 Philadelphia, USA
p.115 Leiden Bio Science Park, Leiden, The Netherlands, 1984
p.118-119 Leiden Bio Science Park, Leiden, The Netherlands, 1984

p.123 Depot Boijmans van Beuningen, MVRDV, Rotterdam, The Netherlands, 2020
p.123 Depot Boijmans van Beuningen, MVRDV, Rotterdam, The Netherlands, 2020
p.121 Ebben multi-stem tree, Cuijk, The Netherlands
p.266-279 The Green Factory exhibition, Hangzhou, China, 2023

Acknowledgements

We would like to thank TU Delft, IAAC and GSAPP Universities and the students of The Why Factory for their contributions to this book; and the European Cultural Centre (Venice, Italy), Dutch Green Building Council (Eindhoven, the Netherlands), and O2 Museum (Hangzhou, China), for exhibiting the results of this research.

Just like every other previous publication by The Why Factory, *The Green Dip* is made of student —non-scientific— work. This book is the result of design speculation with educational purposes.

Book credits

The Green Dip by The Why Factory (TU Delft)
Authors: Winy Maas, Javier Arpa Fernández, Adrien Ravon
Research assistants: Lex te Loo and Anna Sujkowska
Graphic Designer: Selina Landis
Text Editor: Becky Quintal
Copy editor: Leo Reijnen
Contributors: Anna Yudina, Marco Roos, Wim Beining, Sander de Kler, Nicholas Pevzner

Authors: Winy Maas, Javier Arpa Fernández, Adrien Ravon
Research assistants: Lex te Loo and Anna Sukowska
Graphic Designer: Selina Landis
Text Editor: Becky Quintal
Contributors: Anna Yudina, Marco Roos, Wim Beining, Sander de Kler, Nicholas Pevzner
Copy editor: Leo Reijnen
Design of The Why Factory logo + format: Thonik in collaboration with BENG
Printing and lithography: die Keure, Bruges
Paper: Circle Offset, 90 grs
Publisher: Marcel Witvoet, nai010 publishers, Rotterdam

©2024 The Why Factory and nai010 publishers
All rights reserved. No part of part of this publication may be reproduced, stored in a retrieval system, or transmitted in any form or by any means, electronic, mechanical, photocopying, recording or otherwise, without the prior written permission of the publisher.
For works of visual artists affiliated with a CISAC – organization the copyrights have been settled with Pictoright in Amsterdam. ©

2024, c/o Pictoright Amsterdam

Although every effort was made to find the copyright holders for the illustrations used, it has not been possible to trace them all. Interested parties are requested to contact nai010 publishers, Korte Hoogstraat 31, 3011 GK Rotterdam, the Netherlands.

nai010 publishers is an internationally orientated publisher specialized in developing, producing and distributing books in the fields of architecture, urbanism, art and design.
www.nai010.com

nai010 books are available internationally at selected bookstores and from the following distribution partners:

North, Central and South America
Artbook | D.A.P., New York, USA, dap@dapinc.com

Rest of the world - Idea Books, Amsterdam, the Netherlands, idea@ideabooks.nl

For general questions, please contact nai010 publishers directly at sales@nai010.com or visit our website www.nai010.com for further information.

Printed and bound in Belgium

ISBN 978-94-6208-794-1
NUR 648
BISAC ARC000000, ARC018000
THEMA AM

TU Delft

t?f The Why Factory